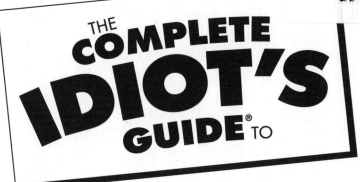

THE
COMPLETE
IDIOT'S
GUIDE® TO

Body Language

by Peter A. Andersen, Ph.D.

ALPHA

A member of Penguin Group (USA) Inc.

To my many colleagues and students with whom I have explored nonverbal communication
for more than 30 years. A special thanks to the three great Andersen women—
my daughter, Kirsten, my wife, Janis, and my mother, Mildred—
with whom I have shared the most beautiful body language.

ALPHA BOOKS

Published by the Penguin Group

Penguin Group (USA) Inc., 375 Hudson Street, New York, New York 10014, U.S.A.

Penguin Group (Canada), 10 Alcorn Avenue, Toronto, Ontario, Canada M4V 3B2 (a division of Pearson Penguin Canada Inc.)

Penguin Books Ltd, 80 Strand, London WC2R 0RL, England

Penguin Ireland, 25 St Stephen's Green, Dublin 2, Ireland (a division of Penguin Books Ltd)

Penguin Group (Australia), 250 Camberwell Road, Camberwell, Victoria 3124, Australia (a division of Pearson Australia Group Pty Ltd)

Penguin Books India Pvt Ltd, 11 Community Centre, Panchsheel Park, New Delhi—110 017, India

Penguin Group (NZ), cnr Airborne and Rosedale Roads, Albany, Auckland 1310, New Zealand (a division of Pearson New Zealand Ltd)

Penguin Books (South Africa) (Pty) Ltd, 24 Sturdee Avenue, Rosebank, Johannesburg 2196, South Africa

Penguin Books Ltd, Registered Offices: 80 Strand, London WC2R 0RL, England

International Standard Book Number: 1-59257-248-0
Library of Congress Catalog Card Number: 2004105324

07   8 7

Interpretation of the printing code: The rightmost number of the first series of numbers is the year of the book's printing; the rightmost number of the second series of numbers is the number of the book's printing. For example, a printing code of 04-1 shows that the first printing occurred in 2004.

Printed in the United States of America

Note: This publication contains the opinions and ideas of its author. It is intended to provide helpful and informative material on the subject matter covered. It is sold with the understanding that the author and publisher are not engaged in rendering professional services in the book. If the reader requires personal assistance or advice, a competent professional should be consulted.

The author and publisher specifically disclaim any responsibility for any liability, loss, or risk, personal or otherwise, which is incurred as a consequence, directly or indirectly, of the use and application of any of the contents of this book.

Most Alpha books are available at special quantity discounts for bulk purchases for sales promotions, premiums, fund-raising, or educational use. Special books, or book excerpts, can also be created to fit specific needs.

For details, write: Special Markets, Alpha Books, 375 Hudson Street, New York, NY 10014.

Publisher: *Marie Butler-Knight*
Product Manager: *Phil Kitchel*
Senior Managing Editor: *Jennifer Chisholm*
Acquisitions Editor: *Mikal E. Belicove*
Development Editor: *Jennifer Moore*
Senior Production Editor: *Billy Fields*
Copy Editor: *Tiffany Almond*
Illustrator: *Richard King*
Cover/Book Designer: *Trina Wurst*
Indexer: *Angie Bess*
Layout/Proofreading: *Angela Calvert, John Etchison*

Contents at a Glance

Contents

Foreword

Imagine for a moment that a court reporter follows you about for one full day. Every word you utter, from "Good morning" to "Goodnight," is typed into an official transcript. At home, at work, at lunch, on the phone, in the supermarket, every word you say is faithfully recorded. Only your own words are written down, without comments or rejoinders from those with whom you speak.

Further imagine that someone who has never met you before—never heard your voice, never seen your face, never looked into your eyes—reads your verbal transcript. After the reading, how are you perceived? Are you seen as male or female? Are you young or old, friendly or unfriendly, pretty or plain? Do you come across as outgoing or shy, caring or indifferent, humble or smug, naughty or nice? Are you self-confident, do you like your spouse, does your boss make you angry?

Answers to these questions are less likely to be found in the wordy transcription than in your body language. Which is to say, much of who you really are—at home, at work, in public, in private—is off the written transcript. The color of your tie, the length of your hair, the shape of your smile, your laugh, your gestures, the softness of your voice, the warmth of your hand, your slight shrug of uncertainty, the tightness of your lips, your lifted eyebrows, the eye contact you give, the set of your jaw, your stance in a doorway, the shoes you wear, your choice of perfume—these are the social and emotional signs others recognize as being the "real" you. Words are important, of course, but your true colors show in the myriad nonverbal signals you send each day.

In this book, Peter Andersen ably explores the nonverbal world you live in. According to anthropologists, speech emerged some 200,000 years ago as the dominant verbal medium of our species, *Homo sapiens*. Yet the nonverbal world is eons older and infinitely more expressive than speech. Words engulf conscious centers of our brain today, such as Broca's and Wernicke's areas, but we still make many of our most important decisions about life and living on nonverbal grounds. We do not need words to define a kiss, decode an Armani suit, or decipher new car smell. A great deal of technical knowledge is transmitted through nonverbal apprenticeships in which we watch and do rather than read a manual. We choose our pets, cars, homes, and mates for nonverbal reasons, and select our wardrobe based on clothing's look and feel. Even scientists, including such notables as Albert Einstein and Stephen Hawking, think in visual, spatial, and physical images rather than verbally in words.

Estimates of what percentage of our total communication is nonverbal range from 60 percent to 93 percent. But the percent of emotional communication that is nonverbal exceeds 99 percent. When it comes to emotions, instead of verbalizing how we feel, our bodies do the talking.

We use body language to convey ideas as well as feelings and moods. Hand gestures called "mime cues" depict shapes, motions, and locations of people, places, and things. Hand and finger positions mimic physical, spatial, and temporal relationships among objects, activities, and events. Mimicking the act of changing a lightbulb uses the same brain modules, and moves the same muscles, as the physical act itself. Brain circuits that underpin mime cues are as complex as those for speech.

The first scientific study of nonverbal communication was published in 1872 by Charles Darwin in *The Expression of the Emotions in Man and Animals*. Since the mid-1800s thousands of research projects in archaeology, biology, cultural and physical anthropology, linguistics, primatology, psychology, psychiatry, and zoology have been completed, establishing a virtual dictionary of nonverbal cues. Discoveries in neuroscience since the 1990–2000 "Decade of the Brain" have provided a clearer picture of what the unspoken signs and signals mean. Because we now know how the brain processes nonverbal cues, body language has come of age in the twenty-first century as a science to help us understand what it means to be human.

Nonverbal messages are potent, compelling, and immediate. They are processed faster than words in ancient brain centers beneath the newer areas for speech. From paleocircuits in the spinal cord, brain stem, basal ganglia, and limbic system, nonverbal cues are produced and received below the level of conscious awareness. They give our days the "look" and "feel" we remember long after words have died away.

Peter Andersen's book will help you decipher the diverse unspoken messages you see, hear, feel, taste, and smell each day as you make your way through our nonverbal world. We invite you to explore and enjoy the adventure!

David B. Givens, Ph.D., Director, Center for Nonverbal Studies

David B. Givens, Ph.D., is the director of the Center for Nonverbal Studies, a private, not-for-profit research center located in Spokane, Washington. The Center's mission is to advance the study of human communication in all its forms apart from language. The Center's goal is to promote the scientific study of nonverbal communication, which includes body movement, gesture, facial expression, adornment and fashion, architecture, mass media, and consumer-product design. For more information, please visit http://members.aol.com/nonverbal2.

Introduction

This book is about your body and how it communicates. Body language, also sometimes called nonverbal communication, includes all the ways we communicate without language, like eye contact, facial expressions, touch, hand gestures, and body postures. It also includes stuff like personal space, the uses of time, scent, territory, physical appearance, and clothing.

Body language is everywhere, but so is a lot of misinformation about it. For instance, contrary to popular belief, you can't read a person like a book. Similarly, there are *no* surefire ways to detect lying, and not all gestures have a dictionary definition.

In this book you'll find thought-provoking information based on scientific research, not speculation. Fortunately, for several decades researchers in communication, psychology, anthropology, and other fields have studied body language. Among the fascinating discoveries that researchers have made are that so-called women's intuition is based on women's ability to read body language, that touch is extremely important throughout our lives, and that eye contact is an integral part of interpersonal communication.

So join with me in an exploration of the human body, how it communicates, and how you can understand the most basic part of human communication.

What's in This Book

Part 1, "The Silent Dialog of Body Language," provides the nuts and bolts for understanding body language. You'll learn about the myths and realities of body language, including why you can't read a person like a book and why you cannot *not* communicate. You will learn about the origins of body language, how it is processed in the human brain, and why body language is so believable. Finally, you will learn whether body language is conscious or unconscious, intentional or unintentional, if it is truly the language of relationships, what role it plays in human intuition, and how you can make body language work for you.

Part 2, "Body Basics: The Codes of Body Language," will discuss how we use the different parts of our bodies—from our eyes to our hands to our armpits to our feet—to send meaningful messages. What is the significance of eye contact, of pupil dilation, eye blinks, and eye movements? What does your fabulous face communicate and how do people control their emotional expressions? What is the meaning of touch, and why does it matter where, who, how, and when you touch? And what about all the gestures people use instead of speaking or while they are speaking? What do people reveal when they sit, stand, or walk? Are attraction and sexual desire communicated through smell? And what does spending time and sharing space communicate? The chapters in this part of the book will tackle all of these questions.

Part 3, "The Power of Body Language," will help you discover the primary purposes of body language, including postures of power and displays of dominance, if and when you can detect deception from body cues, and how liars do and do not give themselves away. And since a primary purpose of body language is to express emotions, we will examine the range of human feelings from love to hate and from joy to shame, and how and why we express and suppress them.

Part 4, "Body Language in Everyday Life," looks at body language in its everyday contexts. After considering youngsters' body language from toddlers to teens, we'll discuss its role in dating and sexual situations, the workplace, politics, within sports, and in the classroom.

Part 5, "Crossing the Boundaries of Body Language," explores the new frontiers of body language. Can body language cross the borders between pets and people? Between men and women? From commercial images to image-conscious consumers? Across continents and cultures? Even between real and virtual people?

Body Language Bonuses

Throughout this book, you'll find additional information about bodies and how they communicate. Here's what to watch for:

Body Talk

In these boxes I explain the jargon of body language and define words you might not be familiar with. You can also turn to Appendix A for a complete glossary of terms.

Bodily Blunders

We have all made minor miscues, frightening *faux pas*, and major mistakes with body language. Here I explain such slip-ups and suggest how you can avoid them in the future.

Positions of Power

Here you'll find tips for reading body language and advice on using your own body language to your best advantage.

Nonverbally Speaking

Look to these boxes for a potpourri of information on how we communicate without words.

Body language is a universal language that cuts across culture and time. Because a lot of body language is visual, this book also contains pictures, from last year and years ago, that attempt to capture body language across time and across culture.

Acknowledgments

Thanks to my excellent editors Mikal Belicove and Jennifer Moore and everyone at Alpha Books who nurtured and honed this project from start to finish. Thanks particularly to my virtual widow and wonderful wife, Dr. Janis Andersen, for her patience and support during this project. A special thanks to my amazing student research assistants who helped locate studies and edit drafts: Kati Armstrong, Mariah Beiber, Carolyn Frank, Shannon Haggerty, Shannon Johnson, Sofia McKenzie, Artesia Taylor, Justin Wixson, Hua Wang, and Liz Yarnall.

Trademarks

All terms mentioned in this book that are known to be or are suspected of being trademarks or service marks have been appropriately capitalized. Alpha Books and Penguin Group (USA) Inc. cannot attest to the accuracy of this information. Use of a term in this book should not be regarded as affecting the validity of any trademark or service mark.

Part 1

The Silent Dialog of Body Language

Talk is cheap! Seeing is believing! You can't believe everything you hear! Are these old wives' tales or important facts about body language? A little of both, and it turns out that those old wives were pretty smart. Research reveals that body language *is* often more revealing and authentic than talk.

The human body is more than bones and blood vessels. It is a treasure trove of information. Most people are fascinated with their own bodies—and with other people's bodies—for good reason. Body language reveals the most important information about our emotions, attractions, relationships, and a whole lot more.

Is a picture really worth a thousand words? Can you tell a book by its cover? Can you hide your true feelings? In this first part of the book you will find out about the myths and realities of body language, where it comes from, and why it's such a vital part of human communication.

Chapter 1

The Myths of Body Language

In This Chapter

◆ Your body communicates loud and clear

◆ Body language isn't a language

◆ You cannot *not* communicate

◆ Meanings are in people, not in messages

◆ Communication may not be intentional

The most idiotic thing about *The Complete Idiot's Guide to Body Language* is its title. Aside from the fact that you're not an idiot, body language isn't really a language. That's right, body language is a misnomer, an oxymoron. Body language is what experts call nonverbal communication or non-linguistic communication. Rather than give you a long and boring explanation of the nuances of language, suffice it to say that body language consists of images, expressions, and behaviors that have no dictionary definition.

Even though there is no dictionary of body language, it's still a form of communication. Some people say it communicates louder, longer, and larger than words. It is a vital form of communication that can be as perplexing as it is enlightening. In this opening chapter, you will learn about the myths and realities of body language and how it affects your every interaction.

So if body language isn't a language, why do we call it body *language?* The same reason we call a peanut a nut when it is actually a legume: Because that's what everyone else calls it. To avoid rocking the boat, I'll use the term that's out there: body language.

Myth #1: Body Language Is Language

I've already said it, but it bears repeating: Body language is *not* a language. But as you'll discover throughout this book, body language is more primary and may be more powerful than language itself. Communication goes way beyond words and symbols. Signs, signals, and symptoms communicate as well.

To understand what body language *is not*, you need to understand what language *is*. Languages are systems of arbitrary symbols that stand for objects, events, processes, and relationships. In other words, languages all use secret codes known only to speakers and users of that language. Example of languages include …

Positions of Power

Body language communicates continuously and commandingly. Occasionally you will read that body language is anywhere from 60 to 90 percent of communication. These numbers are totally bogus. The proportion of body language to language varies in every situation. The bottom line is this: Both language and body language are extremely powerful!

Nonverbally Speaking

Body language evolved long before language. That's why body language is considered more natural and authentic than words.

- ◆ Natural languages like English, Spanish, or Mandarin
- ◆ Sign Languages like American Sign Language
- ◆ Computer languages like Fortran, Cobal, and Java
- ◆ Mathematics: Numbers are a universal language
- ◆ Signal flags such as those used by the Navy
- ◆ Morse code
- ◆ Musical notation

To understand any of these languages, you have to know the code. Each language has an arbitrary relationship with an event of object. *Tak* in Swedish, *Gracias* in Spanish, *Arigato* in Japanese, and *thanks* in English, all mean the same thing, but only if you know at least a little of each language. Unlike a tally such as IIII, there is nothing very *four*-like about the number 4. The word *four* is an arbitrary way of expressing the numeral 4.

Sometime try writing down every eyebrow movement or arm position and say exactly what it means. Can't do it? That's what I thought. Whereas every utterance in a language has a known definition, there is no one-to-one relationship between body language and particular meanings. Body language uses direct representation of things. People have tried to create nonverbal dictionaries but it is impossible.

Body language uses no secret codes. Everybody has an equal shot at interpretation but no single interpretation is necessarily correct. Look for patterns, not symbols, and you will read body language pretty well.

Body language is much less explicit but more authentic than talk. Talk is easy to fake. Unless you are an Oscar winner, you probably can't simultaneously fake your facial expressions, touch behavior, eye behavior, spatial behavior, pupil dilation, vocal tones, timing, gestures, head position, and posture (to mention but a few). You probably aren't even aware at any point in time that you communicate in all these ways. But you're always creating body language, and others are always interpreting it. Which brings me to the next myth.

> **Nonverbally Speaking**
>
> Sign language is a real language. It has everything that real languages have, including words, grammar, and sentence structure. It just uses the hands instead of the voice. So dig it: Body language isn't really a language, but sign language, now that's a language.

Myth #2: You Can Read a Person Like a Book

When it comes to reading, books are simple compared to people. Books use words, and as I just pointed out, words have pretty explicit definitions. People are full of nuance, intrigue, and mystery. Your body language doesn't have explicit dictionary definitions like the words on this page.

Body language is based on images, *analogs*, and icons that are abbreviations of other behaviors. When you pat somebody on the back, you are giving her or him an abbreviated hug—a good thing to do if you don't know the person well enough to hug them. A shaken fist is an abbreviated punch. Smiles in humans and apes originated as appeasement gestures showing closed teeth rather than open ones that can bite! Close distances are signs of close relationships.

> **Body Talk**
>
> An **analog** is a code that has a direct, intrinsic relationship with the thing it represents. A pointed finger is an analog in any culture for sending a person in an obvious direction. Eye contact worldwide is an invitation to communicate. A fist is a simulated punch. When you read body language, you need no secret code like you do when you read real languages.

Is this guy deceptive or just nervous?

(Image courtesy of Robert Avery)

Languages like English and sign language are forms of digital communication. Digital communication indirectly communicates information through arbitrary, discrete codes. Natural language is the most highly organized form of digital communication.

Bodily Blunders

Anthropologist Gregory Bateson claimed that we naturally distrust someone who translates our postures and gestures into words. Posture and gestures are meaningful, but only as patterns, not as explicit symbols. A smile, for example, cannot be reduced to a word like amused, happy, smug, joyful, warm, polite, or pleasant. A smile can mean any one of these things, all of these things, or none of these things.

Bodily Blunders

People often misinterpret body language. Anxiety is confused with deception. Contemplation is often mistaken for disagreement. You cannot read a person like a book. Look for patterns and treat the results as conjecture rather than certainty.

Body language is not a digital communication system but an analog system. Analog communication communicates directly, naturally, and continuously.

Body language is almost entirely analog communication that directly represents the thing it stands for. That's why although we may not be able to understand Swahili, Mandarin, or German, we can understand the body language of people who speak these languages and even the body language of animals.

While you can't read a person like a book, you can read them like a painting, movie, or song. If you look for a one-to-one correspondence between body language and words, you will be lost in linguistic haze. Instead, look for patterns, nuances, analogs, and images.

Myth #3: You Can Not Communicate

Try this. Look directly at a friend and send them no facial expression. Tough, eh? Your blank face communicates! Or try to stand a distance from your friend that is neither near nor far. No can do! You cannot be *no* distance from your friend; you must be some distance—whether it is inches away, across the room, or across the sea.

Is this child's face really blank? What does her face say to you?

(Image courtesy of Peter Andersen)

How about this woman? What does her supposedly blank face communicate?

(Image courtesy of Peter Andersen)

As long as you are alive, you are communicating. Even a person who observes you covertly makes judgments about your unintentional behavior. Even if you are not talking, people are reading your body language and attributing attitudes, emotions, and thoughts to you. It's a little scary because it means that as long as someone can observe you, your body language is making a statement.

As we will discuss throughout this book, people observe and judge hundreds of your intentional and unintentional behaviors. Only researchers make a distinction between the two; ordinary people rarely do. People judge you by gender, physical beauty, race, hair (or lack thereof), hair color, gait, gesture, height, physical condition, and facial expression, and in dozens of other ways. Your intended communication is woven together with unintended body language into a tapestry that cannot be unraveled.

The fact that you can't avoid communicating is a bummer for anyone trying to give someone the silent treatment or trying to withdraw from social interaction.

From eye behavior to gesture, from where you choose to stand to how you smell, from your facial expressions to what you wear, the language of your body is always present. Body language is inevitable. Communication is constant.

Myth #4: Body Language Is Always Intentional

Body language usually is spontaneous. Some body language reveals your hidden attitudes and emotions and is a *symptom*. Symptoms indicate an internal state that is not intended for communication. Just as a runny nose is a symptom of a cold, trembling is a symptom of fear. Let's take smiling as an example. You can smile at a funny e-mail message or a joke in the newspaper. If your spouse sees you smile or hears you laugh, your body language has just communicated. Maybe it stimulated your spouse to smile back, or think you're cute, or wonder "What's so funny?" So most smiles are often symptoms, a form of unintentional but very meaningful communication.

The source of some smiles is *spontaneous* communication. Suppose you're at a party and a good-looking stranger smiles as you. You spontaneously smile in return without even thinking about it. In fact, this is a pretty common phenomenon; smiles are reciprocal, meaning that smiles beget other smiles. You're communicating, but you're doing so unintentionally and without knowing it. Your body is designed to respond spontaneously and mindlessly.

Other smiles are *intentional* body language. Suppose you're about to pick up your girlfriend for a hot date. You really like her, and you want to make a good impression. As the door opens, you smile—a great big beautiful smile. You deliberately want to start the evening off right and you know that smiling will increase attraction and send the right vibes. So body language *can* be intentional.

Body language communicates a rich array of cues, and you should be on the lookout for all of them, whether they are intentional or not.

Distinguishing between intentional and unintentional communication has perplexed communication researchers and philosophers. To only study intentional communication would exclude lots of really interesting and meaningful stuff. Besides, no one really knows which body language is intentional and which is unintentional.

Whether or not something is intentional or what motivated a particular behavior should be treated as a hunch, not a conclusion. Use your senses to understand a person. You can never get inside their head. What you can do is watch people and read their behavior. Take it all in!

Body language will enlighten you if you take the time to watch, feel, smell, and listen.

> **Nonverbally Speaking**
>
> Much of the interesting stuff in communication is the unintentional stuff. Slips of the tongue, double entendres, blushing, deception cues, secret looks, micromomentary expressions, sweaty palms, inadvertent impressions, all disclose and reveal the most interesting things about other people.

Myth #5: Body Language Is a Highly Accurate Form of Communication

Although body language is an extraordinarily powerful and useful form of communication, it isn't very accurate. Like all forms of communication, it is fraught with inaccuracy.

One day many years ago, I was having breakfast at a restaurant near another college I was visiting. A gorgeous girl with a pile of books was sitting in the next booth and staring at me intensely. I was a little taken aback and looked away. When I looked back a few moments later, she was still staring. My heart skipped a beat. She was not looking away, just staring right at me! Was she experiencing love at first sight, I optimistically speculated? Finally, collecting my courage, I initiated a conversation. "How are you on this fine day?" I ineptly inquired. Shaken from her daydream she jumped as if woken from a trance and uttered a slight shriek. "Fine, whoever you are," she replied in a condescending tone and never made eye contact again. My bad! I had eggs on my plate and eggs

> **Bodily Blunders**
>
> People continuously communicate without knowing it. When you are with other people, you are sending messages via body language. You can stop talking, but you can't stop communicating.

on my face. A message received is not necessarily a message intended. Once again I learned that interpreting body language is a perilous process fraught with inaccuracy.

Here's another example: A young man and woman had a wonderful second date and he was walking her up to her front door. Things were going well and both of them were thinking that this would not be the last date—this relationship had a future! As is so often the case, uncertainty and indecision perplexed the young man as he wondered if he should kiss his date goodnight. Feeling good about the positive course of their young relationship, he went for broke and gave her a kiss. He took her heavy breathing as a sign that she wanted to kiss more deeply and longer. When she broke away, pushing him back, he was crushed! "Is everything okay?" he asked. "This darn hay fever" she gasped, "I nearly suffocated. But thanks for a nice evening!" She kissed him again and disappeared inside. Reeling from two body language blunders, he walked home dazed. From mistakenly reading her breathlessness as uncontrolled passion, to incorrectly reading her suffocation as rejection, and back to the welcome reality of nice evening. It had been a tumultuous 15 seconds!

As these body language blunders illustrate, communication is complex and accuracy is elusive. You can't read people like books—heck, even written messages are open to misinterpretation. All messages have multiple meanings. Most importantly, communication is inherently inaccurate and body language always contains ambiguities. Communication cannot be limited to good, accurate, or shared interaction. Bad communication such as misunderstandings, misinterpretations, misconceptions, misperceptions, delusions, false impressions, stereotypes, false expectations, poor listening, noise, lack of attention, and general confusion are all forms of communication worthy of study.

Myth #6: Meanings Are in Messages

The reality is that meanings are in people, not messages. As in the prior examples, a message sent will not be exactly the same as a message received. Even words are somewhat ambiguous. Take the phrase "there was a big cat blocking the way." The word cat could mean different things to different people. The cat could be a Maine coon, a bobcat, a tiger, slang for a dude or man, or a Caterpillar tractor. Meanings are not inherently present in words, and they're certainly not present in body language. Messages are vehicles that carry meaning, but meanings are in our minds, not in the messages themselves.

As we will discuss in detail in Chapter 26, men sometimes misinterpret women's friendly smiles as flirtation behaviors. Conversely, some women think men's blatant come-ons are mere friendliness. And you've probably met people who construe every comment with an obscure, obscene interpretation. There really isn't such a thing as a dirty word, only a dirty mind.

Context is vital for understanding all messages, but especially body language. Body language must always be interpreted in the culture, period, climate, environment, setting, situation, mood, and relationship that provide the context and tell us how to "take" the message.

To make matters more complicated, body language provides the context for other messages. Eye contact with an angry facial expression is menacing, eye contact with a smile is engaging. Saying, "that's really good" while rolling your eyes is sarcastic criticism, saying it with direct eye contact is a compliment. Messages are meaningful only in context, and messages provide context for other messages.

> **CAUTION**
>
> **Bodily Blunders** ___
>
> Talk about misunder- standing. Men are far more likely to read sexual intent in the friendly behavior of women even when women have no such intent. Without a doubt, commu- nication between men and women is occurring; it's just occurring poorly.

Myth #7: The Map Is the Territory

The father of general semantics (the study of the relationship between language, thought, and behavior) Alfred Korzybski said it best: "A map is not the territory it represents, but, if correct, it has a similar structure to the territory, which accounts for its usefulness." Like maps, body language is representational and iconic.

The map is not the territory, the painting is not the landscape, the smile is not the emotion, the gesture is not the object, and the fist is not the punch. All messages are representations.

Unlike real language, which is an indirect and arbitrary representation, body language is a direct representation of feelings, thoughts, objects, or events. This is tricky be- cause the frown looks to us like sadness, so we sometimes forget that it is merely a representation of an expression of sadness and might not actually mean that someone who is frowning is sad.

Now it gets even trickier, because humans can manipulate their body language. For example, our bodies send chemical messages naturally through our pheromones, a topic we will discuss in Chapter 9. But we can use perfume to replace natural smells and still get a positive reaction from our spouse or date. Both the natural pheromones and the commercial scents may be a representation of some underlying emotion, say desire or attraction. But perfume is an intentional representation of another smell. Changing one's smell is a deliberate, planned expression of body language.

In so many respects our communication skills have evolved beyond other animals. We can intentionally as well as unintentionally represent objects, emotions, or events. Such representations can be exaggerated, falsified, denied, minimized, and so on. The trickiest part is that we never really know if body language is authentic and spontaneous or manipulative and planned.

The Least You Need to Know

- ◆ Body language is not a language.
- ◆ You can't read a person like a book.
- ◆ You cannot *not* communicate.
- ◆ Body language is mostly unintentional.
- ◆ Meanings are in people, not in messages.
- ◆ The map is not the territory.

Chapter 2

Unraveling the Mysteries of Body Language

In This Chapter

- ◆ The authentic nature of body language
- ◆ The primacy of body language
- ◆ Understanding your right mind
- ◆ Your bicameral brain
- ◆ Handedness and facedness in body language

We are all body language experts. A lot of what we know about body language we knew before kindergarten. Some of what we know was in our genes, and we picked up other information in our early development. One reason that people find body language so fascinating and mysterious is that we can't remember learning it.

If you are the kind of person who loves to unravel mysteries, this chapter is for you. And these are not small mysteries: How do humans connect and communicate? How did body language develop? Why is body language so different from language?

In this chapter, we will explore the mysterious nature of body language, its origins in the human species and in each of our lives. Finally, we will take a trip inside your head to understand how the brain works with your body in sending and receiving body language messages.

The Authenticity of Body Language

Body language is compelling. Though people don't know why, they trust it more than words. Think about this example: Your spouse has been overseas for two weeks and you are greeting her or him at the airport. Upon seeing your spouse you stand absolutely still, with no touch, and no facial expressions, and say in a monotone, "I love you, I really missed you." Will your partner believe your words? Not likely! That bedeviling body language will probably undermine good old English. What was missing in this airport interaction? Just about everything! The words were fine, but where was the look of joy, the smile, the hug, and the kiss? What happened to running toward your partner or at least moving closer? Where were the vocal enthusiasm and the big hello wave? In other words, where was the body language?

In most cases, when body language contradicts our spoken or written words, we believe the body language. But why? The answer lies in the very nature of body language itself and its spontaneous, multichanneled, redundant qualities that make it very hard to completely fake. There are a number of characteristics of body language that make it authentic and believable.

Multichanneled Messages

Body language is a multichanneled form of communication. Among the many channels are voice, facial expressions, gestures, and touch. Sadness, for example, may be expressed verbally by talking about your sad feelings. Usually however, sadness is accompanied by multichanneled body language that includes various sad facial expressions, quivering lips, sighing and crying, indolent and lethargic postures, apathy about activity, pitiful tones of voice, covering the face, desperate hugging, body clutching, and head lowering, to mention only a few. A key to reading body language is to pick up on a set of such sadness cues. Any half a dozen will do. If you observe a consistent set of half a dozen or so of these cues, you would be pretty safe in attributing sadness to a person's behavior.

> **Nonverbally Speaking**
>
> Try to maintain almost constant eye contact with a close friend during a conversation. See what other changes occur in your body language. Chances are you will naturally smile more and send other positive messages. Body language is naturally designed to be a package of multichanneled messages.

Are these multichanneled messages consistent or inconsistent? The smiles, body position, and toasts send out warm multichanneled messages.

(Image courtesy of Robert Avery)

Similarly, when you want to express love to a person you haven't seen for a while, you say it by moving closer and facing that person directly; by affectionate hugs and warm kisses; by facial expressions of joy, love, and appreciation; by being physically present and spending time with the person; by making loving gestures and meaningful eye contact; and in dozens of other ways we will discuss throughout this book.

Consistent multichanneled messages communicate honesty, sincerity, believability, and accuracy because each additional behavior strengthens and reinforces the overall message. The multichanneled nature of body language, however, is a double-edged sword. Just as a consistent multichanneled message can provide certainty in reading body language, mixed or inconsistent messages result in ambiguity and uncertainty.

Redundant Redundancy

The second reason body language is so powerful is message redundancy. First you need to know that redundancy increases accuracy. Redundancy increases accuracy. Redundancy increases accuracy. Redundancy increases accuracy. Redundancy increases accuracy. Redundancy increases accuracy. Getting annoyed yet? Sorry about that. People don't really appreciate excessive redundancy, at least not with written or spoken words. However, the cool thing about body language is that it is simultaneously and unobtrusively redundant. In an instant I can communicate frustration to you by stomping my foot impatiently, putting my hands on my hips, tipping my head to the side, making an annoyed facial expression, giving you a steely stare, and so on.

The point is this: Unlike speech or text, redundant body language isn't annoying at all; it's actually appreciated because it's helpful. This is the essence of how to read body language: You try to pick up rich redundant sets of messages. You look for a pattern. As I've already pointed out, you can't read a person like a book, one word at time. But you can read a person more like you read a painting or listen to a symphony. You go for the "big picture" and let your intuition be the guide.

Certifying Authenticity?

People know intuitively that body language is hard to fake. Body language is produced in a fraction of a second using dozens of redundant cues, making it almost impossible to completely fake. When all the cues don't go together, it feels fishy. Fishy, sketchy body language makes us suspicious and suspicion, in turn, prompts us to tune in even more closely to body language and to ask probing questions. In Chapter 12, we discuss the whole process of deceitful body language and deception detection in some detail.

Spontaneousness

Verbal communication may be the grandest accomplishment of human history. It allows us to precisely formulate a message and to intentionally communicate it. (The exceptions are slips of the tongue.) Body language, on the other hand, is semi-automatic. It's usually spontaneous and much more likely to be symptomatic of underlying feelings or a spur-of-the-moment expression of one's thoughts, emotions, or attitudes.

> **CAUTION**
>
> **Bodily Blunders**
>
> The best, most believable body language is spontaneous. Posed facial expressions, like the fake smiles on many photographs, look fake. So here is a paradox. You want to look happy, sad, or sincere but you can't plan to be spontaneous. So relax, forget about your body, and let your real feelings show. Trying too hard to send body language is counterproductive.

Verbal communication is richly symbolic, abstract, and planned—all qualities that lend themselves to manipulation. Lying with words is both easy and pretty commonplace, so most of us learn to be skeptical and to use context and body language to validate verbal statements.

Primacy

Finally, as you will discover next, body language is your primary mode of communication, primary in the evolutionary history of the human species, and primary in your life. Body language is a communication system that is collectively and individually more basic than the spoken or written word. That's why we intuitively understand that it's the most basic form of human communication.

Fake smiles, which we often see in pictures, don't look quite right. They look forced and fail to include the lines at the corner of the eye that are a sign of genuine happiness.

(Image courtesy of Peter Andersen)

The Evolutionary Primacy of Body Language

Scholars agree that from an evolutionary standpoint body language developed earlier than language and verbal communication. The earliest animals used body language, and today all animals use various forms of body language as their primary means of communication. Animals use body language to communicate both with members of their own species and with other species.

Nonhuman animals are excellent at body language, and it's a good bet that the ancestors of modern humans were pretty good at it, too. Take your pet cat or dog for example. Fluffy and Fido are pretty good at sending and receiving body language (as we will discuss in Chapter 24). Get out the food and they will bark or meow, rub your legs, or wag their tail. But it's not just food-related movement that they respond to. Try this one with your dog or cat: Say, "You are a wonderful pet," but say it like you are yelling at them. Chances are your pet will react negatively to the tone of your voice, not positively to your kind words. Now try the reverse. Tell your dog, "get out of here you stupid idiot," in a pleasant tone of voice. The silly fluff ball will wag his tail and look pleased even though you just dissed him verbally.

As humans acquired language, it was layered on top of body language as a secondary and often complimentary system of communication. The fact that body language is an older system than spoken language has several important implications. First, linguistics is a poor model for the earlier and more primary method of communication.

So what we know about speech and language is of little use when it comes to making sense of body language. Second, the addition of language has made our other senses progressively less important. For instance, our sense of smell is about the worst in the animal kingdom. And other senses, like sonar, radar, and thermal detectors so prevalent in "primitive" animals, are essentially nonexistent in human beings. Third, the ancient origins of body language, even before the development of cultures, nations, or ethnicities, means that it is a more universal and cross-cultural method of communication.

From the Bodies of Babes

Babies are born users of body language. Their cute little facial expressions and shrill cries communicate clearly without the benefit of words, which are months or years away. We will devote Chapter 14 to a detailed analysis of baby body language, but a few words are in order here. Every channel of body language is available to babies: touch, body movements, gestures, vocalizations, smell, and spatial behaviors are all up and running. Infant interaction sets the stage for an intelligent and communicative adult. The fact that body language develops first and also evolved before language suggests that it is your primary means of communication.

Mysteries of Our Bicameral Brain

The cerebral cortex is the crowning accomplishment of human neural architecture. Sitting atop other parts of the brain that evolved millions of years earlier, the cerebral cortex occupies everything in the head above the eyes and ears. Incredibly, the cerebral cortex is not one, but two, brains! The skull of every human being houses two brains in one, called the left brain hemisphere and the right brain hemisphere. For short we call these the left brain and the right brain. Each brain performs almost completely different functions.

Your two brains are not completely separate; they are connected by a bundle of nerve fibers called the *corpus collosum*. The corpus collosum is like a bunch of cables connecting two extremely sophisticated computers (see the accompanying drawing of the brain). That doesn't mean that each of your brains knows everything going on in the other brain, but they are in touch with each other and able to send information back and forth.

Body Talk

Your **corpus collosum** is a bundle of nerve fibers that connects your right and left brains. This is a good thing: Without it you would never be able to associate a name with a face, label an emotional expression, or talk about body language. It provides coherency to language and body language.

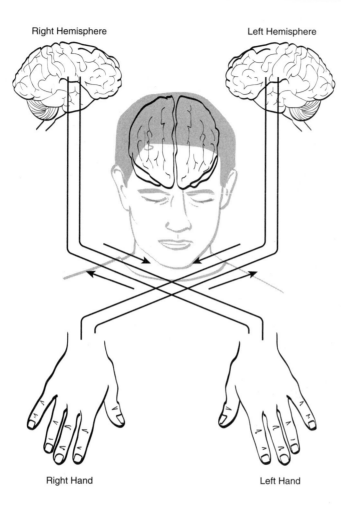

Right Hemisphere

Left Hemisphere

Right Hand

Left Hand

The brain consists the two separate hemispheres connected together only by the corpus collosum. The hemispheres are largely responsible for different types of communication. The right hemisphere controls and understands body language.

Before we get inside your head and discuss what goes on in there, you need to know just a bit more about the wiring of your brain and body. The entire right side of your body, including your right ear, is hooked up to the left brain. Similarly, the entire left side of your body, including your left ear, is hooked up to your right brain. Basically, your entire body has its wires crossed! The eyes are a bit more complicated. The left half visual field of each eye is connected to your right brain and the right half visual field of each eye is hooked up to your left brain. So basically, if you are looking straight ahead, everything you see to your left goes to your right brain and everything you see to your right goes to your left brain.

Now you might be asking, what in the name of neurology does this have to do with body language? The answer is everything. Real language is processed in your left brain and body language is processed in your right brain.

Your Linguistic Left Brain

Your left brain is what this book *isn't* about. It is your linguistic brain. Your left brain is a powerful, biologically-based digital computer that excels at reading, writing, speaking, mathematics, logic, and the use of symbols.

When a person has a severe left brain injury, called *aphasia*, they lose all the functions of language. They may not be able to speak, and have difficulty understanding speech. If the left brain stroke or injury is severe, they will not be able to read or write or do the simplest mathematical or arithmetic problems.

Interestingly, aphasics, or people with aphasia, lose the ability to send and receive all forms of symbols and language. It is not just reading and writing that is lost but all left brained skills including reading, sign language, gestures with a dictionary meaning, computer language, and Braille.

Positions of Power

Perhaps someone you know had a severe stroke and you want to interact with him or her. If they are paralyzed on the left side, their right brain is affected. Talk or write to this person, but don't expect them to understand body language, including the sight of your face. If they are paralyzed on the right side, their linguistic, left brain is affected. Try singing your messages to these folks along with lots of facial expression and touch.

Modern technologies can enable us to listen to and watch the brain in action. Electro-encephalographs can monitor electrical activity in the brain and MRI scans enable scientists to view where brain activity occurs during a given activity. Using these devices, scientists have basically corroborated what brain injury research has found: The left hemisphere is primarily responsible for language, speech, reading, writing, mathematics, and sign language. In short, the left hemisphere governs all forms of symbolic and digital communication.

In Your Right Mind

The right brain is the domain of body language. Your right brain locates your body in space and helps you distinguish up and down from sidewise. It controls the sending and receiving of all tactile (touch) information, except for Braille letters, which are a form of real language and processed in the left brain hemisphere. Your right brain identifies familiar faces and recognizes facial expressions. It interprets tone of voice, melody, and music, including singing. Your right brain interprets all body movements, positions, and gestures. It enables you to recognize environmental sounds including the sounds of nature, machinery, and even nonverbal human vocalizations such as screams, yells, and yawns. It is your right brain that recognizes pattern, art, shape, and space. It is the foundation of spatial and navigational skills. It is the nonverbal hemisphere, the storehouse, processor, and mainframe of body language.

Nonverbally Speaking

People with bullet wounds or severe strokes in the right brain cannot tell the horizontal from the vertical, nor can they recognize the most familiar faces. Once thought to be our unimportant, nondominant hemisphere, the right brain has been found to control the production and perception of virtually all body language.

Internal Communication

The right brain, left brain distinction I've just made is a bit too simplistic. First, about 5 percent of us have totally reversed hemispheric functions, including more than half of all lefties. For these people the right hemisphere processes language and the left hemisphere controls body language. But that is an exception to a general rule.

More importantly, in virtually all people, our two brains are connected via the corpus collosum, which serves as an important internal communication channel. We have one brain, but it has some very specialized parts.

Studies of brain anatomy find that women have larger corpus collosums than men. Some evidence suggests that women excel at tasks where both hemispheres are useful, like interpersonal communication, in which both listening skills and picking up body language would contribute to communication competence. (Chapter 26 explores gender differences in body language.) Men, on the other hand, might have an edge in spatial tasks or math skills, where one specialized hemisphere can problem solve without interference from the other. Some scholars suggest that men's inability to express emotions may be due to reduced communication between the brain hemispheres because of their smaller corpus collosums. Interestingly, several studies have found that gay men have large corpus collosums that are more like those of women than other men. This may explain why, among men, gay men are more emotionally expressive!

I, like many other researchers who study the human brain, believe that humans have modular minds. Think of your brain as housing dozens of smaller brains, each capable of coming to a different decision. These little brains live in two houses that make up your bicameral brain. Each of the small brains can come up with its own attitude on an issue or solution to a problem. But you can't really live with an indecisive brain that comes to five different decisions in response to every problem. We face tough decisions all the time. Think back to a person you were really attracted to but who was kind of an idiot. Part of you was saying, "don't get involved with this person" and part of you was saying, "go for it." But you had to make a decision. In a normal brain one or more modules win the argument and suppress other opinions. This sounds a lot like cognitive dissonance—an internal conflict over what to do—and dissonance reduction—finally making a decision. The modular mind may be the basis of both dissonance and dissonance reduction. A governing module that makes this decision may be what keeps your behavior consistent and coherent.

Nonverbally Speaking

In very severe cases of epilepsy, which cannot be treated, sometimes the corpus collosum is severed, leaving the two brain hemispheres completely separated. While internal communication between the brain hemispheres is completely gone, at least in the short term, it does stop the epileptic attacks. It also enables researchers to communicate with one side of the brain with no information getting to the other. This research suggests that the right hemisphere has little or no verbal abilities and the left hemisphere has little ability to produce or process body language.

Amazingly and amusingly, when a picture of a nude person is projected to a split-brained person, they cannot report seeing it with their left hemisphere, which can speak but has little or no ability to process body language. So they report that the screen is blank. However, researchers know that the right hemisphere sees the nude because the person frequently smiles, giggles, or blushes. The right hemisphere is completely capable of seeing body language and responding with body language. When researchers ask the split-brained person what is so funny, their left brain answers, "I don't know, just a funny screen I guess." This is because their left brain can make no sense of the picture and doesn't have a connection to the right brain, so the right brain, which understands the picture, cannot help out. This illustrates the functional asymmetry of the two hemispheres and emphasizes the right brain's unique skill for understanding body language.

People with severed corpus collosums are literally of two minds. Their left and right brain hemisphere have no communication with one another and make entirely separate decisions. It is not uncommon to have a person try to get dressed with one hand and undressed with the other! Fortunately, in most of us language and body language are unified via the corpus collosum.

The Architecture of Magic

Humans can multitask like no other species. We can tune in to talk and still keep track of complex multichanneled body language. Many researchers think it is the modular structure of the human brain that enables us to accomplish this feat. Starting with the two main modules, the right and the left brain hemispheres, our brains are further divided into many more modules, each capable of solving specialized problems in their own unique way.

The Quantum Leap to the Left and Right Brains

The incredible architecture of the human brain didn't happen by accident, it evolved that way over the millennia. Once humans developed language they had a problem: Does the brain focus on words that provide a new and precise communication system or on the more primitive and accurate body language? The solution was to relegate each form of communication to a different brain hemisphere. But how? Natural variation in the structure of brains and the process of natural selection gave those of us with the new bicameral, specialized brains a survival edge over our unicameral relatives. Humans with two brain hemispheres with different missions had a huge advantage over their ancestors who were less specialized.

But why was the bicameral brain such an advantage?

Many researchers, such as Joseph Jaffe of the New York State Psychiatric Institute and Columbia University, suggest that an efficient division of labor between the two brain hemispheres represented a quantum leap forward in our communication skills. He believes that the overwhelming preponderance of people who process language in the left brain and body language in the right suggests this pattern was so superior in communication that it conferred a selective survival advantage on these new and improved communicators, who could simultaneously process words and body language. Such was the origin of multitasking!

Which face displays happier body language? Most people select the figure on the left. Because they process more information from the left side of the face, the left-sided smile looks happier than the right-sided one.

The Mysterious Evolution of Handedness and Facedness

More than 90 percent of people are right handed. Even lefties tend to gesture more with the right hand. (These right-handed gestures, called illustrators, are linked to speech, and more will be said about them in Chapter 7.) Why would everybody, including lefties, use more right-handed gestures?

The answer lies in our brains and eyes. Earlier you learned that everything you see in your left visual field, which is to the left of where you are looking, goes to your right brain hemisphere. Body language that appears in your left visual field has a much more powerful effect on you than body language in your right visual field since it is transmitted directly to your right brain. This means that other people's right-handed gestures and other people's right-faced expressions have a disproportional influence on us, which has been demonstrated in numerous experiments. In fact, we recognize other people mainly from what their right face looks like. When a composite face is made of the two right halves of a friend's face, that person looks a whole lot more like our friend than a composite made up of two left halves of their face. Our right visual field and left brain are almost retarded in processing body language. Our left visual field and right brain are highly skilled at picking up all kinds of nonverbal communication and body language.

> **Nonverbally Speaking**
>
> Singers, in a group of other singers, will often cup their hand to their ear so they hear the sound and pitch of their own voice. Watch which ear gets cupped! Overwhelmingly it is the left ear. The left ear and the right brain are far better at processing all forms of body language, including music. Interestingly, singers instinctively know that this is the case.

In the course of human evolution, people have adjusted to the bias of the left visual field by providing more body language to the left visual field than the right. All over the world, people use more right-handed gestures that play to our left visual field and right brain. Likewise, the right side of the face, which is seen in your left visual field and by your right brain, is far more expressive and positive than the left side. Studies have found that the left face looks much more sinister; thus researchers call the right side of the face the social side, because it is more upbeat and cheery.

Interestingly, negative emotions seem to be produced more intensely in the left face, not in the more social right face that covers for its more sinister—and sinistral (meaning left-handed)—side. Collectively these facial finding suggest that ...

◆ You recognize other people based on the right side of their face.

◆ You are mainly influenced by emotional expressions from the right side of people's faces.

- People display more positive emotions on the right side of the face to appease others in social interaction.

- People display more negative and perhaps more honest emotions on the left side of the face.

- Good readers of body language should tune in to both sides of the face to get the most complete picture.

Reassembling the Brain

Although it is interesting to dissect the brain, it is important to remember that most people have a single brain with many specialized parts.

Just as all the parts of the brain typically work together, language and body language work together. Both are part and parcel of human communication.

Positions of Power

Body language may be more believable than words, but the same message sent via body language and words work best. So here is a tip: Be consistent. If you want to be powerful, use powerful words and powerful body language. If you want to send a loving message, use terms of endearment as well as endearing body language.

The Least You Need to Know

- Body language is the original form of human communication.

- Body language is multichanneled, redundant, and spontaneous.

- Humans send and receive messages via body language long before they use spoken language.

- Body language is processed in your right brain.

- The right side of the body sends the most body language.

Oblivious Actions: The Unconscious Cues of Body Language

In This Chapter

- ◆ The automatic nature of body language
- ◆ Developing unconscious competence in communication
- ◆ The power of first impressions
- ◆ Understanding intuition
- ◆ Human engineering

Think you're a pretty good reader of body language? Okay, tell me what your boyfriend or girlfriend (or spouse, if you're married) wore on your last date. What was the color of your professor's or boss's shirt last Monday? Did the person you last talked to gesture a lot? What gestures did they do?

Can't remember?

So maybe it's only other people's body language you aren't aware of, but you know all about your own. Okay then, what is the color and design of your socks? When is the last time you smiled? How many gestures did you use during your last conversation?

If you had trouble answering most or all of these questions, you're not alone. People aren't very consciously aware of one another's behavior—or their own. That doesn't mean they don't pick up some subtle cues from one another, they just aren't all that consciously aware of them. Some of the best body language is enacted and received mindlessly and automatically. Even though you're not aware of it, subtle, even unconscious behaviors subconsciously affect you! In this chapter, we will explore the actions that are such a vital—though not always conscious—part of body language.

Mindless Motions: The Langer Equation

One of the most amazing things about the human body is how well it functions on autopilot. Much of what we do and do so well is almost completely mindless. In fact, being mindful of ordinary actions like gestures, facial expressions, or postures can be detrimental in several ways. Mindfulness of our own body language can produce stilted performances that look unnatural, interfere with more important thinking tasks, and make us anxious or nervous.

Social psychologist Ellen Langer of Harvard University has found that reduced mental awareness, called mindlessness, is often advantageous, even essential, in many human activities. Langer's research shows that if some activity, behavior, or communication is very familiar to you, you're better off if you don't think about it.

But mindlessness can be damaging, too, especially in new situations or when novel events require us to be mindful and move beyond habit to conscious decision-making. Consciousness and mindfulness are most important when you are learning and mastering a new activity, and that is certainly true of both sending and receiving body language.

Nonverbally Speaking
Several communication studies show that we are able to recall as little as 10 percent of a conversation after 5 minutes, and we can recall even less body language. We are highly inaccurate even about with whom we interact!

Interestingly, Langer has found that both novices and experts have difficulty explaining a task to another person, whereas moderately competent people can easily explain a task. Novices are pretty clueless as to how to perform a new task, so obviously they have a lot of difficulty explaining it. Ironically, experts also have a lot of difficulty describing how a task is done because they have passively and mindlessly repeated it so many times that the steps are second nature; they do it automatically, but can't remember exactly how. Consciousness is an intermediate step in attaining competence.

Unconscious Incompetence

When we learn a new skill we seem like oblivious idiots.

When you first began riding a bike, driving a car, or giving a speech, you started out mindlessly and incompetently. A new driver may drift into another lane, unaware that he or she nearly wiped out another car. A novice speaker may rock back and forth at the podium and use "uhs" and "ums" after every word, unaware of the ineptitude of his or her delivery. Unconsciously incompetent people remain blithely unaware of their bungling behaviors. Only when a driving instructor or a speech teacher points out these mistakes do novices become aware of their actions and move to a state of conscious incompetence.

Conscious Incompetence

Hopefully, your driving instructor pointed out the most potentially fatal flaws, like not switching lanes without first looking in your rear-view mirror. With any luck your high school or college speech teacher helped you to stop boring an audience to tears with inept speech and bad body language. Instruction makes you conscious of your flaws.

Regrettably, this first flash of consciousness may actually make matters worse! You have moved from a bungling *oblivious* idiot, to a bungling *mindful* idiot, which is not necessarily a good thing. The introduction of consciousness may have made you paranoid, anxious, and self-conscious. The term *self-conscious* is revealing because it means more than self-awareness; it means ill at ease, insecure, and embarrassed. So consciousness can make an incompetent person embarrassed and ashamed, and can actually damage their self-esteem.

> **CAUTION**
>
> **Bodily Blunders**
>
> Embarrassing self-touching behaviors, called *adaptors,* usually occur outside of our awareness. People do not recall if they scratched an itch in an embarrassing spot or picked their nose, for example. But we must be subconsciously aware of adaptors, since we use more of them in private than in public.

Conscious Competence

Fortunately, consciousness is a gift as well as a curse. It enables learning and skill development. If humans are capable of anything, we are amazing learners. Compared to other living creatures that are mainly a network of automatic responses, reflexes, and instincts, human beings are capable of learning almost anything, including a whole lot about their own body language and the body language of other people.

Learning anything requires knowledge and practice. You don't learn how to drive a car, play the piano, or give a speech without knowledge and practice. Same goes for body language. Once you know what to look for, you have to become a people reader. Sit at a sidewalk cafe and watch passersby, look at people on a college campus or pro football game, pay attention the next time you go to a mall. Watch, listen, and feel. Practice your own body language by listening and expressing with your whole body.

Unconscious Competence

Most things you do well, you do unconsciously. That's right, you could almost do these things in your sleep. I'm not even talking about all that involuntary stuff like blood circulation, hormone secretion, and digestion that are entirely automatic. I'm talking about everyday activities like hitting a tennis ball, driving a car, and walking down the street. If you do these things competently, you do them mindlessly. It's only when things get tricky that conscious awareness creeps in to help out, like serving to the backhand of a great player with a mediocre backhand, changing lanes on a strange freeway in heavy traffic, or walking down an icy street. We know instinctively that the greatest performances are mostly mindless. Even basketball announcers describe a great performance by Michael Jordan, John Stockton, or Allen Iverson by saying, "he's unconscious!"

We use the same unconscious process to competently send and receive body language. To be a competent communicator, good body language has to be automatic. Take giving a speech, for example. Outstanding speakers use great gestures, fabulous facial expressions, marvelous movements, and wonderful words without ever thinking about these things. Why? Because, like riding a bike, their practice and experience has made these things mindless. Powerful presentations, inspiring interviews, and dynamic dates come from experience, training, and practice so that these things are completely natural and mindless.

If great speakers, interviewers, comforters, and listeners can be exceptional communicators unconsciously, what role does consciousness play? Why even be conscious? Research suggests that consciousness is the frosting on the cake and should be reserved for connecting with your audience, anticipating and correcting problems, and putting that delicious icing on an already delectable dessert. Consciousness shouldn't be wasted on the routine. The regular, ordinary, and usual should be habitual and unconscious. Consciousness is brought into play to move beyond the routine.

Unconscious Supercompetence

If you have watched hockey legend Wayne Gretzky score a hat trick, virtuoso Yo Yo Ma play the cello, links master Tiger Woods win a tournament, actor Tom Hanks get into character, or any other great performance, you are witnessing unconscious competence. But you are witnessing more than that. These people experience passion, flow, and delight that add a transcendent and inspiring quality to their performances and take those performances to an even higher level. Unconscious supercompetence adds exhilaration, enthusiasm, confidence, elation, and energy to an already competent performance.

The best communicators produce body language that is unconsciously supercompetent. People who communicate brilliantly in any situation—whether it's addressing a national convention, comforting the bereaved, or expressing affection—are relying upon natural instincts that are the essence of charisma. Unconscious supercompetence is the foundation of magnetic body language that others perceive as charismatic communication.

Positions of Power

Excellent, experienced public speakers universally report they are unaware of themselves while speaking. Competent communication requires getting out of yourself. But here's the paradox: If you *try* not to focus on yourself, you think of yourself even more! Instead you should focus on each member of the audience and the content of your talk. This is the path to greater competence.

Mindless Relationships

Research on mindlessness tells us that we become progressively unaware of our spouses' or close friends' body language over time because it becomes part of an everyday routine. One result is that we may think they still do things that they haven't done for years, like interrupting, seething with anger, or looking skeptical. So in long-term relationships we may get blamed for behavior we haven't done in years. We think we know these people so well that we no longer have to pay attention!

Likewise, if a wife has come to believe that her husband is loving or considerate, she may not notice when he slowly stops showing the affection he used to display daily. Research also suggests we take our long-term partners for granted. We may not touch our spouse as much we did years ago, but we aren't aware of the drop-off. Similarly, eye contact may unconsciously decline over the course of a relationship, diminishing connection and preventing the exchange of meaningful body language. Don't be mindless about your most important relationships. Make sure you continue to exchange body language with those you love.

Initial Impressions

Your initial impressions of other people are pretty mindless. It's only when a person is unusually beautiful, incredibly articulate, wildly incompetent, or sickeningly uncouth that we become conscious of our initial impressions of them. Most times, we make judgments and form stereotypes unconsciously and subliminally, based on physical appearance and bits of behavior. These stereotypes and intuitive impressions are both good and bad. Initial impressions are psychological shortcuts that are essential but often inaccurate.

Positions of Power

Habits are ingrained behaviors that save mental resources for other purposes. Ironically, awareness of those ingrained behaviors can produce self-conscious and stilted performances. So once you are satisfied with your body language, forget it! Economy in consciousness is necessary for competence in communication.

Body Talk

Attributions are people's everyday theories about the motives for others' behaviors, including body language. The fundamental attribution error is thinking somebody else's actions are the result of personality traits, rather than unique situations. Thus, it is easy to believe that your own angry reaction was simply due to a difficult situation, whereas your roommate's anger is because he or she is an angry person.

No Second Chance for a First Impression

It is an old cliché with so many implications for body language: You don't get a second chance to make a first impression. What's really bad about first impressions is that they truly stick. Research on *attributions* suggests that we tend to think other people's behaviors are a function of permanent disposition and traits. In other words, people think the way you behave the first time you meet is the way you always behave. Furthermore, people are grudging about changing their attitudes; we are mental misers. Once we form an attitude about someone, it takes a lot to change it. So what's the bottom line? First impressions are significant observations, so watch your body language! On the other hand, as a receiver, it is best to update your perceptions of other people. Their bizarre body language during an initial encounter could have been an anomaly, or they might mature or mellow over time. Impressions of others should be treated as tentative hypotheses, not as established facts. Wise people's impressions are not written in stone.

Halos and Horns

When someone forms a generally positive impression of another person based on an unrelated characteristic, we call it the halo effect. For instance, we tend to think that attractive people are intelligent, or smart people are honest, or famous people are experts. This is another one of those unconscious processes we do all the time. In Chapter 5 we will talk about the fact that physically beautiful people get all the breaks in everything from jury verdicts to job offers, from school grades to political elections. But the halo effect extends way beyond physical beauty. We tend to think that sports superstars actually know the tastiest beer or the coolest cars. We believe that Hollywood movie stars can help us select the best political candidates or mobile phone plans. The scariest thing about the halo effect is how mindless it is. It biases all of us, but we aren't aware of the illogic of our responses.

Lots of body language operates the same way. It is natural to like warm, friendly people, but because of the halo effect, friendly, attractive or socially skilled people get the job because the boss can't tell real warmth or attractiveness from competence. And how many people confuse confidence with ability, or social skill with intelligence?

> **CAUTION**
>
> **Bodily Blunders**
>
> Advertisers exploit the halo effect every day, because we automatically respond positively to people with high status, physical gifts, and good looks. Teach yourself to be media literate. Notice the nonverbal schemes that exploit our natural tendency to be biased by the halo effect.

Physical beauty creates positive initial impressions and halo effects that extend to other types of judgments.

(Image courtesy of Peter Andersen)

Your Incredible Intuition: Tuning Your Sixth Sense

Sometimes you get a feeling about somebody that tells you something just isn't right. It's a hunch, an insight, a sixth-sense, often called intuition. It's not based on analytic, logical skills we normally call intelligence. It's based on a different kind of intuitive intelligence that experts call syncretic cognition or spontaneous communication competence. Many scholars believe that intuition is actually heightened sensitivity to body language.

As you will learn in Chapter 26, legend has it that women are more intuitive than men. Research suggests that women are far more sensitive to body language than men, so legend may be right.

Evidence suggests that the right brain hemisphere, which is specialized for reading body language, excels at understanding patterns, taking in the whole picture, and understanding emotions. This is very different than logical analytic thinking. Indeed, tuning in to body language involves freeing your mind to see complete patterns and not thinking in logical, deductive ways.

Body language is best read as combinations of cues. To detect deception, for example, it is unwise to concentrate just on a person's voice or eye behavior, instead you should process the whole pattern. When detecting warmth, it would be fruitless to concentrate on just the face or gestures when all sorts of body language including, touch, timing, voice, space, and numerous other cues come into play.

Reading body language by using logic is like using words when learning to ski or snowboard. We best learn to ski by visualizing ourselves performing the right movements and actually practicing them, not by following verbal instructions. Thinking about skiing analytically could send you into a tree. Instead of thinking, "plant your pole, turn left, turn right," picture the path hot wax would take if it was flowing down the mountain. With body language, an image, like a picture, is worth a thousand words. Although you probably could learn to ski without visualizing movements, it's not going to generate your best performance.

Nonverbally Speaking
In an experiment, a trained broadcaster smiled when lecturing to one group of students and smiled little to another group. Researchers then asked participants in each group whether the broadcaster was warm and friendly and, if so, why they thought so. The group that saw the smiling broadcaster reported that he smiled, touched, and gestured more, though no touch or gesturing ever occurred! People mindlessly reconstructed that warm people do a bunch of warm behaviors, not just smiling!

When you read body language, tune in to feelings more than logic. I know it seems like a poor fit for Ms. Twenty-something to be dating Mr. Forty-something, and logic may suggest the relationship will fail. But logic is beside the point. Tune in to this couple's body language and ask yourself what kind of vibes you observe. Do they seem to be on the same wavelength, or is their body language completely out of sync? This kind of intuitive information is the data of body language. Which brings us to relationships.

The Silent Language of Relationships

In *My Fair Lady*, Eliza Doolittle says "When we sit together in the middle of the night, don't talk at all, just hold me tight. Anyone who's ever been in love can tell you that, this is no time for a chat." Similarly, anthropologist Gregory Bateson has said that "When boy says to girl, 'I love you' he is using words to convey that which is more convincingly conveyed by his tone of voice and his movements; and the girl, if she has any sense, will pay more attention to those accompanying signs than to words."

The language of relationships is body language. Think about the example from Chapter 2, where I described the various ways people use body language when greeting loved ones at the airport. In that case, actions spoke louder than words. Although natural language is great for abstraction, logic, and facts, it plays a secondary role to body language in relational communication. It is the authenticity and redundancy of body language that makes it so compelling. Talk is cheap and far easier to fake than body language. When it comes to relationships, the unconscious indicators of liking, loving, or loathing send the real messages.

Nonverbal Communication: The Science of Body Language

It's pretty obvious that humans are not random collections of disorganized cells. Take your eye or ear, for example. These sensory organs are meticulously engineered to function perfectly, or at least nearly perfectly. These organs are more than competent recorders: they are nuanced biocomputers capable of providing streams of detailed data that is instinctively meaningful. Humans' ability to generate and receive nuanced signals via body language is equally amazing. Just as scientists study the eyes and ears to figure out what caused them to be the way they are, researchers study body language to explain how we became so adept at it.

The science of nonverbal communication is to make the unconscious obvious, to unravel the mysteries of body language. For the past 30 years communication researchers, psychologists, and other social scientists have been systematically unraveling unconscious processes of nonverbal communication through multiple methods. We watch people in public and carefully record their behavior. Sometimes we observe people unobtrusively and then run up to them and ask questions about their attitudes, behaviors, and relationships. At times researchers have people keep logs or diaries or set off beepers at random times when people disclose their actions. Now and then we observe people in the lab and hook them up to polygraphs and other physiological equipment. We videotape and audiotape people and measure every possible behavior and action. When we are done, we analyze all of the data.

Nonverbally Speaking

If this book whets your appetite, check out the books on nonverbal communication by experts in the field like Laura Guerrero, Peter Andersen, Mark Knapp, Judith Hall, Judee Burgoon, David Buller, Martin Remland, Ron Riggio, Robert Rosenthal, Don Stacks, Miles Patterson, or Valerie Manusov to mention but a few. Or if you want to read original referenced research studies check out the *Journal of Nonverbal Behavior*, where a lot of the original research is published.

Unfortunately, much of what you read about body language in popular books and magazines is bogus. Make sure any book or article is associated with real research done by the most competent research scientists. Unraveling the mysteries of body language takes a lifetime of research and training, not just a job a journalist or a self-appointed body language expert.

The Least You Need to Know

- Most body language is communicated automatically and unconsciously.
- You are most skilled at body language when you are unconsciously competent.
- Initial impressions are mainly perceptions of other people's body language.
- Intuition is heightened sensitivity to body language.
- Body language is the core of close relationships.

Part 2
Body Basics: The Codes of Body Language

Body language is nature's multimedia presentation. Unlike talk, which after all is just talk, body language is a rich form of communication involving every part of your body.

Do the eyes communicate attraction, arousal, and authority? And what about your fabulous face, which is capable of sending hundreds of emotional messages? Is touch essential to human relationships, or does it just rub people the wrong way? Is attraction communicated through smell? Does time talk? And whom do you allow into your personal space bubble?

In this part, we will explore your entire body to see what it reveals to others and how you can read other people's bodies.

Chapter 4

The Eyes Have It

In This Chapter

- ◆ The importance of eye contact in communication
- ◆ Listening requires looking
- ◆ Eye contact and aversion regulates interaction
- ◆ The subtle causes and effects of pupil dilation
- ◆ The significance of eye movements

Your eyes are windows to the world. And they are the primary way you receive body language. You may not have realized it, but it's likely that your eyes are the primary way you *send* body language as well. When you interact with others, you look into their eyes most of the time. You would be considered rude, shy, distracted, incompetent, or catatonic if you fail to make eye contact during conversation.

Your eyes send dozens of other messages, too. Your pupil dilation or constriction makes you more or less attractive. Eye moisture is a clue to your mood. Eye movements are another important source of body language.

An Invitation to Communicate

The eyes send and receive more information than any other organ of the human body. *Eye contact* and *gazing* are essential to communication for both the sender and receiver.

Body Talk

Gazing is the act of looking at another person's face and body. Gazing becomes **staring** when it is done for an extended period of time or in an invasive way. **Eye contact** is a mutual gaze into the eyes.

Eye contact is an invitation to communicate. If you look directly into a person's eyes, I guarantee they will respond in some manner. When a gaze is reciprocal, a friendly interaction often ensues. Other times a person will quickly look away, suggesting they don't want to interact. We use this strategy on elevators, city busses, and airplanes if we don't want to talk to someone. In these cases we adopt a "nonperson" orientation to other people. When you fail to make eye contact, you fail to initiate communication.

Eye contact at any age is an invitation to communicate.

(Image courtesy of Laura Guerrero)

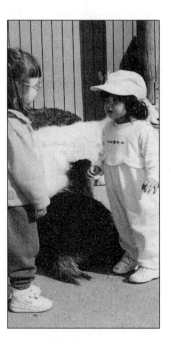

Most people do the same thing with hitchhikers. When a hitchhiker is standing right next to your car at a stop light and you don't want to pick them up, your best bet is to avoid eye contact and treat them like a lamppost, a "nonperson." If a hitchhiker catches your eye, you probably interact by offering apologizing body language or you feel compelled to give the person a ride. The same process occurs on city busses. We read or look out the window to avoid eye contact that would invite interaction. Unfortunately, we treat homeless people the same way. Most of us visually ignore homeless people who are begging on street corners. To look is to communicate, and then we fear we'll be delayed, have to give them money, or feel the need to help.

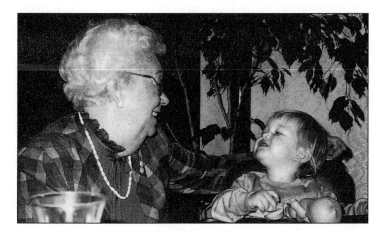

Eye contact sends messages of warmth and intimacy across generations.

(Image courtesy of Peter Andersen)

If eye contact lasts more than a second, people will "connect" and begin to talk, smile, or move closer to one another. Eye contact can be a key to establishing intimacy as well as forming a closer relationship. It is truly a connection that counts.

Eye contact is essential when you're listening. First, it tells your partner you are really tuned in and not distracted by other thoughts or activities. Second, it allows for smoother interaction by managing whose turn it is to talk. Third, and perhaps most importantly, it enables you to read your partner's body language. Without eye contact you have difficulty detecting emotions like fear or sadness, happiness or joy, shyness or excitement. Without eye contact you can't detect indecision, deception, empowerment, insecurity, decisiveness, or a host of other cues. Try this: Tonight really look at your partner when they are talking and don't interrupt except to ask leading questions. Something wonderful will happen!

Establishing Immediacy

Immediacy behaviors signal approach and availability, and send warm, stimulating messages to other people. A whole set of behaviors, including touching, smiling, nodding, facing others, showing relaxation, leaning toward others, and synchronizing our conversations, to mention but a few, are immediacy behaviors. Eye contact is at or near the top of the list of the most important immediacy behaviors. Flirting between new acquaintances always includes eye contact as a powerful immediacy behavior that strengthens their bond and communicates that courtship is occurring. Friends connect during conversations by looking at one another. Even long-term married folks maintain closeness and intimacy with eye contact and smiles.

Body Talk

A nonverbal **immediacy behavior** is any action that signals approach rather than avoidance and sends warm, friendly messages to others. Eye contact is one of the most powerful immediacy behaviors, but so is smiling, touching, sitting closer, or spending time with another person.

In new relationships, using immediacy behaviors will initiate communication and establish connection as long as these behaviors are not too warm or too intimate. Escalating immediacy is delicate development. Too slow and your new acquaintance may think you lack interest. Too fast and you may seem threatening or desperate.

Immediacy behaviors are the primary way we develop closeness and connection to other people. And the warm, immediate behaviors don't make you less powerful. In fact, these warm actions operate in concert with power behaviors to create the most effective leaders. Effective managers, parents, teachers, and doctors, use both warm *and* powerful body language.

In the classroom, eye contact is the most important immediacy behavior. Teacher eye contact shows confidence, controls classroom interaction, and enables teachers to read the body language of their students. Research by Dr. Janis Andersen of San Diego State University shows that increasing immediacy behaviors like eye contact dramatically improves motivation in the learning process. In classes with immediate professors, ones with expressive body language, students are motivated to read more, are more likely to follow the professor's advice, give higher evaluations of the instructor and the class, take other classes in the same subject, and pay closer attention in class. Amazingly, students' liking of a class and willingness to follow a teacher's recommendations increase by 60 percent or more in teachers who use immediacy behaviors like eye contact.

Positions of Power

If you want a powerful connection with your partner, stare into her or his eyes more intently than usual. You will pick up cues you never saw, and the connection will be significant.

A young lawyer, perplexed because she lost so many clients, contacted me one day. She had graduated high in her law school class, had won some of her first cases, and outside the courthouse seemed reasonably competent. As a communication consultant, my first goal was to assess what she did right and wrong and then offer some advice or training to improve her style. I entered her office and sat down on a soft chair opposite her desk. Lining the front of her desk was a whole set of law books, evidently placed there to enhance her credibility. Her voice emanated from behind the row of books, but all I could see was the top of her head. Quickly I removed the law books so we could make eye contact and establish some immediacy. Even with books gone she buried her nose in a legal pad and wrote furiously as I role-played a client with legal problems. I asked her to put the pad away and look at me. She complied and awkwardly began to make eye contact. She was uncomfortable without her pad and books, but gradually warmed up. We ended our first and only session with me reminding her to make eye contact with everyone she talked to, including clients, juries, and judges. For many of us, eye contact is a normal thing. But for others, looking at people is a divine revelation!

Positions of Power

Eye contact is an invitation to communicate. If you want to strike up a conversation or initiate a relationship, look at someone and smile. Their body language will tell you instantly if they want to communicate with you or not.

Elation Dilation

A lot of body language is pretty obvious if you look for it. But some body language is very subtle and even unconscious.

One of the most subtle and unconscious cues is pupil dilation. The pupil is the little black center of your eye that expands, or dilates, in dim light to let more light in and contracts in bright light to protect the eye.

Which woman is more attractive? More approachable? Most people pick the woman on the right, though few folks can identify pupil dilation as the reason.

(Images courtesy of Janis Andersen)

Your pupil unconsciously dilates to objects and events that you find attractive or interesting. Thirsty people's eyes dilate to pictures of cola or orange soda, unlike people who have just had several drinks. Hungry people's eyes dilate to pictures of hamburgers or french fries, but not the eyes of people who have just had a large meal.

Sex and gender differences also affect pupil dilation. Women's eyes tend to dilate to pictures of men, especially partially clad men but also nude men! (This dispels the notion that women do not like nudity, though it may be politically inappropriate to admit it.) Of course, men's eyes dilate to pictures of women, especially scantily clad or nude women! Most gay men don't display pupil dilation when viewing nude women but rather when viewing nude men, suggesting a pretty deep biological basis for homosexuality. In controlled settings, the pupils can provide clinicians with a diagnostic tool for sexual preference.

Virtually all women's eyes dilate to pictures of babies—even women who have no present desire to have children! This suggests that women have a deep affinity for infants. Men's eyes show little dilation to pictures of children, unless the men are fathers! Men's, but not women's, eyes dilate to landscapes, perhaps suggesting the more adventuresome nature of men.

Our eyes constrict to objects or scenes we dislike. Pictures of garbage, burn victims, or rotten food produce pupil constriction. If your boyfriend's pupils or girlfriend's pupils constrict when they look into your eyes, you may be in big trouble. But be careful—pupil dilation is difficult to consciously detect. Scientists have developed a device to measure pupil dilation called a pupilometer and a science of pupil dilation research called pupilometrics. Advertisers and marketers have used these devices in the marketplace to test unconscious attitudes toward products and advertisements.

It has been noted that blue-eyed people sometimes look less warm than brown-eyed or black-eyed people. Studies show that while many blue-eyed people are perceived as very attractive, they are thought to be less warm and loving than brown-eyed people. Get some pictures and compare Nicole Kidman to Jennifer Lopez. While both are extraordinarily beautiful women, J-Lo looks warmer, almost certainly due to the fact that her entire iris (the colored portion of the eye) appears to be one giant dilated pupil.

But the most amazing thing about pupil dilation is that other people instinctively detect dilation and constriction and unconsciously respond to these cues. Hordes of scientific studies have found that people with dilated pupils are perceived as more kind, attractive, and approachable. In my own research, I've found that women in identical photos with retouched pupils were perceived as more socially and physically attractive with dilated pupils than constricted ones! Interestingly, pupil size did not affect ratings of skill or ability to do a job, suggesting that the pupils are used as the basis of social and sexual interaction but not in work-related domains.

Which girl sends warmer and friendlier body language?

(Images courtesy of Janis Andersen)

Ekhard Hess and his colleagues at the University of Chicago conducted the most extensive series of studies on pupil dilation. In the most interesting of these experiments, Hess showed participants two pictures of a mother holding her baby. The photos were identical in all respects, except in one photo the mother's pupils were retouched to show contraction while the other showed dilation. Participants were showed the two photos and asked, "Which mother loves her baby more?" People unanimously chose the mother with dilated eyes but virtually none could say why! Most misattributed the source of their judgments and said things like, "Her face is more pleasant," "She has a warmer smile," or "She is holding her baby closer." This suggests two important points about body language. First, people form interpersonal impressions without knowing how or why they formed such impressions. Second, people are great rationalizers—they will make up reasons for things they believe even when they don't know why they believe them.

Nonverbally Speaking

Your pupils may give you away during interpersonal interaction. Research shows that your pupils expand when you are attracted to someone and constrict when you dislike somebody. Worse, others unconsciously detect these cues and find you warm and attractive when your pupils are dilated and cold and unattractive when they constrict.

Today we are justifiably proud of the sophistication of scientific research on nonverbal communication, including the research on pupilometrics. However, our ancestors were pretty smart, too. Many generations have known about pupil dilation even though they lacked the tools and the vocabulary that social scientists have today. Hundreds of years ago in Italy, wealthy women used a drug called belladonna, which is made from the poisonous, mildly hallucinogenic, but deadly nightshade plant. When these courtesans administered small amounts of belladonna to the eye, their pupils dilated, making them appear more attractive. Interestingly, the name for drug comes from ancient Italy and means "pretty woman" in Italian!

So here's how your pupils work. When you are attracted to or aroused by something, your pupils dilate. Other people unconsciously detect pupil dilation, which causes them to believe you are nicer, warmer, and more attractive. This is how a lot of your body language works: subtly and unconsciously, but powerfully.

> **Nonverbally Speaking**
>
> The green eyeshades traditionally worn by poker players do more than shade player's eyes from casino lights. They prevent other players from detecting the pupil dilation that would accompany a straight flush.

Ocular Organizers

One of the most important functions of eye contact is controlling and organizing interaction. When you fail to make eye contact with someone, you are treating her or him as a nonperson and inviting that person to *not* communicate.

Yet even when you choose to interact with someone, your eyes help regulate their behavior. Looking at someone is a nonverbal handoff that tells that person it's her or his turn to speak. If you are leading a meeting or teaching a class, looking directly at a person is a powerful turn-taking cue—it tells that person that you're giving him or her the floor. Similarly, some teachers can get students to stop talking merely by staring at them, without having to interrupt their lecture.

> **Positions of Power**
>
> When speaking to a group, make eye contact with every person in the room. You and your audience will feel the connection. Always start by looking and smiling at a positive person with a happy face. They'll smile back. You'll start a spiral of success. As you appear more connected and confident, the audience will become more attentive and connected, which in turn will bolster your confidence. Avoid making eye contact with the scowlers and skeptics at first. Once you and the positive people have connected, you can slowly pull in the negative folks.

Across the world, eye contact connects a speaker with an audience.

(Image courtesy of Peter Andersen)

Looking away at the end of a sentence helps you keep the floor. This is especially true if you keep the pitch of your voice steady and if you take a noticeable and audible breath. Similarly, if you cannot get a word in edgewise and want a turn, stare intently at your interaction partner as they are speaking. If the speaker pauses and makes eye contact, go for it—it's your turn. It may not have been an intentional handoff, but the exchange will be smooth and won't be considered an interruption.

Many of us use body language to turn-take naturally and mindlessly. But many people get interrupted easily because they have bizarre body language that defies normal interaction rules. One insecure colleague of mine would pause at the end of a sentence and look the people he was interacting with in an effort to elicit agreement. People would often chime in, believing that it was their turn to speak. My colleague often said, "Let me finish" due to his inept and confusing ocular turn-taking cues. Likewise, you probably know people who are always interrupting others. Many of these people fail to recognize the soft handoffs provided by eye contact and other body language cues.

Positions of Power

You can prevent people from interrupting you with this easy device. When you pause briefly at the end of a sentence, look away. Other people will find it difficult to take their turn. On the other hand, if you want someone to speak, pause at the end of the sentence and look directly at that person. Chances are he or she will take the soft handoff and feel obligated to speak.

The Look of Authority

Every successful person is occasionally perplexed with self-doubts and anxiety. This is particularly true for public speakers. Speaking in public is an extremely scary activity for many people. Indeed, public speaking ranks as the top fear of Americans in most opinion polls—topping terrorism, spiders, and even death itself. Eye contact is one of the keys to successful communication, and especially to competent public speaking.

> **CAUTION**
>
> **Bodily Blunders**
>
> Looking at someone with a direct stare and a blank facial expression can be a deadly combination. Positive facial expressions should accompany eye contact. Poker-faced stares are threat signals and can invite a fight, particularly if you stare at a stranger or a rival.

First and foremost, eye contact communicates confidence. Especially when combined with a slight smile, directly looking into the eyes of the audience makes you radiate strength and self-confidence. Second, the audience connects with you personally and it feels like you are directly communicating to each individual, not to some amorphous mass.

CLEM-ming Inside Your Head

Your eye movements can send messages of deception and truthfulness. One common stereotype is that "shifty-eyed" people are deceptive and untrustworthy. Although this is a widely held belief, shifty eyes are not one of the better deception cues, as you will find out in Chapter 12. But remember, from a communication standpoint, perceptions *are* realities. So, regardless of whether direct eye contact is really a deception cue or a truthfulness cue, people believe that shifty eye movements are deceitful and sneaky and treat shifty-eyed people accordingly.

> **Body Talk**
>
> When your eyes move left or right together, nonverbal communication researchers call these **conjugate lateral eye movements** or **CLEMS** for short.

In reality, scientists have found that shifty eyes— what they call *conjugate lateral eye movements*, or *CLEMS*—are signs of mental activity. In fact, the direction of your CLEMS is associated with the side of the brain you are using. Rightward CLEMS indicate left-hemispheric activity and are usually associated with real language, computing mathematical problems, and logical thinking. On the other hand, leftward CLEMS are associated with visual, spatial, and nonverbal communication.

Try this. Have a friend sit facing you. Ask him or her to spell Mississippi—chances are that they will look to their right (your left) while searching for the spelling. Next have your friend describe how to get from her or his house to work and back. Chances are your friend will look to their left (your right) during this task. Research suggests that this works particularly well for males, because they are more likely to use one side of the brain or another during these sorts of tasks than females. Women often use their entire brain when solving problems.

Some people habitually look one way or the other. People who look to their left when solving just about every kind of problem are thought to be "right-brained" and are the sort of people who rely on visual cues, spatial information, and body language. Right lookers may be "left brained" people, who are more likely to use logic and language and rely on talk rather than body language.

Nonverbally Speaking

A few years ago I was negotiating the purchase of a house from a man who always looked to his right. Suspecting he was a logical, verbal man, I carefully crafted my coldest, most logical arguments, and wound up getting my price. In this case, reading his body language as a guide certainly seemed to help me to negotiate the best price, but be careful about generalizing from a single event like this.

Eye movements while thinking are pretty common, and there is some evidence that they stimulate mental processes. This means that teachers should be careful not to misinterpret their students' CLEMS during test-taking as attempts to cheat. Rather, classroom CLEMS often stimulate mental activity and should be encouraged. Be a good body detective and learn the difference between devious glances at another student's test and CLEMS.

Likewise, novice speakers may use numerous CLEMS. They may look around the room as though their notes are written on the ceiling and walls. Over time, speakers should try to minimize CLEMS and use their eyes to connect with the audience, but CLEMS are okay when people are learning to do public speaking. In fact, calling attention to a beginner's CLEMS might produce even more anxiety than the person was already experiencing!

The Least You Need to Know

- Eye contact is an invitation to communicate.
- Listening requires looking.
- Eye contact and eye aversion can be used to regulate conversation.

◆ Eye contact establishes warmth, immediacy, and friendship.

◆ Pupil dilation subconsciously makes you more attractive to other people.

◆ Eye movements are signs of mental activity.

Our Fabulous Faces

- ◆ The halo effect: What's beautiful is good
- ◆ Your face reveals and conceals
- ◆ The universal nature of facial expressions
- ◆ How we manage facial expressions of emotion
- ◆ Characteristic of emotional expressions
- ◆ Internalizers and externalizers

When you face the world, it's crucial to put your best face forward. It's not so important to put your best foot forward, for in the era of the image, beautiful faces rule!

Like our eyes, our faces are keys to our emotions. They are also a way of communicating with body language across cultures and languages. People around the world recognize facial expressions and the emotions they display. Throughout our lives our faces go to management school for training more crucial to success than any MBA. We learn rules about how, what, when, and where we should show our emotions. But be careful— overmanagement can be injurious to your relational and personal health.

What's Beautiful Is Good

Ever since childhood you have been told "Don't judge a book by its cover." Well, it didn't work. Most of us still judge people by what we see. And when the cover is beautiful, we believe the person possesses all kinds of positive traits. What's really interesting is that, as noted in Chapter 3, beauty extends to all sorts of characteristics unrelated to physical appearance. Worse, most people are totally unaware of the extreme unconscious bias they have toward a beautiful face.

Sad but true, we don't give unattractive people a chance. From childhood through retirement we tend to avoid the fat, the ugly, the geeky dressers, the handicapped, and people who look old. Is it any wonder that the youth and beauty industry—from health clubs, to hair salons, to plastic surgeons—is booming?

Positions of Power _____

Here is some advice. As a reader of body language, look past looks. If you look beyond looks, you'll have better employees, better friends, and better marriages. As a sender of body language, however, realize that looks rule! Fashionable clothes, a nice-looking face, good makeup, and attractive hair will help make friends, obtain contracts, get dates, land jobs, and even help to get you acquitted in court!

It starts early on. Even in the lowest elementary school years, teachers believe that handsome, clean, and neatly dressed students are smarter than their less attractive classmates. And research shows that this produces a powerful self-fulfilling prophecy. Teachers see intelligence and initiative in the pretty kids and stupidity and sloth in the unattractive ones. This leads to an academic death spiral for some students, who come to believe they will fail and end up as failures as a result.

We believe that pretty people have nicer personalities even though there is no research that suggests that personality and looks are meaningfully correlated. We *think* pretty women are less hostile, more honest, better adjusted, more sexually responsive, smarter, and better educated. We *think* more handsome, bigger men are born leaders, more intelligent, harder working, more ethical, better lovers, more mentally healthy, and more skilled workers. As a result, more attractive people get more dates, more job offers, and higher starting salaries. As noted in Chapter 3, more attractive people profit from what is called a "halo effect," a process by which people generalize from one positive quality to other totally unrelated qualities. In our minds having angelic looks leads to angelic behavior, heavenly profits, and divine talents.

Studies from several countries, including the United States, have shown that more attractive male political candidates usually win. In the United States during the past century, only twice has the shorter presidential candidate prevailed. The recent election of a political novice, Arnold Schwartzenegger, for governor of California is the result of people's belief that good looks, a muscular body, and a charismatic image signify leadership qualities regardless of experience, morality, or competence. However, the same might not be true for female candidates; a few studies show that attraction makes little difference, and one study shows beautiful women are at an electoral disadvantage. Yet so few women hold high office in America that we don't really know if looks are an advantage or disadvantage. Until we have a larger group of females running for the senate, governorships, or president, we won't be able to undertake studies to find out.

Beautiful people even get breaks from juries. Researchers have shown that, even controlling for other factors, good-looking defendants were less likely to be convicted than their unattractive counterparts. Not surprising that Ted Kazinski fared a lot worse than O. J. Simpson! Even when they are convicted, sentences tend to be lighter for more attractive, better-dressed defendants.

When you need assistance, like money for a phone call or a jump for your car, it helps to be attractive. Studies show that such assistance is more easily obtained by good-looking people than less attractive ones, and this was true of both cross-sex and same-sex assistance. Handsome and attractively dressed petition-gatherers obtain more signatures, and people are more likely to follow a well-dressed man across the street against a red light than the same man in casual clothes.

It should come as no surprise to learn that the advertising industry exploits the halo effect many times each day. Sports heroes and supermodels tell us what cars to drive or what beers to drink. Quality department stores hire beautiful people to sell you products, and good restaurants employ attractive waitresses to give them a better image regardless of their service skills. Aren't you just a tad tired of beautiful bimbos—male and female—who read the TV news but have no idea what they're talking about or even how to pronounce the words on the teleprompter?

Darwin's Universal Faces

Long ago, Charles Darwin proposed that facial expressions are universal the world over. Like lots of other claims Darwin made, he was right on track with this one. There really are no unique emotional displays like Australian anger, Saudi surprise, Jamaican jealousy, Samoan sadness, or Danish delight (although, being Danish, I do delight in a good piece of cheese Danish now and then).

Years ago Crosby, Stills and Nash sang it well: "If you smile at me I will understand 'cause that is something everybody everywhere does in the same language." And they hadn't even read *The Complete Idiot's Guide to Understanding Body Language!*

Around the World with Universal Expressions

So how can you be sure that people show facial fear or happiness the same way all over the world? Paul Ekman and his colleagues at the University of California in San Francisco designed one of the best and most clever research projects to test this idea. Ekman and his associates traveled to places all over the world showing people pictures of facial expressions. Regardless of the culture, the races of the people, whether the cultures were literate or preliterate, or whether they were urban or rural, people everywhere identified the same emotions in the same facial expressions.

Could it be that people all across the world saw the same facial expression from television and movies? This hypothesis was disproved with data from isolated preliterate cultures in Asia and New Guinea who matched the same facial expressions with the same emotions as did people from all the other parts of the world. Now you know that New Yorkers can recognize the smiles of Somalians and Japanese can recognize fear in the faces of Frenchmen.

> **CAUTION**
>
> **Bodily Blunders**
>
> If you're from a big city don't be surprised if, when visiting a small town, strangers smile at you on the street. They are just being friendly and probably aren't going to try to swindle you or sell you drugs. And you small town folk, be careful of smiling at strangers in the big city—it may invite the wrong kind of interaction.

When an expression is universal, it probably is a biological, inherited behavior. Chimps, our closest cousins in the animal world, have really similar expressions to you and me. Check out ape expressions next time you're at the zoo. Pretty fascinating! And don't be surprised if some of the ape expressions remind you a lot of Uncle Scott's scowl or Grandma Gerty's grimace. Ape expressions are hardwired to their emotions the same way yours are.

How many innate, cross-cultural, universal facial expressions are there? Researchers agree there are at least six: anger, disgust, happiness, sadness, fear, and surprise. Other scholars add interest, shame, contempt, confusion, and excitement to this list.

Are there any differences in facial expressions across cultures? The answer is not many, though a few differences are worth discussing. The biggest variation across cultures is in display rules, which are instructions people learn in a given culture about when and where it is appropriate to display emotional expressions. But cross-cultural similarities in facial expressions dramatically outweigh the differences.

Looking Like the Blind

The universality of facial expressions strongly suggests that the production of emotional expression is a genetic characteristic shared by all members of the human race. What if we could observe the facial expressions of people who had no opportunity to learn facial displays? By studying children who were born blind and deaf, we can do just that. Children who are blind and deaf from birth have never seen a facial expression and have had no opportunity to observe other people's facial expressions and to learn from them.

German researcher Eibl-Eibesfeldt studied the facial expressions of a group of children blind from birth. Amazingly, when the facial expressions of these children were compared with normal-sighted, normal-hearing children, nearly identical facial expressions were produced for sadness, crying, smiling, laughing, pouting, fear, and anger. Could such expressions have been learned through touch? Not very likely, since even severely retarded babies display similar facial expressions to normal babies! (One difference was observed between blind and deaf versus sighted children: The blind and deaf children produce fewer facial expressions than sighted children.) Thus, another body of research seems to confirm that our expressive faces are part of human nature rather than collective learning.

Aping Expressions

So research indicates that facial expressions are genetically inherited rather than learned behaviors, but how far back do facial expressions go? Is this a development of human evolution, or do other species have facial expressions, too? If they exist in several similar species, they probably existed in our common ancestors, too.

Although pet owners think their dogs' and cats' facial expressions communicate the same emotions as humans (see Chapter 24), not too much research has been done on canine or feline expressions. But apes are another story.

The best bet in a search for facial expressions is to look at our long-lost cousins, primates. These apes bear the closest genetic resemblance to humans and had common ancestors fairly recently—recently, that is, if you think like geneticists and archaeologists, who consider 10 million years to be recent! Do apes have the same expressions you and I have? Without boring you with the scientific details, let me take you on a brief tour of research that's been done on two of my favorite emotional expressions, smiling and anger.

Sometime, watch two adolescent apes playing/fighting with one another. They will chase each other around the enclosure jumping on each other, wrestling, and making menacing sounds, which is why it's hard to tell if this is playing or fighting. Body language researchers call these "mock aggression displays," and adolescent humans do these, too. Anyway, at some point the larger teenage ape gets the upper hand in this play fight. The winner engages in an angry dominance display, which includes jumping up and down over his opponent, angry vocalizations, and a wide-open mouth bearing angry teeth about to bite the vanquished adversary. I think I actually saw an identical display by a wide receiver in a recent NFL game. Anyway, this body language, whether by ape or human, says "You are defeated, but instead of killing you I will just jump on you for a while to display my dominance!"

Meanwhile, the defeated ape is cowering beneath the dominant victor making pathetic little monkey whimpers. Zooming in on his pitiable, tiny monkey face, we see a giant smile with bared, closed teeth. His body language screams, "Don't hurt me, don't hurt me, I'm no threat, I don't bite!"

Scholars pretty much agree that the smile is a part of submission displays that evolved in ape and human ancestors and that say, "I am friendly, happy, and pose no threat." In many cultures smiling is more than just happiness; it signals appeasement, politeness, and friendliness. So even though we clever humans follow display rules for when and where to smile, the smile is there in our genes. Nobody had to teach us to smile.

Anger and dominance, on the other hand, involve aggressive supremacy displays in both humans and monkeys. During mock aggression displays, dominant moneys will engage in bogus biting and "gnaw-wrestling," with powerful postures, and a fierce facial expression that resembles a bite about to happen. These facial expressions are so easily recognizable that you can identify them in a dog or cat or scare the heck out of a three-year-old by simulating an angry face.

Your Innately Social Smiles

While smiling is an innate behavior, it is almost always displayed socially. Smiling in private is relatively rare compared to social smiling, which is relatively common. Robert Kraut of Carnegie Mellon University designed several imaginative experiments to test the notion that we are more likely to smile in social situations. First, he placed cameras at both ends of a bowling alley and watched bowlers' expressions. He found that after strikes, most bowlers' faces were pretty expressionless—that is, until they turned and looked at their friends, when they smiled.

Kraut also took pictures of fans at hockey games after their team scored a goal. When they were looking at the ice, even if their arms were raised in celebration, they remained pretty poker-faced. But when they turned to the fan beside them, huge smiles appeared on their faces. So here is the bottom line: Your face is programmed to send emotional body language messages *to other people*, not merely to reflect your internal emotional state. You are built for body language, and your face gives you a large vocabulary.

Your Emotional Motions

Your face produces a veritable cascade of emotional expressions. Rarely is the face still; even your motionless "blank" face looks like it is expressing boredom or displeasure. Your face is in virtually constant motion expressing one emotion after another.

Let's take a closer look at these six universally recognized facial expressions.

Happiness

Any child can produce a happy facial expression either in a drawing or with his or her own face. Of course, one characteristic of a happy face is a smiley mouth that is upturned at the corners. Interestingly, studies show the upper face, with raised cheek muscles and upturned lines at the corner of the eye, is even better at communicating happiness than the lower face. And research has shown that real happiness is more apparent at the corners of the eyes than the mouth. Deeply felt rather than forced smiles produce these characteristic wrinkles at the corner of the eye, and the absence of "smiling eyes" makes a smile seem a bit forced.

Sadness

Any kindergartener knows that a sad face includes a mouth that is turned downward at the corners. But sad faces are also composed of eyes that look like inverted almonds, turned down at the corner. Like happiness, sadness is actually more identifiable from the eyes and eyelids than the mouth. Sad faces, especially the faces of sad kids, look pitiful and seem to elicit comfort from other people.

Despite the happy Christmas context, this child is showing a classic unhappy face.

(Image courtesy of Peter Andersen)

Fear

Fear is a rapid expression, sometimes starting as surprise and quickly morphing to fearfulness. When you express fear, your eyebrows are raised, your eyes are open wide, and the corners of the mouth are drawn back, stretching the lips and sometimes revealing your lower teeth. The eyes have a creepy, distant, ominous look about them. Fearful expressions are highly contagious, and when one group member shows fear, fearful faces can reverberate around the room!

The fear expression is easily recognized regardless of age or culture.

(Image courtesy of Peter Andersen)

Anger

Anger is recognizable by knit, lowered, cantankerous-looking eyebrows, narrowed eyes, and a tense jaw, sometimes with the mouth open and the teeth exposed. It looks a little like a bite has occurred or is about to occur. What is really scary is that in some big cities nearly everyone has this angry look frozen onto their face, probably as some sort of preemptive display to ward off the angry people who are clearly everywhere. An angry face often produces an appeasement display or a retreat from others, but it can also provoke anger and even violence.

> **Nonverbally Speaking**
>
> Angry people make me mad. And research shows that they do the same to you. Given that facial expressions are contagious, I have a theory that certain cities and countries are caught in virtually endless spirals of anger expression.

Angry people, like other angry animals, look scary and vicious.

(Image courtesy of Robert Avery)

Surprise

Surprise is the most fleeting of facial expressions; it flickers across the face in less than a second. Think about it—it's hard to be continuously surprised! You can be intermittently surprised, but surprisingly, even that gets routine and unsurprising after a while. The surprise face is composed of rapid opening of the eyes, a rapid raising of the eyebrows such that the area above the iris, called the sclera, is exposed. Usually the mouth opens, the jaw drops, and the teeth are slightly parted. In about a second, pure facial surprise turns into surprised fear, surprised anger, surprised happiness, surprised embarrassment, or one of a number of other unexpected emotions.

The surprise facial expression is the most rapid and fleeting.

(Image courtesy of Peter Andersen)

Nonverbally Speaking

All over the world people perform a rapid eyebrow flash as a greeting. Try this: Catch the eyes of total strangers and quickly raise both eyebrows. I'll bet more than half the strangers greet you in return either verbally or nonverbally. Since this is a universal sign of recognition, don't be surprised if some people look confused as they try to remember where they previously met you.

Bodily Blunders

Twenty years ago, Mr. Yuck, a disgusted-looking cartoon-character with his tongue hanging out, appeared on medicine bottles and poisonous products to warn preschool kids about the danger of ingesting what was inside. Today Mr. Yuck is out of business. Most likely his disgusting little face was too yucky for the marketing departments of the pill companies.

Disgust

Not surprisingly, the yuckiest-looking facial expression is disgust. This expression originated with foul tastes and smells, but has become body language we save for foul people and foul actions. In the disgust expression the eyes are squeezed nearly completely shut, the nose is wrinkled, the mouth is turned downward, and in the most extreme cases, the tongue protrudes out and down. If your face was a turtle, disgust would result in pulling all your sensory organs (except maybe your tongue) into your shell.

Disgust is a universal, spontaneous facial expression.

(Image courtesy of Robert Avery)

Finding Differences Among the Similarities

Even though people around the world share many of the same facial expressions, there are vast differences regarding when it is considered appropriate to display those emotions. In the individualistic United States we tend to be externalizers, expressing whatever we feel. We let the communicative chips fall where they may and less frequently consider the consequences of our expressiveness. Other cultures, especially Asian cultures, find this individualist expressiveness to be odd, shocking, and even childish. Asians tend to use display rules and internalize most of their emotions. There is one exception: Asians smile a lot! But for Asians, smiling is a universal sign of politeness, not happiness. Americans are apt to think of Asians as incomprehensible, inscrutable, and uptight.

Going to Management School

Infants and small children show everything they feel, but as we grow up we learn to more carefully guard our emotions. Adults, especially adult men, tend to manage and internalize emotions rather than express them. Human societies are "management schools" where we learn to control our emotions and to display them strategically.

Internalizers and Externalizers

You all know the kind of person I am talking about: Erin Expresser! To Erin, an emotion felt is an emotion expressed. Life is one big drama. Her body language communicates excitement, sadness, joy, shame, and jealousy to any onlooker. Erin is what researchers call an externalizer, a person who shows all his or her emotions on the outside. And I'm sure you also recognize this guy, Inexpressive Ian, who throughout his teens never frowned or smiled and just recently, in his mid-thirties, has begun to show a clue or two that he even has emotions. Ian is an internalizer, a person who keeps his emotions inside, to himself.

Nonverbally Speaking

Now I know that it seems a skosh sexist to say that men are typically internalizers and women are usually externalizers. But, in reality, this pattern seems to prevail worldwide, suggesting biology may be at work. Your male ancestors may have evolved as more poker-faced because revealing emotions could be dangerous, especially emotions like fear, weakness, or guilt. Your female ancestors may have benefited from emotional expression, especially in communicating with infants and toddlers. (We will discuss sex difference in body language in Chapter 26 if you are still along for the read.)

According to communication professor Ross Buck of the University of Connecticut, externalizers are much easier to read and adjust to. Their body language is highly accessible and researchers view these folks as skilled and accurate senders. Externalizers make better initial impressions, are easier to talk to, and may have an easier time establishing relational closeness.

Internalizers manifest few facial expressions but show much higher indices of internal responses on measures like heart rate, blood pressure, and electrodermal response.

Positions of Power

This is a tip for men: Failing to use facial expressions may be associated with heart disease, stroke, and even cancer. So start to retrain your face. When you're talking to your wife or girlfriend, use facial expressions when both speaking and listening. And here is a bonus: Your partner may feel closer to you as you begin to use your face expressively.

Given that little boys tend to be emotionally expressive, it is likely that the internalization predisposition of many males is more learned than innate. Internalizers are perceived to be emotionally unavailable, a comment that is often made by women about their male partners. Now really, can you imagine many men complaining about their partners' emotional unavailability? But the lack of facial body language is a real issue for women who associate love and intimacy with emotional sharing. So guys, give it up a little. Express yourselves a tad, especially with your partner. And women, don't expect a male partner to be as emotionally available and focused as your closest girl friend.

Finally, here is an important item about your health or the health of your loved ones. The internalizing body language, which men are more likely to employ, raises most physiological responses such as heart rate, blood pressure, and stomach acid. Could this lead to health risks and early death? Research suggests that the answer is yes! Internalizers have more coronary disease, heart attacks, and strokes! And evidence also suggests internalizers may be more cancer prone, likely to develop arthritis, and have more dermatological problems. Using body language as well as speech to express your emotions is vital for good relational and physical health. This is particularly true for men, who are mostly internalizers and have more heart disease and strokes. The fact that male life expectancy is nearly a decade shorter than women may, in part, be due to emotional internalization. So learn to express yourself. Your relational and personal health may benefit greatly.

Display Rules

Check out the face of a two-year-old sometime. What they feel is what they express. There is no control of facial expression whatsoever. You don't have to be a mind reader to know what the child is feeling—the face says it all. Research shows that with each year from kindergarten through the end of high school people show fewer and fewer emotional expressions. We call this maturing, growing up, decorum, and good manners. As an adult, I'm sure I don't make the disgust expression at the taste of my hostess's asparagus soufflé, even though I might really want to!

The conventions regarding when it is appropriate to make an expression are called display rules, and though these rules differ from culture to culture, each culture expects that adults have mastered them. While it may be deceptive not to show your true feelings all the time, it is part of communication competence. People who randomly display their feelings via body language in any situation are thought of as incompetent, unskilled, childish, or just plain nuts. Competent facial management is so well learned that you probably never think about how many hours each day you spend controlling your face and concealing your true feelings.

Unlike today, when people say cheese and smile for photos, these 1911 immigrants to America reflect the seriousness of their venture.

(Image courtesy of Peter Andersen)

Dislay rules are mastered in each culture as children mature and develop. Most display rules are versions of the following five types of emotional presentations:

- **Social simulation.** The is when you express feelings you don't have, like smiling at your mother-in-law's new polyester dress (a blue-light special and bought on sale), looking sad over an enemy's misfortune, or surprised at the not-so-surprising surprise party you knew about for months. Every day you unconsciously and competently simulate expressions of interest, happiness, surprise, or sadness that you just don't feel.

- **Intensification demonstrations.** This is when you show more feelings than you actually have. Sometimes you feel an emotion but need to produce an even greater emotional display than you actually feel. Examples might be getting teary-eyed at your long-lost Uncle Louie's funeral when you barely knew the guy, or looking happy and surprised at the cool clip-on tie Aunt Alice gave you for Christmas. We look interested during boring speeches and look worried over a friend's trivial troubles, all in the name of social appropriateness.

Body Talk

Micromomentary facial expressions are fleeting facial expressions that last less than a fifth of a second—a fleeting smile or smirk leaked during a serious moment, for instance. These expressions can be subconsciously processed by observers, leaving them with lingering questions about our insincerity. We often call these lingering questions intuition.

- **Expression inhibition.** This is giving the appearance of having no feelings when you really have feelings. Little boys learn to "be a man" and show no fear, while little girls are taught it is not "ladylike" to act out anger. You may try to keep a straight face during your boss's pratfall or try to show no happiness over the firing of an inept colleague. But complete inhibition is hard, and our feeling may leak in the form of *micromomentary facial expressions.*

- **Motion miniaturization.** Sometimes you want to lessen or de-intensify an emotional expression. An enraged parent might tone down his or her act to mild dissatisfaction in response to a child's misbehavior. Your desire to laugh turns into small smirks, jealous rage transforms to a dirty look, total lust becomes a flirtatious smile, or complete panic is transformed to mild worry. Preserving your image and maintaining face is so important that you deftly miniaturize your expressions, often with no awareness you have done so. On the other hand, you may deliberately understate emotions as part of your effort to be a more strategic communicator.

- **Emotional masking.** Masking is the most deceptive of the display rules. Here you cover an emotion with a totally different expression. Sadness at a colleague's undeserved promotion is covered by elation. Pleasure in a minister's faux pas is covered by looks of religious reverence. Fear of speaking in public is covered by confident looks and proud smiles. Of course, when you see through an emotional mask, you tend not to trust the person.

Facial Styles (Your Signature Style)

So now you know that emotional facial expressions are inherited. Psychologist Paul Ekman has shown that facial expressions are basically the same all over the world.

Furthermore, this genetic trait must go back a long way, because our closest cousins in the animal world, chimps, have really similar expressions to you and me. Ape expressions are hardwired to their emotions the same way yours and mine are.

The Least You Need to Know

- ◆ Beautiful faces tend to be successful faces.

- ◆ Your face reveals and conceals.

- ◆ Facial expressions are innate and culturally universal.

- ◆ Display rules tell us how to manage our emotions.

- ◆ Each emotion has a unique expression.

- ◆ Internalizers and externalizers display emotions differently with dissimilar consequences.

Chapter 6

Digital Communication: Reach Out and Touch Someone

In This Chapter

- Therapeutic touch across the lifespan
- Sexual signals via tactile communication
- Types of tactile body language
- Getting under the skin: the risks of touch
- The language of touch in your close relationships

It's really "touching" to think that, in your loving relationships, touch is your most intimate form of body language. But touch has a bright side and a dark side. Touch can compel or repel, comfort or threaten, sexually stimulate or sexually harass. The power of your touch to create lasting bonds in your closest relationships is unmatched by other forms of body language.

Tactile body language, technically called *haptics*, is a multifunctional action. It plays a central role when you communicate tenderness, sexuality, reinforcement, love, threat, and support. In this chapter, I'll try to help you understand your own tactile behavior and the touching behavior of others. We'll consider tactile transgressions as well as the power of touch to heal, attract, and create loving connections.

From Cradle to Grave

Throughout life, touch is your deepest and most intimate connection to the ones you love. When you were an infant, touch was an essential connection for comfort, nourishment, warmth, love, and, as research shows, for life itself. Researchers have found that *tactile deprivation* is terrible for a child and can actually be life-threatening. Numerous studies of children living in orphanages, kids who are isolated due to immune system problems, and children living in abusive homes show that depriving a child of touch can retard and even kill them. These studies show that children who are deprived of touch are usually sickly, socially maladjusted, quiet, overweight, devel-opmentally disabled, and have difficulty learning. In Chapter 14, we will discover that it is difficult to touch a baby too much. Babies totally deprived of touch experience failure-to-thrive syndrome, which involves weight loss and eventual death.

Body Talk

Technically, the study of tactile communication is called **haptics.** Studies have shown that tactile communication is psycho-logically and physically benefi-cial. A hug a day may keep the doctor away. So be healthy, be happy, be haptic.

Body Talk

Being denied sufficient touch is called **tactile depriva-tion.** This is a serious situation that can leave an adult lonely, desperate, stressed, and in ill health. It's even more serious for babies, sometimes even causing death.

Your sense of touch develops earlier than your other senses. While your recollection is probably a bit hazy, your first sensations of body language were in the uterus.

If you are a mother, the physically closest you will ever be to your child is before your child was born, followed only by breast-feeding. Though breast-feeding has gone in and out of vogue at various times in America, there is little doubt of its benefit to Baby or Mom. For Baby, what form of body language could be more comforting, intimate, and bonding than feeding from Mom? And research shows some amazing long-term effects of breast-feeding, such as a stronger immune system, better psychological adjustment, and higher reading scores. Of course, when Baby is fed from a bottle it can still be an inti-mate body connection that even Dad can enjoy!

Hugs communicate warmth for all people at all ages.

(Images courtesy of Peter Andersen)

Babies thrive on stimulation, so touch is vital to their world. Watch a six-month-old as you hand her or him an object. The baby will look at it, feel it, shake it, and, of course, taste it. Tactile body language is a central part of the baby's ability to process and understand the world he or she lives in, especially their social world. (We will examine baby body language in more detail in Chapter 14.)

In infants as well as adults, touch centers of the brain occupy a disproportionably large part of the cerebral cortex, suggesting that humans are predisposed to comprehend the world through the tactile body language of oneself and others.

By the time a child reaches school age, their world of touch is changing. They still need and like a parent's cozy and comforting touch, but at the same time they are starting to rebuff some parental touch. When I was six or seven, I would sit on my mother's lap in our car (yes, this really was before seatbelts!). As soon as we got near home, I would quickly leap off my mom's lap so my little baseball and football buddies wouldn't think of me as a momma's boy. Such is the life of kids torn between two tactile worlds.

In the early school years, some kids reject opposite-sex touch. During this so-called latency period, girls may find boys disgusting and vice-versa. Kids are developing space boundaries and often don't like touch from other kids. At the same time, kids still need a lot of touch. Ask any kindergarten or first grade teacher and they will tell you they are proxy parents. When I used to tutor second-graders, each morning I would arrive before class to read a book to them. Immediately two or three would hop up onto my lap and another five or six would crowd around, all in tactile contact with one another. It's truly a storybook dog-pile that you would never find among 10- or 12-year-olds, who are way too cool to touch that much. Teen touch is a whole different story, one we will discuss in more detail in Chapter 15. Suffice it to say that touch takes on whole new meanings and challenges for teens.

Youth is cherished in America, even worshipped. Youthfulness is considered beautiful, and unfortunately, the loss of youth is stigmatizing and dishonored in our culture. Instead of being revered and respected, as elders are in some cultures, in America the elderly are frequently shunned, sequestered, and avoided. Studies of the elderly, especially those in nursing homes, suggest that their lives are often devoid of touch. The very small amount of touch that the elderly receive is mostly functional and instrumental touch, not soothing or intimate touch. As a result, the elderly experience severe tactile deprivation with negative consequences to their emotional, relational, and physical health.

Touch Types

All touches are not created equal. We use different kinds of touch to convey different meanings: a pat and a squeeze are used to communicate different things. The location of the touch also makes a difference in its meaning: A touch on the shoulder is not the same as a touch on the chest. Likewise, touch is used for different purposes: An examination from a doctor is not the same as flirtatious touching by a lover. Let's look more closely at where and how touch communicates.

Location Is Everything

Research suggests that the location of your touch is a critical element of body language. Generally, the safest place to touch men is on the shoulders, hands, or arms. Depending on the nature of your relationship, touching a man in other areas may be taboo. Opposite-sex friends can touch most men anywhere above the waist, but same-sex friends better stick with the shoulders, hands, and arms.

The safest place to touch women is on the shoulders, arms, small of the back, top of the head, and hands, but this also depends on the relationship. In addition to these locations, opposite-sex friends can usually touch the knee but not the thigh. The most taboo regions are obviously the genital regions, the chest for women, and the thighs and the buttocks for both sexes.

Purposes of Touch

Communication scholars and psychologists have studied the many ways we use touch. Touch is a versatile form of body language that we use in many ways, including the following:

◆ **Professional touches.** No, we aren't talking about prostitutes! Many professionals— from chiropractors to dental hygienists, from hair stylists to surgeons, from athletic trainers to tailors—touch you as part of their professional roles. Just because it's professional doesn't mean it can't be pleasurable, though. Getting your hair washed, a massage, or a chiropractic adjustment might be functional, but it can also feel really good.

Professional touch, which includes hearty handshakes and shoulder touching, conveys positive initial impressions.

(Image courtesy of Peter Andersen)

◆ **Tactile etiquette actions.** Frequently you touch because good manners and civility require it. You shake hands at a business meeting. You help Aunt Hilda with her coat. You give a teammate high fives after a basket. These are virtually mandatory touches, and their absence is an interpersonal indiscretion. Most important is the handshake, which should be firm and confident but not macho or injurious. Handshakes are a crucial kind of body language that creates powerful interpersonal impressions.

◆ **Influential actions.** Requests accompanied by light touches on the shoulder or arm are great for gaining compliance. Studies of petition-gatherers, doctors, waitresses, moms and dads, strangers asking for change, or any persuader show that light touches make requests harder to refuse.

Bodily Blunders _____

Handshakes create lasting impressions. The three biggest body bungle handshakes are as follows:

- ◆ The nonshake: communicating disrespect and poor manners.
- ◆ The Myron Milquetoast, limp-wristed, or dead-fish handshake: communicating weakness and apathy.
- ◆ The bonecrusher: communicating insecurity or rudeness.

◆ **Haptic healing.** Research reveals that touch can heal. People, especially children, who get a lot of touch, are much more likely to be free of illness. Likewise, the arts of massage and acupressure can soothe, relax, and heal. Chiropractic alignments and exercises by physical or occupational therapists are other kinds of healing touch. Although more research is needed in this area, there can be little doubt that touch can heal.

◆ **Playful touches.** Like our distant cousins, the chimpanzees, a lot of our touching is playful. Most boys, and even some men and girls, engage in "mock aggression displays" or play fighting. Fake punches, play wrestling, teasing touches, tickles, and feigned affection are all actions designed to frivolously connect with others while sending messages that the actions aren't serious. Of course, fake affection and mock aggression can be mistaken for the real thing, so it's important that your body language says "play in progress."

◆ **Closeness cues.** Our friends and family are usually the recipients of frequent hugs, cuddles, high fives, and comforting strokes. These behaviors are the glue that holds close relationships together by communicating warmth and intimacy. But be careful! Too much tactile intimacy with friends may signal romantic interest and destabilize the relationship.

◆ **Loving touches.** Loving touches are warm, involving, and intimate forms of body language. Snuggling with your spouse, holding your grandchild on your lap, or hugging a close friend are examples of warm, intimate touch that sends loving messages in our most important relationships.

◆ **Sexual touches.** Sexual touch is designed to arouse and should only be used in romantic relationships that have mutually arrived at the stage of sexual desire and consent. Similarly, even with a long-term sexual partner, such touch should be reserved for the right moments, in the right frames of mind, in the right contexts. As the saying goes, timing is everything!

The Ties That Bind

Touch connects you with other people. Field observations by anthropologist Desmond Morris and his team have discovered 457 types of body contact that can be summarized in 14 categories of "tie signs." Tie signs are tactile body language that signals an interpersonal relationship or social intimacy. Let's look at the 14 tie sign categories:

♦ **The handshake** is the most formal and least personal of tie signs but one of great importance in your initial interactions and after long absences. It is amplified and personalized by secret handshakes, variations like high fives, and handclasps that use the left hand squeeze-play as an intensifier. If you're really into it, a handshake becomes an embrace, which is another kind of tie sign.

♦ **The body-guide** is an intimate version of pointing or showing someone the way. Typically the guider places her or his hand on the small of the other person's back and steers them forward lightly. While originally considered polite, the fact that adults often use it with children sometimes makes it a pushy or condescending gesture when used with other adults. So beware of these haptic hurry-ups and controlling contacts!

♦ **The pat** is primarily a parent-child touch, but a pat on the back also can be used as a reward for a job well done. Some affectionate pats are actually miniature hugs. Be careful of pats on the head. They are okay for Rover, Fluffy, or even a small child. But adults, especially women, hate pats on the head because of their condescending connotations.

♦ **The arm-link** is a sign of coordinated walking and most typically used with the aged or infirmed. Often the female hooks her hand through the bent arm of a male to communicate closeness. Younger healthy couples rarely use the arm link unless they are arriving at a formal place such as a banquet, church, or award ceremony.

♦ **The shoulder embrace,** an arm around another person's shoulder, is a tie sign mainly employed by males. Given that the shoulder is not a taboo or highly sensitive area, males can use the shoulder embrace for both female friends and male buddies. Some people believe it is a possessive behavior, so depending on the relationship, it may be loved or loathed.

♦ **The full embrace** or hug is used in your close relationships, especially during greetings or farewells. Young lovers may use this tie sign at any time as a romantic and even sexual signal. Slow dancing is a socially sanctioned form of the full embrace.

- **Hand-in-hand walking** is a significant tie sign for couples, who use it to signal that they're romantically linked. It is also used with children and with people of any age in a crowd or crossing a busy street. Hand holding is an egalitarian action since nobody has "the upper hand" unless someone takes the lead or gives someone "a hand" by pulling them uphill or through a crowd.

- **The waist embrace** is a mobile hug that signals more intimacy than walking hand in hand. A more intimate version of this occurs when young, strolling lovers slide their hands into the back pockets of their partners!

- **The kiss** comes in many forms, but the location, duration, pressure, and depth of kiss send crucial body language messages. Kisses range from "French" or tongue kisses of young lovers to brief, light "pecks" on the lips or cheek with a relative. In some cultures, light kisses on the cheek or lips occur between friends, even same-sex friends.

- **Hand to head touching** is indicative of an intimate relationship because the head is a sensitive and personal area. Head pats can be condescending, but head strokes or massages are sensual, intimate, and even sexual. Confine these touches to intimate relationships. You can touch a stranger on the shoulder, but don't touch them on the head.

- **Head to head touches** are intimate behaviors used by lovers and spouses. On occasion, this posture is also used in close relationships when two people are tired and use one another's shoulders and heads as human pillows.

- **The caress** is body language that is sometimes sensual but usually sexual. Caresses generally rub, stroke, squeeze, or explore part of your partner's body. It is the central tie sign of young lovers. Caresses must only be used in your closest relationships; this is a form of body language that can literally "rub someone the wrong way."

- **The body support** is used by the able-bodied to support children, the sick, or elderly. When used by teens or adults, it is a playful, intimate form of body language. A ritual form of this behavior is carrying the bride over the threshold of a new home. A playful form is carrying your partner over a puddle or riding "piggy-back." Carrying a person who has fainted or supporting a drunk who cannot stand are rescue behaviors that are very socially supportive forms of tactile body language.

Positions of Power

Most touch in close relationships communicates warm and intimate body language. However, some touches, such as head pats, pushes, pokes, or tugs, can be perceived as very condescending or controlling. Watch out for these touches to avoid being a tactile tyrant.

◆ **The mock attack** is a playful form of body language generally used among male friends, although women may do this with their fathers, brothers, or husbands, and even lovers may tease and titillate with mock attacks. These include arm punches, hair ruffles, ear nibbles, grabs, mock headlocks, pushes, and even tackles.

Avoiders and Approachers

I have always been fascinated with this question: Why do some people love to be touched and others can't stand it? For 25 years I have been doing research on *touch avoidance* with colleagues and graduate students. Interestingly, my fellow researchers and I have found that touch avoidance comes in two forms: same-sex avoidance and opposite-sex avoidance.

Researchers know that touch avoidance is partly genetic, since little babies only a few days old will seek or shun touch. Much of touch avoidance, though, is cultural and climatological. People from the Northern Midwest; Northern Europe; much of Asia, but especially Northern Asia; and former British colonies such as Canada and Australia tend to avoid touch. People who are descended from the Mediterranean or the Caribbean and even the southernmost parts of the United States tend to be touch approachers. Religion, too, plays a part. Women from Muslim and Hindu countries and fundamentalist Protestant men and women are more likely to be touch avoiders, whereas Jewish people and agnostics tend to be touch approachers.

Body Talk

Touch avoidance is a personality trait that determines the degree to which you like or dislike touch.

The roles and life stages through which you are passing also determine your degree of touch avoidance. Older people are more avoidant than younger people, married people are generally more avoidant than single people, and people with parents who did not touch—especially fathers—are more avoidant than those with touchy-feely folks. Likewise, parents who used a lot of spanking and hitting have more touch-avoidant offspring.

Research has shown the deep-seated nature of touch avoidance. In one experiment, slight touches were used on both touch avoiders and touch approachers during an interview. Touch avoiders disliked the experiment and the experimenter when they were touched and liked both when they were not touched. Conversely, touch approachers liked the experiment and the experimenter more when they were touched and less when they were not touched.

In another experiment, participants were asked to pick up a chair and set it up near an interviewer. Touch avoiders set up the chair significantly farther from the interviewer than the touch approachers. Literally, touch avoiders stay "out of reach" and "out of touch." This and other studies suggest touch avoidance represents a deeper-seated avoidance of intimacy. An approach orientation and comfort with touch are associated with higher self-esteem and better interpersonal relationships.

Positions of Power

If you carefully observe the nonverbal reactions of friends and loved ones, you can learn whether they like or dislike touch. Touch approachers stand closer and purr like cats when you touch them. If you touch approachers, they will not only like the touch, they will like you much more. But your relationship will go downhill if you touch a touch avoider more than absolutely necessary.

Tactile Transgressions

Your touch can be compelling but also repelling. Tactile transgressions are touches you really should avoid. Using a little common sense will help you avoid offending others, tainting your reputation, and bungling relationships.

Rubbing Someone the Wrong Way

Your tactile body language can literally rub someone the wrong way. But how do you know when this is happening? The answers to the following six questions will help you out:

◆ **Is this person from another culture that has different touch rules?** Culture is a force as powerful as human nature itself. Many people from other cultures think our culture is weird: materialistic, individualistic, and unruly. But we tend to think that other cultures have pretty weird body language, too. The body language of central Asian men kissing each other's beards, topless women in some isolated tribes, veils or burkas worn by Moslem women, and men in the South Pacific and Africa in what look like dresses seem pretty odd to most Americans. What is normal to one culture can be really weird to another. Jimmy Carter, our friendly, smiling southern president, once kissed Mrs. Sadat, the first lady of Egypt, on the podium before a speech. Her retreat and revulsion represented pretty clear body language. Make sure the types of touch that are okay in your culture are also okay in other cultures. And if you aren't sure, ask.

◆ **Does this person like me?** Most people really like touch from people we find rewarding. Research by myself and by Professor Judy Burgoon of the University of Arizona has independently revealed that we like close distances and touch from people we find rewarding and attractive. This includes people we find physically attractive, high-status people like presidents and celebrities, socially attractive people like our closest friends, and clean, well-dressed people. By contrast, think about how little you like being touched by filthy people. Attraction is in the eye of beholder, so you need to honestly assess how much someone likes you before you touch them.

◆ **Does the person I'm interacting with like touch?** As we discussed previously, some people just don't like to be touched. But short of a complete psychological inventory, how do you know? Here are a few clues! Does a person have closed rather than open body language? Do they stand far rather than close? Do they avoid touching you? If the answer to these questions is yes, take it slow. Your friend may not like touch and will take a longer time to warm up to it than most people.

◆ **Is this the right situation?** Kissing your wife in the bedroom or even the living room is just fine, but kissing her in the office or the boardroom may be the wrong place or the wrong time. Be sensitive to situation and context. Similarly, be careful of public displays of affection. Some people are uncomfortable with it, and it's not always considered to be socially appropriate.

◆ **Is my partner in the right mood?** If your spouse says, "Not tonight dear, I have a headache," take his or her word for it. People might not want a back rub if they have to get up in four hours, might not be sexually responsive when they are all stressed out, might not be very lovey-dovey when they are angry, or might not be in the mood for playful touch when they are sad. Reading a partner's body language is critical to assessing their mood, and their mood is a key to whether touch will be considered appropriate or inappropriate.

◆ **Is it the right relationship?** As we will discuss in the next section, relationships are the key. If you have a warm, consensual, loving relationship, most touch will be okay.

> **CAUTION**
>
> **Bodily Blunders**
>
> Touch creates a wonderful bond between people, but be careful! What you think is playful, your partner may think is painful. What you think is teasing, a co-worker might think is harassing. What you think is friendly, a friend could find embarrassing. No form of body language requires more discretion and other orientation than touch.

Relationship Realities

Relationships rule! Research on body language and relationships is making clear that relationships trump other forces, even the individual, when it comes to determining whether touch is appropriate or not. In several studies I conducted on unwanted intimacy, the relationship was the key. People were asked to write about experiences in which they felt someone had been too intimate with them and why. The majority of participants said that it was the relationship that made the touch inappropriate. People said things like: "My boss at the restaurant has no right to touch me like that. This isn't a personal relationship, it's a work relationship." "My girlfriend's roommate had her hands all over me. Maybe she was just being friendly, but heck, she is NOT my girlfriend and it made me really uncomfortable." "I really like this guy a lot but on our second date he was all over me. Now, maybe I am old fashioned, but I like to get to know a person for a while before we do that stuff." The relationship holds the key. Any of these behaviors would have been fine in the right relationship, at the right relational stage.

Nonverbally Speaking
Most tactile transgressions occur in new or professional relationships where touch just isn't appropriate. Always err on the safe side. Until you have become close to another person emotionally, relationally, and psychologically, avoid body messages that appear harassing or excessively intimate.

In studies of sexual harassment and sexual assault, relationship boundaries once again took center stage. In the right relationship at the right time and place, almost any kind of touch is potentially okay, so long as it doesn't hurt or injure. But most sexual harassment complaints come about not because people hate touch, not because they find the person unattractive, and not because he or she isn't a nice person. Sexual harassment usually occurs because it crosses the boundary of an appropriate working relationship.

The Least You Need to Know

◆ Touch is essential for health throughout life.

◆ The location and type of touch is central to its meaning.

◆ Not everyone likes touch. You need to know if a person is an approacher or avoider.

◆ Don't rub people the wrong way.

◆ Touches are "tie signs" that connect people.

Chapter 7

Nice Gestures: Communicating with Your Hands and Arms

In This Chapter

◆ Sign language: a body language that is a language

◆ Emblems: gestures with dictionary meanings

◆ Talking with the hands: speech-related gestures

◆ The meaning of self-touching behaviors

◆ Synching together: matching others' gestures

Like so many things about people, hands and arms are unique in the animal world. Not only are hands handy for holding tools, they are perfect for communicating.

The focus of this chapter will be on gestural body language, gestures that have no dictionary definition but that are highly meaningful nonetheless.

Though they differ slightly from culture to culture, gestures are a universal form of human communication. But before we look more closely at gestural body language, let's take a minute to consider sign language. As noted in Chapter 1, unlike body language, sign language is a true language.

A Body Language That Is a Language

People have been using signs for thousands of years. In fact, some linguists believe that sign language may have evolved before spoken language.

Sign language is a true language.

(Image courtesy of Robert Avery)

Some scientists claim that the vocal apparatus to support language evolved long after humans were using language, suggesting that the first form of language was sign language. We may never know the true origins of human language, but sign languages today work just about as well as spoken languages.

Sign languages occur naturally in cultures throughout the world and were often used to communicate among different tribes or cultures. Diverse groups that range from Native Americans to Benedictine Monks used sign languages for centuries. Native American children in many tribes were taught to sign before they were taught to speak.

Sign language has most of the same characteristics as speech, such as grammar, vocabulary, structure, and syntax. And today signs bear little resemblance to what they stand for—like words, signs are arbitrary symbols.

It's Emblematic, Stupid!

Emblems are close cousins of sign language. An emblem is a gesture with a dictionary definition. These gestures are really part of language and, like signs, are processed in the left brain hemisphere—the same side of the brain that processes spoken language. Because emblems have specific dictionary definitions, they generally differ from culture to culture, just like language.

Here are some common emblems used every day in North America; without looking at the answer on the right, can you guess what each emblem means?

Making a fist and holding the thumb straight up	Need a ride
Making a circle with the thumb and index finger while holding the rest of the fingers straight up	Okay or good
Sliding an index finger across throat	Kill
Making a "V" with the index and middle finger	Peace or victory
Extending the middle finger upwards	Up yours
Holding one or both thumbs straight up	Okay, affirmation
Sliding one index finger over the other	Shame on you
Bouncing the heel of the hand off the forehead	Forgot or stupid
Circling an index finger next to the head	Crazy
Holding two arms high in the air	Touchdown
With palm facing body, pulling an index finger toward face	Come here
Waving an index finger at someone	Bad or scolding
Holding an index finger to the lips	Quiet
Holding the thumb straight down	Bad or no

These are just a few examples of hundreds of emblems with dictionary meanings you have in your vocabulary. In sports, umpires and referees use emblems to make all kinds of calls to officiate games. In everyday life, Americans regularly use more than 100 emblems.

*The thumb-down emblem
signifies negativity or disagreement.*

(Image courtesy of Peter Andersen)

But here is the problem. Like words in English, Italian, or Mandarin, emblems
only work in their own culture. In Chapter 27, I discuss some interesting, even life-
threatening, problems that occur when emblems are used cross-culturally. Forming a
circle with index finger and thumb means okay in the United States, worthless in
France, money in Japan, homosexual in various Mediterranean islands, and the same
as an upraised middle finger in Latin America.

Few emblems are universal. Perhaps a raised and open palm, which is a sign of peace or
greeting, is most cross-cultural and universal. The hand shrug is another fairly universal
gesture indicating, "I have no idea" or "I don't understand." Various hand-to-mouth
gestures mean quiet or silence. Patting the belly or pointing to the mouth indicates
hunger in many cultures, and the mock shiver with the hand around the body is a sign
of coldness in most places. Likewise, waving is a fairly universal sign of greeting or
farewell, but cross-cultural variability exists even among these widely used gestures.

*The open palm is a universal
sign of greeting or peace.*

(Image courtesy of Peter Andersen)

Illustrators: Talking with Your Hands

Perhaps the most important gestural body language is the illustrator, a type of gesture that accompanies speech. These gestures are essential to getting your point across, but they also help you synchronize your body language with other people and with other aspects of your own body language.

Although some cultures, including many Mediterranean and the Middle Eastern societies, are widely recognized as using many illustrators, almost everyone uses some gestures while speaking. Not all illustrators are alike, however, as the following sections will, er, illustrate.

Batons: Beating the Cadence of Speech

Perhaps the most important kind of gesture is the baton, a naturally occurring gesture that beats the rhythm of speech. They are call batons because, like an orchestra leader's baton that keeps the musicians on the same beat, these gestures keep the beat for the speaker and the audience. They also help us to keep the rhythm of our own speech flowing fluently. These are chopping, punching, or conductor-like gestures, directing the "melody" and rhythm of our words. These gestures flow almost constantly in most conversations but are especially employed by public speakers. In conversations, big batons are almost always used when the speaker is making an important point, disagreeing, or telling something exciting.

Watch a good public speaker. Their biggest gestures occur simultaneously with the most stressed and accented words. This is a powerful speaking style that looks well coordinated and spontaneous; however, using big gestures incorrectly communicates weakness and even deception. Former president Richard Nixon and former California governor Grey Davis were often criticized for uncoordinated gestures that lost them credibility with voters.

Batons can add dynamism and power to a speech. Great speakers from Martin Luther King, Jr. to John F. Kennedy, from Jesse Jackson to Bill Clinton, from Ronald Reagan to Jay Leno make (or made) extensive use of gestures. It's hard to put much passion in a speech without them. Think of your favorite teacher or college professor. I bet he or she made extensive use of gestures.

> **Nonverbally Speaking**
>
> Watch somebody talking on the telephone, especially in a heated or important conversation. It is not uncommon to see them gesture! It seems like a strange thing to do, since the listener can't see them, but it isn't. The gestures, which are generally right handed, stimulate the speech centers in the left brain and facilitate speech.

Competent speakers use a large number of illustrators. They are essential to communicating strength, competence, confidence, and enthusiasm. They also help speakers coordinate their body movement with their words. Some great speakers even give a gesture or two before they speak, which may rev up the language centers in their brain.

Ideographs: Airborne Ideas

Another gesture that accompanies speech is the ideograph, a gesture that sketches an idea. For example, if you were to say the stock market fell drastically, accompanied by a downward gesture as though you were tracing a line, you'd be using an ideograph. Here are some other examples of ideographs: While saying "there is a negative relationship between inflation and recession," you move one hand up and the other hand down. While saying "from the past to the present," you move your hand from one side to the other. While saying "All Americans must unite in this time of danger," you start with the hands out to the sides and bring them together.

> **CAUTION**
> ### Bodily Blunders
> If ideographs are overly planned they look staged and contrived. Planning to be spontaneous isn't easy! Many quality speakers just free their hands and let the gestures flow.

Pointers: Directional Gestures

Pointing is a common gesture that serves many functions. If you watch a teacher in class or the president at a press conference, they will call on people by pointing. Since pointing with the first finger is considered rude, and very insulting in some cultures, it's best when pointing at somebody to use the entire hand or fist with the thumb on the side.

Pointing directs attention or indicates direction.

(Image courtesy of Peter Andersen)

Pointing gestures also indicate directions, command people go to in a specific direction, or direct attention to a particular task. Pointing suggests status and is most likely to be used by people in more powerful positions. Often people will point to indicate the location of an object while providing verbal information such as, "it's over there."

Pointing can also be used to warn others of danger. A hiker might exclaim "Look out," while pointing at a rattlesnake, or a baseball fan might point to a foul ball flying toward him. If several people simultaneously, point in the same direction, they will quickly get other people's attention. Want to draw a crowd? Get a couple of friends to stand on a busy street and start pointing up.

Positions of Power

People point when giving directions. I've learned that the directions people give with their hands are often more accurate than their verbal explanations, especially if the gestures are precise. Remember that gestures are a more right-brained form of communication, which is where spatial memory is stored.

Pictographs

Pictographs are movements that draw a shape or object in the air. "It was a giant wave," the surfer gasps while illustrating with his hands the size and motions of the wave. "The valance extends all across the window," a woman tells her friend while spreading her hands apart. "She had a great body," sighs the young man as his hands trace an hourglass figure.

Pictographs are spontaneous gestures that literally paint a gestural picture for listeners. Like much of body language, they complement verbal messages, increasing their accuracy and providing additional meaning.

Spatials

Spatial gestures are hand movements that indicate size or distance. "The fish he caught was this long," the fisherman's wife reports as she holds her hands seven inches apart. Of course, her husband is holding his hands about two feet apart, but that's another fishy story.

We use spatials to describe ski jumps, buildings, boulders, and near first downs. We communicate far away distances by throwing open our palms.

Spatials often accompany words when communicating across great distances or when it's noisy. A football coach yelling "spread the defense" over the noise of a large crowd will gesture by rapidly pushing his hands apart. On a noisy city street, an employee may help a fellow truck driver back up by holding her hands apart and bringing them together to show how far the truck is from nearby objects.

> **⚠ CAUTION** **Bodily Blunders** _____
>
> Gestures can easily be misread across culture. Years ago, following a summit meeting with President Johnson, Soviet Premier Nikita Khrushchev joined his hands together high over his head and pumped them up and down. The American press was outraged, because this is a triumph gesture used by victorious prizefighters in the United States. Khrushchev's intended meaning? International solidarity and cooperation. Oops!

Gestures, including spatials, are learned early in life, as indicated by this baby's "so big" gesture.

(Image courtesy of Peter Andersen)

Bodily Reproductions

Speakers frequently use a kind of gesture called a *kinetograph* to reproduce bodily actions. They are often used to embellish a story and captivate an audience. For

> **Body Talk** _____
>
> Bodily reproductions are technically called **kinetographs,** gestures that recreate a bodily or physical action.

example, when describing a fight a person might say, "and then the little guy slugged the big guy," while throwing a roundhouse punch to imitate what happened. Or a speaker might say, "He dribbled down the court and as the buzzer went off he took the shot," while shooting an imitation jump shot. A woman might say "and he snuck up behind me and scared the heck out of me" while showing surprised and scared facial expressions.

Bodily reproductions can also be used to describe inanimate events such as avalanches, car accidents, and bee attacks. They are an essential part of storytelling and add excitement to any narrative.

Triumphant Displays

Gestures are often used to signal victory, success, or triumph. End zones in football are a veritable showcase of triumph displays. Fists in the air, mock touchdown signs, finger-wagging at an opponent, and a dozen varieties of spiking the football frequently follow touchdowns. Prizefighters will often raise one or both hands in the air after winning a decision or knocking out their opponent. Baseball players will circle the bases after a home run while clapping their hands or raising one hand in the air with a clenched fist.

Watch a high school tennis match or a Little League baseball game, and you will see players pumping their fist after serving up aces and driving runs in. Track stars and football players may not even cross the finish line or the goal line before starting their triumph displays.

On election night, political candidates will wave or raise one or both hands up over the head, or one of their supporters will grab the candidate's hand and hold it high like the referee does with a winning fighter. Triumphant waves to the audience accompany a candidate's entrance.

> **Nonverbally Speaking**
>
> Of course the V-sign is a triumphant display that is a victory emblem. First pioneered by Winston Churchill as an emblem of hope for victory in war, it has been adopted by triumphant candidates, quarterbacks, lottery winners, and spelling-bee champions.

A fist raised in the air is a sign of power or triumph

(Image courtesy of Peter Andersen)

Punctuators

Punctuators are forms of body language that disrupt or interrupt an interaction or accentuate or stress a particular message.

One set of such gestures are leave-taking cues. Just before a departure, it is fairly common to witness punctuating gestures. The most common leave-taking punctuators are the handclap, the knee slap, and the desk smack, which are often accompanied by statements like "well thanks for coming by" or "I gotta be hitting the road."

People often punctuate their anger or frustration by stomping their feet. Small children are notorious for stomping their feet during temper tantrums. Foot-stomping also is part of the body language of disappointment when, for example, losing a contest, missing an appointment, or forgetting something at home.

Sometimes punctuators accentuate a point while speaking. For example, a parent may turn both hands upward and slap the back of the upper hand down on the other while saying things like, "If I have told you once, I have told you …" or "Let me make myself clear," with a hand slap accompanying each word.

Punching one hand with another can be used to emphasize a phrase while speaking, such as "we must be strong in the face of adversity," or "I promise profits will be restored in the next quarter." Hand punches have a strong and sometime aggressive quality and should be used appropriately since they have a faintly violent flavor.

Getting That Syncing Feeling

Synchronous gestures send messages of rapport, alignment, and affectionate feelings. In Chapter 16, I describe synchrony as an important way of communicating affection, immediacy, intimacy, and closeness. It is really important to get in sync with other people and to reciprocate their gestures.

In fact, failing to reciprocate certain kinds of gestures is a real taboo. Let's start with gestures of hello and good-bye, including hand waves, finger flutters, and handshakes. You already learned in Chapter 6 that failing to reciprocate a handshake is likely to be taken as a snub or an act of complete social incompetence. Even young children begin to recognize that waves, handshakes, and hugs are reciprocal.

> **CAUTION**
> ### Bodily Blunders
> It's really lame when someone holds up their hands to give you a high five and you reach to shake their hand. It's all about alignment. Recognize the gesture! To be in sync with others, give them the kind of flesh they give you.

Even in very large groups, body synchrony is a sign of unity and solidarity. Think of University of Texas fans doing the "hook 'em horns" gesture with the index finger and pinky extended, University of Southern California fans making the "fight on" victory sign, or Florida State University fans doing the "tomahawk chop." While these group gestures can be really annoying to opponents and nonfans, they produce powerful group solidarity between the school, the fans, and the team.

When juries are sworn in, they hold up their right hands as signs of the oath of honesty and diligence. When Americans say the Pledge of Allegiance, they place their hands over their hearts. Group prayers in church use folded hands and other sacred signs to show solidarity and commonality in the worship of God.

Postural and gestural mirroring or mimicry is a sign of respect or rapport even in the very young.

(Image courtesy of Laura Guerrero)

Group synchrony and gestural matching send powerful cues of closeness and alignment through groups. It is important not to take these rituals so seriously that they substitute for individual thought. One element of brainwashing is getting people to engage in ritualistic behaviors that commit them to groups that may turn out to be crazy cults, political extremists, or dangerous hazing.

Nonverbally Speaking

While group synchrony is a powerful sign of solidarity and group rapport, it can also be chilling! Think of the German people during World War II mindlessly "sig heiling" with their arms extended at a 45° angle. Gestures can contribute to group contagion and conformity and other destructive actions.

One wonderful and synchronous behavior is the toast. It is accompanied across the world by raising a glass in the air, touching the glasses together, and saying stuff like "to your health" in English, "Skol" in Danish and Swedish, "Compai" in Japanese, or "Salud" in Spanish or Italian. This ritual is performed at weddings, before special meals, and at holiday dinners. It is a form of body language a lot like the rituals we perform during greeting and leave-taking, but in a sense it is more special because it takes place in the middle of an interaction when good "cheer" can literally and figuratively prevail.

The toast is used in many cultures as a gesture of good tidings.

(Image courtesy of Peter Andersen)

The Least You Need to Know

- ◆ Sign language is a real language, not a body language.
- ◆ Emblems are gestures with dictionary definitions.
- ◆ Illustrators are gestures that accompany speech.
- ◆ Gestures are often used to signal triumph or victory.
- ◆ Gestural synchrony is important for group solidarity.

Chapter 8

Portable Positions: Walking, Sitting, and Standing

In This Chapter

- ◆ The body language of your "walk"
- ◆ Reading seating
- ◆ What does standing stand for?
- ◆ Avoiding the body language of crime victims
- ◆ Tie signs that link people together

We communicate with our body whether we're walking, sitting, or standing. Remember, your body always sends messages; one cannot not communicate!

People infer information about your mood, power, vulnerability, gender, age, ethnicity, health, and personality from the positions you assume and the way you assume them. So what are your positions telling others about yourself?

Do the Locomotion

We don't always realize it, but from infancy to the golden years our walk sends body language signals that are interpreted by other people. So let's talk the walk.

Baby Steps

The crawl is a body language milestone in a baby's development. It is more than a reminder to parents to childproof *everything*; it's baby's new window to the world. Crawling is like going from snapshots to movies, from staring at the ceiling to truly exploring. Neurologists believe crawling plays an important role in stimulating both sides of the brain and even acquiring language. Some infants, however, slither rather than crawl, and some kids skip both slithering and crawling and go straight to walking with no adverse effects.

Adults crawl, too. Crawling with your baby is an important way to connect with your child. It lets you interact at baby's level and creates a special rapport. Kids of all ages love adults who join them on the floor.

Many babies start to cruise—standing while holding on to chairs, tables, or whatever—around the room long before they can walk. When a child starts cruising, he's starting to send off the body language of a child, not a baby. And of course, baby's first steps are a big deal. Those lurching, wobbly steps are a marker of the change from infancy to childhood, or at least toddlerhood. Most babies like the adventure of walking, especially if someone is there to cheer them on.

Walk Like a Man (or Woman)

Men and women have distinctly different walks. Seen in silhouette or even in computer-generated stick figures, a person's gender can usually be easily distinguished by their walk. Men's bodies are almost motionless when they walk, especially the hips and torso. Men walk with their feet nearly a foot apart and swing their arms significantly. The arm swing counterbalances the legs and prevents the torso from twisting.

> **Nonverbally Speaking**
>
> It's not just genetics and training that make women walk like women—it's clothing. Tight skirts and uncomfortable shoes, especially high heels, help produce the sway in the hips characteristic of women's walking. Several surveys show that the hips are the body part with which women are least satisfied, but it is the hourglass figure and wide hips, particularly when in motion, that communicates womanly body language and is attractive to men.

Women add motion to their locomotion. Their hips move significantly more than men. This additional motion is partly due to women's biologically wider hips, but not entirely, in view of the fact that men can walk this way, too, and sometimes do. Women are much more likely to put one foot in front of the other when walking, which sets their hips in motion.

Out of the Gait Impressions

Your gait says a whole lot more about you than just your gender; it says a bunch about who you are and what you are up to. Like it or not, people scope out your gait and make judgments about you based on it.

Power-Strides

Lots of people move quickly today because it seems so necessary. The trademark of the new millennium is the stressed-out lifestyle that you will read more about in Chapter 10. Given how much we do, it is not surprising that we are rushing to meetings, dashing to work, hurrying to class, scurrying off to soccer practice, or just bustling around the house. Fast walkers look competent and busy, although a bit frazzled. Ratcheting up the pace of life is the price of living in a productive, materialistic society like America.

Others rope us into power-striding. We want to talk to a colleague who is late for a meeting and suddenly, there we are, power-striding at their pace. Adjusting to the pace of others is an important skill that sends messages of connection and adaptability. Leaving another person in the dust is pretty rude body language and usually requires an explanation—"Hey, I'm really late picking up the kids; catch you later," or some such accounting.

Falling behind may also require an explanation, even a feeble one like, "Well, see you tomorrow." Failing to keep up can also be damaging to one's image, suggesting you are too unmotivated or out of shape to match your partner's pace.

One of the most chilling power strides is the goose-step. This unnatural, but dominant walking style with the legs and arms straight is still associated with deranged despots like Hitler and Stalin. In part it is the painful, inept, and ridiculous nature of the goose-step that gives it additional power; it is all form and no function.

Not only does the goose-step have dictatorial connotations, all angular movements are less pleasing to the eye and inherently associated with power and masculinity. So the angular

Nonverbally Speaking
After World War II, like many relics of the Nazis, West Germany outlawed the goose-step. To my knowledge it is the only ambulatory body language banned anywhere in the world. North Korea's military still employs this reviled relic of past dictatorships.

nature of the goose-step may be innately rigid and authoritarian. The sound of the goose-step in military boots is additionally unsettling but also awe-inspiring.

Walking Ways

Lots of body language is communicated by your style of walking. Putting a little spring in your step is an old cliché, but research supports that light-footedness, a moderate to long stride, swinging arms, and an erect posture are associated with happy moods and positive self-esteem.

Strolling—the act of slowly ambling along, seemingly with little purpose—sends a totally different message and in some ways is almost more like sitting than striding. We rarely stroll alone, except maybe in formal gardens or in museums. Strolling is normally done in pairs and is actually a very companionate and even conversational mode of locomotion. Strollers are not going anywhere in particular; strolling is an end in itself.

Shuffling, the doddering gait of the aged and infirm, sends messages of dependence, weakness, and frailty. This is the absolute opposite of the power stride on a body language scale. The one benefit of the shuffle is that it might elicit nurturing and caregiving from other people. Shuffling is a submissive form of gait. Years ago, blacks were encouraged to shuffle to signal subservience.

Marching, purposefully striding in unison with others, has always had a military flavor to it, and the act demands coordination and concentration. Marching bands are a great form of unified body language.

Seated Signals

Sprawling postures are signs of power and masculinity, which we discuss in more detail in Chapters 11 and 26. Powerful men and some powerful women occupy lots of space in classrooms, boardrooms, and living rooms by spreading out, scattering around possessions, sitting with their legs spread and the elbows away from the body.

Unlike men, women sit with their legs together. Research shows that even when they are wearing slacks, women sit with their knees together. This "ladylike" position, which originated with skirts and dresses, may outlive the skirt. While overexposure is not an issue in pants, the spread-leg position still has negative connotations and is avoided by most women.

The sprawl position with arms and legs apart is a classic male gender cue.

(Image courtesy of Peter Andersen)

Women typically sit with their arms close to the body and legs together in the "ghost skirt" position.

(Image courtesy of Robert Avery)

Positions of Power

Many people adopt symmetrical, mirror image, or at least similar sitting positions when they interact with others. Such positions communicate rapport and closeness and facilitate interaction. While mirroring is typically an unconscious process, try deliberately mirroring another person while you're sitting. If it isn't too obvious what you are up to, you may find that it increases rapport and connection.

Don't Stand for It!

Standing is often considered to be a position of domination, but there are lots of ways to stand and not all of them are dominant postures. Perhaps the most powerful stance is spread-legged and hands on hips, also called the arms akimbo position. Folding your arms while standing is also a dominant position that communicates coldness and unapproachability.

While the hands on hips position is masculine and powerful, reversing the hand so that the thumb is forward and the fingers are back give this a much more delicate and feminine flair. Combined with a slight hip tilt, this body language gives off distinctly feminine cues. A related behavior is the pelvic roll, a movement frequently used by women and rarely by men. When shifting weight from one foot to the other women frequently do it in a circular motion, by rolling the hips. This is a very feminine and even somewhat seductive form of body language, if you have ever seen this movement done well.

In formal speaking situations, how one stands is vital. Standing tall with an erect posture is the body language of competence, confidence, and power.

> **⚠ CAUTION**
>
> **Bodily Blunders**
>
> Sometimes when people, especially women, are chilled, they will fold their arms. Although they aren't intentionally sending negative signals to others, this thermally chilly body language turns out to be interpersonally chilly as well. Closed body language makes people seem less warm, immediate, and friendly.

Standing with your hands on your hips, also called the arms akimbo position, is powerful and dominant.

(Image courtesy of Robert Avery)

Formal speeches require powerful positions, including standing tall, a straight posture, and purposeful gestures.

(Image courtesy of Peter Andersen)

Bodily Blunders

Here are some types of body language to avoid when public speaking:

- ◆ Rocking: Don't rock out when speaking—it could make your audience seasick.
- ◆ Slouching: It looks lackadaisical and uninterested.
- ◆ Resting: Podiums are for notes, not bodily support.
- ◆ Pocketing: Creepy! Use your hands for gesturing.
- ◆ Reading: Look at the audience most of the time; only briefly glance at your notes.
- ◆ Touching: Avoid self-touching; it's disturbing
- ◆ Manipulating: It's distracting to watch a speaker play with a pocket pen or other objects.

Good public speakers connect with the audience by standing tall, looking confident, and speaking well. Be sure to look at every person or area of the room. Gesture, smile, and then forget about yourself. Look for the positive people and focus on them. Confidence begets confidence. People respond well to a confident and interesting speaker, and they give the speaker positive feedback.

Criminal Intent

Victims of crime are usually not randomly chosen. Like vultures looking for a wounded animal, muggers, robbers, and rapists look for certain body language in a potential victim. Obviously, failing to fit a mugger's profile would be a good thing. Nothing said here is in any way intended to blame the victim of a crime. Nonetheless, holding rare meat up to a grizzly or carrying honey near a beehive might not be the best idea.

Several researchers, including David Messakappa and myself, have consulted with crime victims as well as imprisoned criminals to try to find out what cues criminals might look for in a victim. The following list is assembled from these studies:

- **Jewelry and fine clothing.** While these expensive artifacts are success and status symbols, ironically they are also a bit like waving meat in front of a hungry tiger. Assess where you are going and ask yourself if it is wise to look too "well heeled" in certain situations, neighborhoods, and countries. On the contrary, several studies found that looking dirty or disheveled reduces your chances of being mugged.

- **Looking fearful.** Ironically, looking fearful is associated with being selected as a victim. Just like a pit bull can sense fear and is more likely to attack an apprehensive person than a bold one, looking paranoid is like holding up a banner asking to be victimized.

- **Short stature.** Not surprisingly, short people are more likely to be victims than taller people. There's not much you can do about being short, but you can be aware of when and where you travel. Police have reported for decades that criminals overlook larger and tougher-looking people.

- **Weak walking style.** Muggers select victims who look weak, slow, and feeble. Short steps, a slow pace, and lack of arm swings are associated with weak walking. Walking faster, taking longer strides, and swinging arms are cues less likely to attract a mugger. Confident walkers ranked near the bottom of potential victims.

- **Weak body language.** Muggers told us that they were least likely to select people as victims who looked strong and/or fast. Obviously, muggers want to increase the odds of a successful heist or assault. Walking stooped over, looking stiff and tense, and appearing to be physically weak are associated with being a potential victim. One mugger told us, "I wouldn't try to rob a body builder, linebacker-type dude. I would probably get my ass kicked, and robbed myself."

♦ **Submissive behaviors.** Studies of both rape and robbery victims suggest that people who look weak, cowering, or frail appear less able to defend themselves. One robber told us, "You want somebody that looks like they would not put up a fight. Like a pack of wolves picking out the smallest deer, you want it as easy as possible."

♦ **Revealing appearance.** Several studies of rape victims report that revealing clothing was associated with being a rape victim. Obviously, in certain situations wearing such revealing clothing may be unwise. Once again, this finding is not intended in any way to blame the victim of such a brutal and demeaning crime.

♦ **Elderly appearance.** Not a shocker, but the elderly are prime candidates for muggers. Looking old, having white hair, a halting gait, stiff movements, and a stooped posture were some of the cues used by muggers. Perhaps coloring one's hair and going to the gym has an additional benefit beyond weight loss or heart health: looking youthful deters muggers.

♦ **Looking away.** Data show that looking away and, especially, looking down are associated with being a victim. People who look happy, confident, and stare back at others are less likely to be targets. But be careful, because long or menacing stares can provoke an attack.

♦ **Appearing drunk or high.** Drunks have always been more likely to get rolled. Looking intoxicated is an invitation for criminals who correctly believe that an intoxicated person may not be able to defend him- or herself. Likewise, lots of sexual assault victims are intoxicated at the time of the assault. So here is a word to the wise: Know your limits.

> **Positions of Power**
>
> Any time you feel that someone is trying to harm you, use your full body language arsenal. Yell "No!" and "Help!," scream, blow a whistle, or throw a shoe through the nearest pane of glass. In cases of sexual assault, yelling "Fire!" tends to be taken more seriously than yelling "Rape!"

The Ties That Bind

Now we move from lies and crime to a tender topic: The ties that bind. Tie signs are the body language of relationships. So how does a couple's body language say they are a couple?

♦ **Handholding.** This is a big commitment, especially for teen-agers who are making a public statement that they are a couple by clasping hands.

◆ **Standing close.** In the '80s the rock band the Police sang "Don't stand, don't stand so, don't stand so close to me," to reflect the concerns of a male teacher who worried about a young female student who had a crush on him. As a form of body language, closeness counts!

◆ **Matching outfits.** Though his and her shirts are a bit cheesy, many groups— from high school cliques, to sororities, to businessmen—wear similar clothing. While short of an actual uniform, matching is a tie sign.

◆ **Body contact.** All forms of touch communicate togetherness and bondedness. See Chapter 6 for more on these types of cues.

◆ **Food-sharing.** Drinking from the same glass, eating from the same plate, and feeding each other are powerful tie signs. These rituals are performed in intimate relationships by families, lovers, and spouses, but never by strangers. The cake-feeding ritual performed by brides and grooms is a powerful symbolic tie sign.

◆ **Body symmetry.** When people are closely connected they adopt similar postures and positions. If imitation is the highest form of flattery, body symmetry is the highest sign of connection.

This young girl's pose echoes the statue of the little mermaid in Copenhagen. When people are in rapport with others they adopt similar, symmetrical positions.

(Image courtesy of Peter Andersen)

Note how the hand positions of the audience mirror the gestures of the speaker.

(Image courtesy of Peter Andersen)

Anthropologist Desmond Morris claims that hotel doormen, who see thousands of couples come and go, can easily tell if the couple is married, one person is married, or they are both single. Unmarried couples manifest many more tie signs, whereas married couples are generally less affectionate and more complacent about checking into a hotel. Conversely, some unmarried couples overcompensate by acting like total strangers.

Eye contact and handholding are clear ties signs communicating that these two are a couple.

(Image courtesy of Robert Avery)

Groups use tie signs, too. From sorority sisters and sports teams to motorcycle or street gangs, groups display body language and adornments that communicate membership. Other groups, be they preppies, goths, greasers, or jocks, wear the same style of clothing to signify group membership. Some groups, like the Hell's Angels and high school letter earners, wear matching jackets. Similarly, matching tattoos signify membership in many groups or gangs (which also makes it a tad harder to switch groups).

Secret signs are important to group membership and widely used by street gangs, religious groups, military organizations, Masonic lodges, fraternities, and sororities. These include secret handshakes, secret gestures, and secret ornaments. We don't really know too much about secret signs because they are, well, secret.

The Least You Need to Know

- ◆ Walking styles communicate body language about age, gender, ethnicity, and mood.
- ◆ Seating positions signal mood, power, and gender.
- ◆ When you are speaking in public, stand tall and don't rock, slouch, rest, use your pockets, or play with objects.
- ◆ Crime victims' body language often signals profitability and vulnerability.
- ◆ Tie signs are a form of body language that signal connections among people.

Nose, Nose, Anything Goes: Olfactory Communication

In This Chapter

- ◆ Smell as a neglected body language
- ◆ The nostalgic nature of smell
- ◆ The evaluative nature of smell
- ◆ Pheromones as sexual attractants
- ◆ You might not smell what I smell

Americans, as well as some Asians and Europeans, have become aroma-phobic! To err is human; to smell is a crime. Each day Americans shower, wash, anti-perspirize, deodorize, freshen, perfume, and generally cover any trace of our natural odors.

In this chapter, we will examine the role that body aromas—artificial and natural—play in body language. If you're ready for a whiff of what goes on in our brains when we smell body aromas, read on.

Aromaphobia

A central finding of research on olfaction is that there are no neutral odors. That's right, smells are something we love or hate. Think of the wonderful scent of a fresh bakery, a chocolate factory, your wife's favorite perfume or your husband's favorite cologne, or the smell of plumeria or honeysuckle. Most of us (though not all of us) love those scents.

Now think about the "wonderful" odor of road kill, your workout clothes after a long session, the cat's litterbox, or the garbage you forgot to take out last week. You probably find these smells pretty rank, repulsive, and revolting.

Now think of a totally neutral smell. Tough, huh? It is plenty easy to think of smells that attract and repel, but pretty hard to think of a middle-of-the road smell. That should tell you something about the origins and purposes of smell. Smell is all about approach and avoidance.

We are attracted to smells we like and repelled by smells we dislike. That's because smell evolved as a defense mechanism. The smell of smoke, rotten food, or a predator made our ancestors fearful and cautious. The smell of fresh food, clean air, or their loved ones attracted our ancestors.

Smells produce automatic reactions: There are no neutral scents.

(Image courtesy of Robert Avery)

Our natural avoidance of certain smells has expanded to many natural smells. In the United States and a few other places, like Japan, virtually any body odor is a bad odor, and we cover ourselves in perfumes, colognes, scented soaps, and deodorants to keep those odors covered over. However, in many periods of our history and in many cultures today, some body odors are quite acceptable—even attractive. But there is little or no chance for this natural form of body language to operate in our contemporary society. Instead, we send olfactory messages strategically by using artificial chemical odors and the natural smells of other animals and of plants.

Nosing Into Your Past

Your nose tells you what to approach and avoid, and it does the same thing for other animals.

So where does our picky, evaluative sense of smell come from, and what good is it? As humans evolved, we practically lost our sense of smell. Our eyes became more important in navigating, picking up body language, and reading text. As our eyes, ears, and brains evolved, our olfactory sense diminished. In fact, the surface of your smell membrane is about the size of a postage stamp, whereas a dog or a monkey has a smell membrane over 100 times as large, about the size of a man's unfolded handkerchief. As humans developed world-class brains and we started having things like parental training, schools, and culture, we needed less of the automatic stuff like a world-class nose.

So our nose is pretty obsolete but not yet entirely useless. The olfactory cortex still processes smell since it is handy to have other types of input in addition to our most important senses like vision, hearing, and touch. Smell is also linked to the limbic system in our brain that detects and governs basic emotions and is one of earliest developing memory centers. So our noses still tell us what to approach and avoid, regulate our endocrine system, and interact with our hormones, and they are still important receivers of other people's olfactory body language.

> **Nonverbally Speaking**
>
> Studies show that babies can easily pick out the scent of their mother from any other woman, and that they have a real preference for the comfort and scent of their real mom. This finding indicates that humans have a remaining vestige of our ancestors' smell identification capability.

> **CAUTION** **Bodily Blunders**
>
> Find a fragrance you just love? Be careful. It may smell great to you but not so great to others, particularly the opposite sex, who react to different pheromones. Better to take your spouse or an opposite-sex friend along when shopping for a scent. Select something you both like!

Your Nostalgic Nose

Have you ever visited the home you grew up in or your old high school many years later? Nostalgia city! For most of us, walking into our old home or school is a trip down memory lane. We become flooded with the smells of yesteryear. And each smell evokes scenes and events of long-gone days.

Positions of Power

Since smells are nostalgic, take a trip with your spouse or special friend down memory lane. Go back to the town you first lived in, the beach you went to in the summer, the place you first met. Go ahead, be a sentimental sap! Drawing in the sights and smells of those early, romantic days when love was new may rekindle forgotten feelings.

Even the smell of a childhood neighborhood can bring back wistful memories. A few miles from my boyhood home, adjacent to our favorite baseball field, is a coffee factory. Objectively, it smells pretty bad—not the smell of fresh ground coffee that so many people cherish, but more like severely burned coffee beans. A single whiff of that awful smell and the wonderful baseball games of my youth come flooding back! A friend stealing second base while screaming the "wipe out" laugh. Tagging a runner out at home plate. Climbing a tall fence to get to our secret field, which was actually a huge lot between two warehouses. Smell is a sense that connects us with the past.

Two of my friends who grew up in the polluted industrial smoke of Hammond and Gary, Indiana, outside Chicago, always felt these immensely nostalgic, melancholy, and evocative emotions when returning to this region. The fresh air of a Canadian camping trip paled by comparison with the olfactory reminiscences brought to mind by the smells of oil refineries and steel mills.

Does the smell of pine trees in the summer bring back memories of summer camp or backpacking trips? Pines always remind me of summers in Wisconsin, Christmases past, or skiing through the trees in the Sierras or Rockies. Along with these memories are the people of our past and the relationships we had, each with their distinct olfactory profiles.

Body Talk

The language of olfactory body language is **pheromones**. Pheromones are external chemical messengers, just like hormones are internal chemical messengers. Some pheromones are perceived and processed consciously, but some affect your behavior without you even knowing it!

Perhaps the cruelest smell is the scent of your ex-boyfriend's or girlfriend's cologne or perfume. Floods of memories come back—not just nostalgic ones, but memories of an era gone, a relationship departed.

Perfumes and natural scents of our loved ones are very meaningful to us. The olfactory body language of courtship, romance, and sexual arousal are more than fleeting impressions. In the next section you will come to appreciate one of the most elemental and ancient of the human body languages, the sexual scents of human *pheromones*.

Sexual Signals: Our Fabulous Pheromones

The sense of smell is one of the primary forms of body language in the animal world. Bears, dogs, cats, chimps, gorillas, and most other animals use smell as a primary channel of body language. Animals are constantly smelling for food, danger, changes in the weather, and most important, sexual signals.

Unlike humans, who can have sexual relations at any time during the year, animals only mate when the female is in heat or estrus. Animals signal that they are available for mating in several ways, but the principal communication channel is smell. A male dog, cat, or monkey will not mate unless the female emits certain sexual pheromones that signal her readiness for mating.

Humans rely principally on other communication channels for attracting mates, including physical appearance, flirtation cues, eye contact, facial expressions, and conversation, while smell plays a somewhat less important role in courtship and mating rituals.

Nevertheless, olfactory body language still plays an important role in human hormonal, sexual, and relational communication. Women are extremely sensitive to male hormones and pheromones. For example, only women, not men, can smell testosterone acetate, a derivative of a male sex hormone. Another clue: Female smell is far more sensitive during ovulation—when women are fertile—than during menstruation and pregnancy. Females are particularly sensitive to male pheromones during ovulation, when olfactory body language cues could make them more receptive to sexual attractants.

> **Nonverbally Speaking**
>
> Several studies report that smell disorders are frequently accompanied by a lack of sexual desire. That really stinks!

Women living together often have their menstrual periods at the same time. Research has shown that this menstrual synchronization is the result of pheromone forces. Much like sharing hormones, women who share one another's pheromones via olfactory body language establish cycles that are coordinated with other women's body clocks. Recent evidence also suggests that pheromones can induce or impede ovulation. The fact that reproductive readiness is influenced by pheromones suggests that our olfactory body language plays an important role in the mating process.

Research also suggests we may select mates based on their scent, and that this process plays a role in the natural selection of diverse genes that are different from our own. We smell better to people of the opposite sex whose genetically based immunity to disease differs significantly from our own. Likewise, these genetically different people smell better to us! Thus, olfactory body language that is different from our own may assist with the process of natural selection.

Some evidence also suggests that certain pheromones cause people to engage in more affectionate and sexual encounters. The rash of websites selling pheromone-based products is a testament to people's desire to enhance sexuality through olfaction. But be careful: Most of these products are unregulated, and both their effectiveness and side effects are unknown.

> **Nonverbally Speaking**
>
> Studies show that most people are attracted to pheromones of the opposite sex—with one exception. We tend not to be attracted to pheromones of opposite-sex close-blood relatives. This mechanism may be an innate defense against incest!

> **Nonverbally Speaking**
>
> In many tribal cultures, smell is used to detect emotions much as we use facial expressions. Before wedding engagements, families might smell the bride and groom to detect negative emotions. Far-fetched? Doctors in America are trained to diagnose diseases, including schizophrenia, with smell.

The chemical exaltolide, which is a human pheromone, is frequently used as a perfume base. Likewise, many of the other ingredients in perfume and cologne contain plant and animal pheromones, including musk, from the musk deer; ambergris, from the stomachs of whales; and castoria, obtained from the sweat glands of the Canadian beaver. The fact that so many perfumes contain plant and animal pheromones tells us a lot about their potency for human body language.

Of course, one of the ironies of modern American society is that while we wash away all our own pheromones, we replace them with "better" pheromones from other species. It is a bit like substituting a Gwyneth Paltrow or Ben Affleck mask for your own face. It could be an improvement, but it would seem pretty constraining and artificial. But that is what we do with our pheromones, and, in doing so, we reduce the possibility of communicating with natural olfactory body language.

Do You Smell What I Smell?

For years we have known that people differ dramatically in their ability to smell. There's a good chance that you and your neighbors will disagree about what something smells like, if it smells at all, or if it smells good or bad. To take just a few examples, Swedish Ivy, Sage Brush, and Queen Anne's Lace are very aromatic to some folks, and have virtually no smell at all to others. And those who can smell these plants can't agree whether they like the smell or not. To me Swedish Ivy has a pungent smell, to my wife no smell at all. Furthermore, studies show that some people are vastly more sensitive than other people to certain scents like green peppers, onions, cinnamon, coffee, and carnations.

Often these differences in olfactory sensitivity, definition, and evaluation split between males and females. Research shows that females are generally more sensitive to smell than males. We are not sure if these are genetic variations or differences in socialization. Like so many things, it is probably some of both.

Studies show that women outperform men in the identification of most smells, especially perfumes, foods, and other stereotypically female smells. Surprisingly, women do better than men in identifying many stereotypically male smells, too. Men, however, outperform women in identifying Crayola crayons, Brut aftershave, horseradish, rubbing alcohol, soap, and Vicks VapoRub. Research has also found that women find most odors to be stronger and more memorable than men. These findings are consistent with the general principle that women are generally more sensitive perceivers of many forms of body language.

Nonverbally Speaking

While numerous individual differences exist in smell sensitivity, some people suffer from *hyposmia*, an extremely weak sense of smell, and a few suffer from *anosmia*, having virtually no smell at all. These syndromes can be congenital defects or can be caused by certain viruses and even nasal polyps. Reduced smell sensitivity is associated with loss of interest in food, because a large part of taste is actually smelled. To realize what individuals with these smell disorders experience, think back to the last time you had a very severe cold and virtually no taste at all. You probably had no desire to eat and when you did eat, food was pretty unappealing. Anosmia is also associated with depression and with reduced interest in sexual behavior. Two parts of the brain associated with emotion, the amygdala and hippocampus, are understimulated in anosmics, resulting in depression, less emotional experience, apathy, and even greater rates of unemployment.

As with other forms of body language, research suggests most scents are received unconsciously. In fact, the all-important pheromones that affect our social and sexual behavior are often not associated with a particular smell at all, but frequently do produce a specific feeling or emotion.

The bottom line is this: Unlike other kinds of body language where there is considerable agreement about the presence or absence of a given gesture or expression, people do not agree about smell or whether it is positive or negative. So if your friend says that something has a strong odor, take their word for it. Chances are it does smell strong to them. And the same goes for odor evaluation. The smell of hay, green peppers, or coffee might smell great to you, but it might not smell so good to your friend. Your nose is not a good barometer of what another person's nose smells.

Each day we use numerous products to smell better.

(Image courtesy of Robert Avery)

The Olfaction Industry

We are supposed to believe that smell is a relic of our past, our forgotten sense. If you believe that actions speak louder than words, smell might be our most important sense. Each year Americans spend billions of dollars to smell better. Surveys show that Americans use numerous odor-enhancing products each day. The list of products to enhance our smell is imposing: perfumes, colognes, deodorants, anti-perspirants, foot powders, chewing gum, and breath sprays—the list is almost endless! And the advertising industry targets almost every area of our bodies as a potential olfactory offender: mouth, neck, intestines, underarms, cheeks, crotch, vagina, hair, and feet.

One communication-consulting firm I have worked with actually does seminars on selling with food, taste, and smell. Their research shows that gourmet tastes and smells create moods much more conducive

Bodily Blunders

Like it or not, body odor is taboo in America. If a friend has extreme body odor, tell them privately. They may have little smell sensitivity or be from a culture where no smell taboos exist. Body odor can result in interpersonal avoidance and even unemployment. It reeks to be spurned. So help out a putrid pal!

to agreement and hence to business deals. Of course, the great prevalence of business lunches suggest that people intuitively know that taste and smell sell. (A cocktail or glass of wine probably doesn't hurt business, either.)

Some real estate agents understand the power of smell. A common suggestion for making your house feel like home to a prospective buyer is to make it smell good. The first thing to do is neutralize any household smells. If it smells like other people's bodies, pets, or cooking odors, a prospective buyer will subconsciously think they're in somebody else's home, not their own home. But if it has wonderful, nostalgic smells, it will make the prospective buyer feel right at home. Try putting some cinnamon in a pan of water and boiling it slowly on the stove. The result is sensational. The entire house smells like apple pie. In the mental images created by olfactory body language, apple pie is all about childhood, motherhood, baseball, and home.

> **Bodily Blunders**
>
> Your home is an extension of your body, and a smelly home will lead to stinky home sales. Real estate agents report that terrible turn-offs include body odors, tobacco smoke, strong disinfectants, insecticides, cat box odors, and smelly pets.

The Least You Need to Know

- ◆ The sense of smell is inherently evaluative.
- ◆ Olfactory body language is part of sexual attraction.
- ◆ Smells are inherently nostalgic and emotional.
- ◆ Humans send and receive external chemical messengers called pheromones.
- ◆ The huge olfaction industry suggests that smell is an important form of body language.

Space and Time Relations: Communicating via Territory, Time, and Distance

In This Chapter

- ◆ Understanding your territorial nature
- ◆ Your personal space zones
- ◆ Defending your space and territory
- ◆ Your personality and personal space
- ◆ Approaching and avoiding the maddening crowd
- ◆ Timing is everything

You've all witnessed party fouls like these: Katlyn is a pretty, well-built young woman who really likes Mike, a shy but attractive young man. In an effort to get more intimate with Mike, she keeps moving closer, invading his space bubble. Mike appreciates the attention, but Katlyn is way too close and keeps moving closer until Mike is in the corner, desperate and a bit embarrassed by Katlyn's behavior. Most of us don't like space invaders—even attractive ones from planet Earth. Party foul!

Here's another one: The invitation says the big party is to start at 6 P.M. You arrive at 5:45 and find a shocked and desperate hostess in her slip. Another party foul!

Two of the most important components of your body language involve time and space. Time and space provide the context for every message you send, but they do way more than that. They are messages in their own right that often speak far louder than words.

The Territorial Imperative

Like most of our animal relatives, humans are territorial creatures. Most wars are fought over two issues, religion and territory. Much civil litigation is over property rights, boundaries, and ownership. Some of the biggest environmental battles are conflicts over land preservation or land development.

You would quickly become aware of just how territorial you are if a stranger entered your house or car. Indeed, humans have an elaborate and explicit system of deeds, contracts, and titles to unambiguously reserve their territory. Our home territories are an extension of our bodies, and the ways we mark our territories are an extension of our body language.

At the borders of your territory, you may communicate ownership explicitly with signs that say "private," "no trespassing," "beware of dog," or "no soliciting" and a number of other explicit "boundary markers." In recent years, the ubiquitous home security sign has been widely adopted to serve notice to potential intruders that the home is protected. Some homeowners have posted pseudo-security signs that are not really accompanied by security systems at all. These homeowners recognize the importance of communication; the real benefit and deterrent of home security systems may be in the sign, not in the system.

Most of us put up nonverbal features that extend our body language and protect our territory. Most homeowners and apartment dwellers use locks to protect their property against intrusion or theft. We erect walls, gates, and fences to clearly communicate the boundaries of our territory. Recently, gated communities have become popular and are often accompanied by armed guards. Again, the effect of these may be more psychological than real since the entire perimeters of these properties are rarely secure and it's relatively easy for pedestrians to penetrate them.

Of course we are protective of property we own, but we are also very protective of our temporary territories. Your seats at football games and concerts, your blankets in parks and on beaches, your table in a restaurant or library, your seat in a theatre or classroom are guarded with an elaborate body language that is universally understood but rarely discussed.

The objects around this shopping mall table reserve space.

(Image courtesy of Robert Avery)

Marking Your Territory

Animals mark their territory in a variety of ways, usually by leaving bodily scents or droppings on their home spaces. Most people are discouraged by their families from marking territories in these ways. However, many teenagers and even some bachelors ignore these familial admonitions and mark their territory with dirty clothes and foul olfactory cues. The rest of us have far less obnoxious territorial marking methods.

One of the primary ways we establish territory are with object markers. As you arrive in a classroom, a cafeteria, a football stadium, or theatre, you are likely to mark your territory with objects such as coats, hats, books, or backpacks. The amazing thing is that other people recognize these are territorial markers and almost never relocate

Positions of Power

You can save your table in a cafeteria by using territorial cues called object markers. Jackets and full drink cups are effective markers. But be careful of half-full drink cups. They are usually considered garbage and are ineffective territorial markers.

such objects. And this silent language is quite universal. Removing markers is considered rude and often provokes verbal retaliation from others.

Disputes sometimes occur when markers are abused. Have you had the experience of arriving early in the bleachers at football or baseball games only to find the best seats are all covered by 40-foot-long blankets? Markers that overclaim territory may be considered a breach of body language etiquette, and provoke other interesting forms of body language and even antagonistic arguments.

Spreading out objects marks territory.

(Image courtesy of Robert Avery)

Setting Up Camp

When students arrive at my college classroom, they quickly mark their territory with books, coats, and backpacks. When they leave, of course, they take these markers with them, leaving the territory unmarked. The following week, they return to the same territory even though there are no assigned seats. Over time students establish territorial tenure, the right to a space because you have occupied it in the past. This is similar to "squatter's rights" in the old West, a claim that occupying a territory for a time gives you property rights even in the absence of a deed.

Territorial tenure is tricky because, unlike markers, there is no visible indication that the territory is taken. Students who come to class and find someone in "their seat" are angry and frustrated, and communicate it through their body language; dirty looks, rolling of the eyes, stomping off to a new seat, and deep sighs are common reactions. Sometimes they will go beyond body language and say, "Hey, you're in my seat," which always stimulates an interesting dialog.

Similar examples of territorial tenure can be found in school and company cafeterias, in boardrooms, and on outdoor benches where people habitually congregate. Often members of the same ethnic group, sorority, work group, or friendship network will occupy the same table each day fending off intruders with dirty looks and other forms of protective body language.

Your Home Is Your Castle

People regard where they live—whether it's a house, apartment, or dormitory room—as sacred, private space. Visitors are welcome, but only by invitation. Even the Fourth Amendment to the Constitution explicitly secures our homes, possessions, and our selves when it states: The right of the people to be secure in their persons, houses, papers, and effects, against unreasonable searches and seizures shall not be violated.

> **CAUTION**
>
> **Bodily Blunders**
>
> In North America, personal space zones are carefully prescribed. If you stand or sit within 1½ feet of another person, you are a space invader who is thought of as weird and pushy. The exception, of course, is in close or intimate relationships where close distances and even touch is okay, even desirable.

Inside Your Personal Space Bubble

Wherever you go, your personal space goes with you. It's an invisible bubble that you carry around with you and that extends about 3 feet out from your body. Actually, your personal space bubble is pear-shaped and extends over 3 feet in front of you and a little less than 3 feet on the sides and back. People are more approachable from the side than the front. That's because your cold shoulder isn't nearly as sensitive as your nice warm front. Similarly, we turn our back on those we want to avoid while reserving our front for those we love and value. We are most careful to protect our front from invasion because 90 percent of our nerve endings are oriented toward the front of the body, including face, lips, mouth, nose, breasts, genitals, and ears. Frontal approaches are most stimulating and may seem overwhelming.

> **Body Talk**
>
> Our closest zone of interaction is called **intimate distance**. This interaction zone, which extends from actual tactile contact out to about 1½ feet, is reserved for our most intimate relationships: spouses, children, romantic partners, and our closest friends.

Interpersonal Distances

Years ago, anthropologist Edward Hall noted that Americans use personal space zones that correspond to the type of relationships they have. Today little has changed. The most remote zone, called public distance, extends from 8 feet away from your body and beyond. This space is reserved for important speakers, Hollywood stars, sports celebrities, and famous political figures like presidential candidates and the president himself. The Secret Service becomes discernibly nervous when the president wades into a crowd to press the flesh.

Public space is a form of high-status body language for speakers and celebrities, because it makes them the center of attention and a scarce resource with whom the "common folk" are lucky to rub elbows.

Elected officials and company executives can easily lose contact with the public and their organizations, resulting in executive isolation and poor information flow. Executive isolation occurs when the spatial isolation and privacy of company executives and elected officials puts them out of touch with their organizations and the public. Often, lower-echelon employees who have more contact with ordinary people are more in touch than upper-level managers.

The second zone of interaction, social-consulting space, extends about 4 to 8 feet away from the body. Salespersons, teachers, business people, professors, and consultants typically maintain this distance, which is somewhat personal but professionally detached. Think how annoying it is for a salesperson to get into the closest zone of personal space as though he or she were an intimate friend or relative. Similarly, sitting down in a meeting 5 inches from a colleague when other seats are available is weird and intrusive. Observe your own behavior during a nerdy colleague's invasion. It is likely to say "Give me some space."

The third zone of interaction where most of our interpersonal exchanges occur is called causal-personal distance. The zone extending from about $1\frac{1}{2}$ to 4 feet away from the body is between one and two arm lengths away, close enough to shake hands but far enough to prevent more intimate tactile interaction. At this range it is also easy for people to read one another's body language.

Not coincidentally, the closest, warmest zone of interaction is called intimate distance and extends from actual contact out to about $1\frac{1}{2}$ feet from the body. Intimate friends, romantic partners, and family members are the only people allowed into this zone, with one exception: toddlers. Young kids, because they haven't yet learned adult rules about personal space, are likely to use anyone they encounter as a road, a rug, or a security blanket!

Professionals around the world interact within the social-consulting space.

(Image courtesy of Peter Andersen)

Individual Distance Differences

Not all people understand or use these same rules of personal space that we overlearn in North America. People from other countries—especially those from contact cultures like Greece, Egypt, or Italy—may violate these rules of personal space, making them seem very weird to us. These mutual misunderstandings in body language will be explored more extensively in Chapter 27, where we explore the codes of culture.

Men have bigger space bubbles than women. This is especially true for same-sex relationships. You can remember the difference this way: Women sit and stand within an arm's length of just about everybody. Men sit and stand within an arm's length of women but not other men.

Age is another factor that influences interpersonal distance. Studies show that as they mature, children's personal space bubbles expand, finally reaching adult size in early adolescence. Likewise, studies found that we tolerate special invasions from 5-year-olds much better than invasions from than from 10-year-olds, suggesting that adults play a role in such socialization.

Another factor influencing space is attractiveness or reward value. According to research by University of Arizona Communication professor Judee Burgoon and her associates, people high in reward value are more easily able to invade other people's space. This includes physically attractive people, higher-status people, well-dressed people, people who are similar to us, or people with just about any positive quality. And as rewarding people invade your space, they actually increase their credibility, attractiveness, and persuasiveness.

People with different personalities also use and perceive space differently. A series of my own studies suggest that touch avoiders, people who dislike tactile interaction, adopt far greater interpersonal distances than touch approachers. They keep people beyond arm's length and are literally "out of touch." Likewise, socially conservative, shy, and paranoid individuals have larger personal space bubbles.

Studies of violent prisoners suggest that they have highly exaggerated personal space bubbles. People in jail for violent crimes, but not those in for nonviolent crimes, exhibit defensive arm positions called body buffers, and also retreat when someone else enters the room. These reactions are the kind you would exhibit if a menacing stranger stood two inches from you. This neurotic, paranoid quality may have caused their violent behavior to begin with. Or maybe it is a case of projection; they believe that others behave the same as they do.

The Maddening Crowd

In case you haven't noticed, the world is filling up with people! In just my lifetime, the world population has doubled. Farmers' fields have become condo complexes, the woods you played in as a kid are now subdivisions, and you frequently sit in traffic on streets in cities and suburbs. While some folks have headed back to the country, most people are still flocking to cities or burbs. Is this a good thing? What are the effects of overcrowding? And how does our body language change as a result?

The Demons of Density

Half a century ago, John Calhoun observed that rat populations stabilized in a quarter-acre outdoor pen at about 150, not growing or shrinking. He decided to design a controlled experiment, called the behavioral sink, that examined what happened to rats who were put in overcrowded cages compared to their less crowded counterparts. What he found was stunning. Compared to uncrowded ones, many rats in the crowded cages displayed the following traits: Total withdrawal from social and sexual relations, random mounting of other rats regardless of sex, disorganized or nonexistent nest-building, fighting near the food bins despite an abundance of food, numerous miscarriages, complete disregard for spatial boundaries, and cannibalism.

Do these findings apply to people? Not precisely, but the best answer is unfortunately yes, to some degree. Studies suggest that overcrowding has a number of detrimental effects.

Studies of overcrowded dormitory rooms by psychologist Jack Aiello and colleagues at Rutgers found that students in the high-*density* rooms felt more *crowded* and stressed, and less satisfied with school than those in lower-density rooms. Worse, work productivity declined and physiological stress tests showed much greater stress for the students in high-density environments. Other studies of high-density neighborhoods found that density produces more juvenile delinquency even when controlling for other factors like poverty and education. Overall, a whole series of studies has shown that the effects of higher density include …

Nonverbally Speaking

Density is an objective measure that refers to the number of people per square foot. **Crowding** is perceived density, a feeling of too many people in a given space.

♦ Decreased cognitive and work performance.

♦ Increased physiological and psychological stress.

♦ Additional accidents.

♦ More deviant behavior, including crime.

♦ Less satisfaction with living conditions.

♦ Fewer relationships and reduced association with neighbors.

♦ More verbal aggression.

Far from the maddening crowd, we seek solitude on vacations and in remote places.

(Image courtesy of Peter Andersen)

People act to reduce the negative effects of crowding in a number of ways. First, in crowded cities, neighborhoods, and dormitory rooms, people cope by spending less time in the most dense area. This suggests that parks, beaches, and nature preserves will become increasing valuable as you and I experience more crowding. Second, people shift the responsibility to other people and technologies to cope with crowding—they hire secretaries and doormen, screen calls, have unlisted numbers, and communicate by e-mail. Third, in crowded environments we adopt a "nonperson orientation." We step over passed-out drunks, ignore beggars, reduce eye contact with strangers, and stay in the safety of our homes.

When Crowding Is Chic

Despite the negative effects of crowding, in certain instances most people actually seek crowding. If you are a young person looking for excitement, you would be mighty disappointed if you went clubbing and nobody was at the club. Uncrowded sorority invites just aren't much fun. Going to a pro sporting event with a tiny crowd can be kind of depressing. In fact, an important part of the Superbowl is the crowd: the scarcity of your ticket, the loud cheers of the crowd, the endless tailgates outside the venue. These grand gatherings are part of the attraction of sports that you can read more about in Chapter 18.

In some settings, we expect and even like crowding.

(Images courtesy of Peter Andersen)

Time Is Money

Tune in to how people around you talk about time: *Time is money. Spend your time wisely. It was a waste of time.* Of course, time isn't really money, and you can't literally save time. Nevertheless, in our society time is a commodity. How we use time communicates clearly to other people.

The study of how we use and treat time is called *chronemics.* Researchers in this field have come to understand that in the United States and Northern Europe, waiting time for business and social engagements should be kept to a minimum. An American businessman in Latin America might be kept waiting all day for a meeting only to be told to come back tomorrow. This might be a major affront to the American but his Latin American counterpart has no idea this is offensive. In the United States, being more than 10 minutes late is considered very rude and requires an apology.

In the same vein, how much time we devote to an activity or relationship indicates its importance to us. I am always amazed by people who tell family members how much they love them but never spend any time with them. Their body language speaks louder than their words. When you spend time with someone you are telling them how important they are. Our research suggests that spending time with someone, may be the most important nonverbal message you send for building or maintaining a relationship. Think about how you spend your time. Do you spend it on the important stuff?

Positions of Power

Chronemics is the study of people's use of time and the meanings we associate with time during interpersonal interaction.

Bodily Blunders

In America, time is money. So avoid wasting people's time and, in particular, avoid late arrivals. They are a rude and inconsiderate form of body language.

Timing Is Everything

The study of chronemics has also found that timing is everything in conversation. First let's talk about talk time.

You have probably encountered uncouth, boorish people who only talk about themselves and dominate all of the talk time. Similarly, we've probably all attempted to carry on a conversation with people who won't talk—talk about frustrating! Here's a rule of thumb. In a two-person conversation, if you talk more than two thirds or less than one third of the time you are out of conversational balance and should adjust. And here are some rules of thumb for group behavior. If you never talk, maybe it's time to participate. People perceive noncontributors as shy, dimwitted, and lethargic. And if you want to be perceived as a leader, here is a final rule of thumb: talk your share plus 10 percent. So in a two-way conversation, go for 60 percent; in a five-person group, go for 30 percent. Obviously, what you say is also important, but no more so than how much you say.

Nonverbally Speaking

Are you a sparrow or an owl? Sparrows are early risers, and the early bird supposedly catches the worm. Night owls, on the other hand, have disdain for both worms and sparrows and prefer to sleep in and stay up late. Teenagers and young adults are more likely to get up late and stay up late. Senior citizens are more likely to be the early-to-bed, early-to-rise types, and think sleeping in is lazy and decadent. Urban dwellers colonize the night in the bright lights of the city. Farmers and ranchers are likely to be up before the crack of dawn. There is no right or wrong time to rise or turn in, but the chronemic body language of owls and sparrows sends powerful messages that create influential interpersonal impressions.

The Least You Need to Know

- Humans are territorial creatures.

- Your personal space goes where you go.

- People defend their space and territory with tenure, buffers, and markers.

- Crowding has negative consequences.

- In America, time is a commodity that is spent, wasted, and saved.

- Timing is everything.

Part  3

The Power of Body Language

Body language is powerful stuff. In fact, a primary purpose of body language is displaying dominance and presenting powerful postures. What is the voice of authority? How can you increase your power through eye contact? What positions are associated with higher status?

People use body language to get an upper hand in devious ways as well—they send deceptive body language messages. Do you have the power to detect others' lies? You'll get some tips on how to (and how not to) go about detecting deceptive body language in this section.

Finally, I'll tackle the topic of feelings, and how communicating your emotions—including happiness, love, fear, embarrassment, pride, and sexual desire—can help you connect with people.

11

Postures of Power

In This Chapter

- ◆ The power of position and stature
- ◆ Ocular influences
- ◆ The voice of authority
- ◆ Tools and rules of touch
- ◆ The power of resourceful relaxation

More than a century ago, barnyard biologists observed that the "top" chicken could peck on every other chicken in the pen, but the lowliest chicken couldn't peck on any other hen. Called "dominance hierarchies," these pecking orders exist in every animal species, and humans are no exception.

But how are human pecking orders established in a country such as the United States where everyone is said to be "created equal"? Equality is a great legal principal and a foundation of our civil rights, but we are not all equal. Physical power, economic power, political power, and perceived power differentiate us from one another.

Power, in part, is a self-fulfilling prophecy. If you think you are powerless you definitely will be powerless, because your body language will reflect your lowly status. Acting as though you're powerful is no guarantee of power, but the perception of power is an essential power prerequisite. Powerful body language is a key to gaining control over your life and achieving success and status.

Standing Tall in Advantageville

It all started with physical power. The larger, the stronger, the person with the better club and superior spear was the ruler of the family, tribe, or kingdom. Today, physical power has largely been replaced by economic power, political power, legal power, and occupational power. Actual wrestling matches have been replaced by legal, corporate, and political bouts. Nonetheless, the recent elections of live "superhero" action-figure governors Jesse Ventura and Arnold Schwartzenegger make us all realize that muscle power still counts in the power perception game. That is the central point of this chapter: Power is a perception, and body language creates powerful perceptions.

There is little doubt that physical size is still a potent part of personal power. Though bigger people may not actually have more power in a civilized society, they do communicate more powerful body language.

Tall, muscular, athletic men are perceived as natural leaders.

(Image courtesy of Peter Andersen)

When Randy Newman sang that short people "got little baby legs, that stand so low, you got to pick 'em up, just to say hello," we all giggled. Yet the song left most of us vaguely uncomfortable, since the stereotype was very real, the song was demeaning, and the consequences of being short can be dire. Plus, there is little one can do about being short, other than to pick tall parents with long genes.

Listen carefully to the language of elevated body language: "That was *big* of you," as opposed to "That was a *small* thing to do." When we're successful we feel "10 feet tall" or "on top of the world." Our prototypic male hero is "larger than life," "stands tall in the face of adversity," will always "stand up and be counted," and is never "small minded," "small time," or a "small fry." We "look down" on the actions of incompetent people who never "rise to the occasion." The so-called "Napoleonic Complex" is allegedly based on overcompensation for inadequate height.

Positions of Power

If you are a diminutive public speaker, set the stage for success. Put a platform behind the podium and adjust the microphone before you start speaking. Peeking over the podium and straining to speak into the microphone are not positions of power.

From the time we start school, we are lined up according to height. Teachers select taller boys for the more important jobs. A dozen studies show that bigger kids with more muscular bodies are preferred by other kids as friends, playmates, and leaders. The short and the scrawny are the last to be picked for teams and the "biggest" heroes in school are the largest athletes, who play football and basketball.

For men in particular, height is powerful plus. Tall, dark, and handsome is the traditional stereotype of the ideal man. Studies show that taller men are thought of as leaders, but it works the other way, too; leaders and celebrities are thought to be taller than they are. For men height and power are joined at the hip. Taller presidential candidates overwhelmingly prevail, and taller male job applicants get higher salaries.

It's not easy for a man to increase his height, short of minor adjustments like wearing elevator shoes. But it's not only a matter of height. More muscular men are perceived as being more credible and powerful. Working out and bodybuilding is about so much more than health; it is about status. Muscular men look like leaders. They are "pumped up" with pride as well as muscle.

Slouching and slumping make people look shorter, and standing tall increases perceptions of power and status. People who are depressed, downtrodden, and defeated all stoop and droop, further decreasing their power and contributing to their beleaguered and defeated situation.

Traditionally, petite women were the ideal female stereotype. After all, a diminutive damsel was fit for any broad-shouldered knight! Tall women were considered gawky, gangly, and geeky. This stereotype is changing, and today stronger, taller women do get more respect, as the ideal height for women has moved above the average. Still, people find it a bit odd when a woman is considerably taller than her boyfriend or husband. Likewise, muscular builds have become the high-status look for women as well as men.

Positions of Power

Now here's a paradox. Seated people are more powerful because it's uncomfortable to stand. But the higher position trumps the less powerful, lower position. Resolution? Put high-status people on raised platforms—like the queen's elevated throne, the looming judge's bench, or the towering podium at a national political convention.

Submission rituals have always involved lowering, kneeling, covering, prostrating, or bending. Women curtsied to show respect and politeness. Men bowed, tipped their hat, or took off their hats or helmets entirely. People still kneel at the feet of high priests and monarchs. Bowing to royalty is an age-old custom emblematic of people's submissive lower positions. In Japan, bowing is still customary, much like pleasant hellos or handshakes in the United States. The depth of the bow in Japan indicates the status of the other person.

This graduation speaker holds a position of power communicated with attire, elevation, and space.

(Image courtesy of Peter Andersen)

Eye Eye, Sir

Direct eye contact intensifies interactions. In close relationships, eye contact connects and bonds. Similarly, in pleasant conversations, along with pleasant facial expressions, eye contact deepens friendship and warmth; whereas with a mean expression it intensifies anger and serves as a threat. Eye contact is most powerful in communicating confidence. Direct eye contact intensifies confident expressions and communicates power, particularly for a speaker.

Penetrating eye contact along with a stern face and the arms akimbo position is powerful body language.

(Photo courtesy of Robert Avery)

Try this exercise. Practice a speech with your spouse, friend, or secretary, and while doing so maintain constant eye contact. Don't look away, glance around the room, look up to think, or blink. Pretty tough to do, eh? If you can pull it off, the effect is compelling; the listener will perceive that you exude confidence and power.

Studies of dominance suggest that prolonged gazes are powerful and intimidating. This probably goes all the way back to our primate past when a direct gaze was a display of dominance. Any playground tough guy can tell you that to flinch is to lose in schoolyard scraps. Absence of eye contact gives the impression of shyness and submissiveness, particularly for women.

Likewise, people react differently to direct gaze. Shy and submissive people tend to back off and break eye contact when confronted with direct gaze, whereas dominant people tend to move closer when they're the recipients of direct gaze. Shamed, apologetic, or submissive individuals will lower their eyes to avoid direct eye contact with a more powerful person. In addition, people don't break off eye contact randomly; the more submissive person looks away first. Dominant people rarely break eye contact first, whereas passive people are usually quick to break eye contact. Blinking, which is a very submissive signal closely akin to flinching, is done a lot more by women than men.

Business attire, a muscular build, direct eye contact, and an elevated podium create a position of power.

(Image courtesy of Peter Andersen)

Audience eye contact is also an index of a public speaker's power. Commanding speakers receive almost continuous eye contact from the audience. Speakers who are gazed at by visually attentive listeners are far more powerful than those who are visually ignored.

The late Ralph Exline, a psychology professor at the University of Delaware, developed an index of visual authority called the dominance ratio. It is computed by taking the amount of time spent looking while listening (a respectful, submissive behavior) and dividing it by the length of time spent looking while speaking (a confident, dominant behavior). Lower scores indicate more dominance and higher scores more submissiveness. It is a useful tool that can be used to determine whether your visual body language is powerful or powerless.

A study of ROTC officers showed that those with lower visual dominance scores (more looking while speaking than listening) had higher leadership rankings. Visual dominance is a key aspect of commanding presence. Leaders almost always look more while speaking than while listening.

The Voice of Authority

The sound of our voice is an essential aspect of body language. Research shows that more fluent, deeper, louder, and faster talk comprises the voice of authority.

Unfortunately, women are at a disadvantage when it comes to vocal power. However, the flip side of males' deeper, harsher voices is that they are less able to communicate intimacy and may be downright scary to small children. But in the power game, deeper, louder voices rule. And women are faced with another somewhat sexist predicament. Loud women are often perceived as shrill and even "bitchy." Women can effectively compensate by using the lower register of their voice when asserting themselves. This is totally counterintuitive, since the voice tends to rise when we are insistent, angry, or frustrated. But with a little practice women can use a lower vocal register effectively.

Faster speech, up to a point, is perceived as more credible and powerful. Research by Dr. David Buller of the Cooper Institute suggests that up to around 375 syllables per minute a speaker's competence increases, then plateaus, and declines at faster rates. In short, we do fall for fast talkers.

Regional accents have been shown by research to carry less weight, except in one's home region. When Georgian Jimmy Carter campaigned in Alabama, he often jokingly asked the audience, "Isn't it great to have a person running for office with no accent?" Outside the south, southern accents may have "redneck" or "hillbilly" connotations. New York accents play well in the Bronx, but elsewhere may sound "low class" or too rough and tough. Chicago accents can have a working class flavor, and the Southern Californian dialect may give the impression of being an "airhead." Certainly every region has an accent. However, the upper Midwest is perceived to be almost accent free, which is why many national newscasters have come from Iowa, and most 800-number operators are in Nebraska.

Positions of Power

Many of us can turn on and off our accents, which is a terrific skill. Situationally appropriate vocal body language will maximize your credibility.

Once again, celebrities and highly attractive individuals are exceptions to the findings on accents. Research suggests that if a person is attractive, high-status, or a celebrity, an accent may attract our attention, causing us to focus on a person's positive qualities. The ghetto accents of Eminem or Ice Cube, the Prussian accents of Henry Kissinger or Arnold Schwartzenegger, the Latin accents of José Feliciano and Gloria Estefan are testament to the fact that accents *can* be more advantageous than disadvantageous.

Clear articulation and enunciation also communicate power and status. When you speak well, you sound well bred, educated, and intelligent. Several types of speech are especially damaging to credibility and status. Poor pronunciation like *dese*, *dem*, and *dose* undermine perceptions of a person's competence and good image. False starts or incomplete sentences send signals of low confidence and anxiety. Vocal interjections or filled pauses are really, uh, like, ya know, like, uh, totally, ya know, annoying!

Bodily Blunders

One blatant body bungle is the filled pause, such as *ahs*, *ums*, *likes*, and *ya knows*. When you feel the urge to uh or um, do it silently. The result is a silent pause that sounds thoughtful and composed.

One nonverbal vocal cue that has received relatively little attention is laughing. Laughing is generally considered a friendly and appeasing behavior. For instance, laughing at your boss's or father's jokes is generally considered a polite and subordinate behavior. Likewise, the nervous laugh bolsters the confidence of a person with low power in an anxiety-provoking situation. However, laughs are highly contextual, and laughing at another person's misfortune or at an extremely embarrassing situation is dominant, mocking behavior.

Tactile Tools and Touch Taboos

In the 1970's, several popular books suggested that touching others was a display of dominance that was subjugating and controlling. Although touch does have power implications, recent research indicates that touch has more to do with intimacy than power. And, contrary to many popular books, males do not touch females more than females touch males.

Clearly, powerful people touch more than powerless people. Kings can touch commoners, doctors can touch patients, police can touch suspects, but the reverse is rarely acceptable. Touch doesn't give people actual authority; rather, authority gives people the right to touch. Touchers are perceived as dominant and in control of the situation and, certainly, powerful people touch more. Managers touch employees more than the reverse, teachers are more likely to do the touching than be the recipient of the touch, and doctors are more likely to touch patients than the reverse.

In romantic relationships, holding hands or walking with arms around each other's back are signs of possessiveness and togetherness. Studies show that the person who initiates these tactile connections is the more powerful. And the person who cuddles to the partners touch is more submissive.

Here are a few rules of thumb when it comes to touch:

◆ **Location counts.** The safest places to touch another person are on the shoulder or upper arms. Avoid areas perceived as sexual or sensual.

◆ **Relationships matter.** I give my secretary backrubs that she loves, but we have been good friends for over a decade. Touch is toxic when inappropriate in the wrong relationship.

◆ **Touch communicates to observers.** Huggy bear and kissy face are games best played in private.

◆ **Controlling touches are perilous.** Most people will not appreciate being pulled, tugged, or restrained.

◆ **Reactions matter.** You can usually tell whether another person likes touch by reading their body language. If you are unsure, ask them if they mind casual touching.

◆ **Verbal communication is key.** Date rape, assault, and sexual harassment often can be avoided by good verbal communication.

Stanley Jones, a communication professor at the University of Colorado, has identified four ways in which touch is used as a power move.

In the first, called the *affection-to-compliance sequence*, one person softens up the other person with affectionate touching that pleases the recipient. An example of an affection-to-compliance sequence would be if, in the middle of cuddling and kissing her boyfriend, a pretty young woman asks him to take her on a vacation.

A second tactile power sequence is the *seduction-and-rejection-game*. Here a person will initiate touch but reject tactile escalation. For example, a woman will stroke her date's knee but when he tries to kiss her she says: "I'm not ready to get involved." In this sequence, the initiator uses touch as a power move to turn on and to turn off affection.

A third touch power sequence is the *power-matching move*. Friends may punch each other in the arm or play wrestle. Willingness to play signals relational closeness and power equality.

Finally, in the *irritate and mollify sequence*, an initiator uses an aggressive or intrusive touch that irritates or interrupts another person. When the recipient shows displeasure, the initiator follows with affectionate touch to compensate. Young lovers use these, and they are really pretty sickening to watch.

A big beware is in order here. Be careful of manipulation in close relationships, especially tactile manipulation. You don't want to be perceived as exploiting touch in your closest relationships just to get your way or to get attention. Touch can be playful, but when it gets harsh or is unappreciated, consider toning down your act a bit.

Kinesic Clout

You learned earlier that, traditionally, taller people command more power; likewise, standing over someone is a power position. But body language is rarely simple and, as it turns out, standing can be both submissive and dominant.

This man is more powerful because he is standing but also because someone else is serving him.

(Image courtesy of Robert Avery)

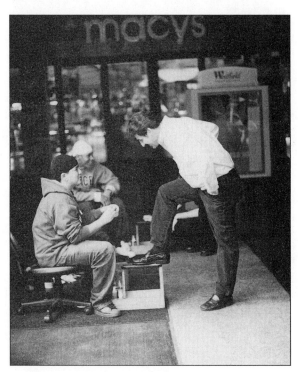

Nonverbally Speaking

Kinesics is the technical term for the study of body language, or more precisely, body movements. Coined half a century ago by nonverbal communication pioneer, Ray Birdwhistell, kinesics is to body movement what linguistics is to language.

Relaxation Rules

In the realm of body language, relaxation rules, whereas tension and rigidity subordinate. Studies show that higher-status people are permitted to display their power with relaxed body language that includes arm and leg asymmetry, sidewise tilts, leaning back on a chair, elevating one's feet, sprawling, slouching, and slumping. By contrast, subordinates' body language is upright and uptight. Subordinates are more likely to have their feet flat on the floor, their limbs closer together, and to stand and sit in more erect, uncomfortable positions. While the powerful can afford to relax, the weak must remain watchful. In the animal kingdom, rodents are the most tense and attentive since they are avoiding becoming somebody's dinner. The majestic relaxation of the grizzly or lion, except during an attack, is the body language of calm, confident power.

Contradictory cues? The uniform and standing position give this person power but also subordinate him since he is constrained by the task and must stay in an uncomfortable position.

(Image courtesy of Peter Andersen)

Rigidity communicates subordination, whereas movement signals dominance. Think of the Marine Corps drill sergeant who can move wherever he likes while the recruits must stand rigidly at attention. Superiors in any organization can act while subordinates can only observe. Superiors can lean in, invade space, and even selectively touch subordinates, while the reverse is not true.

Powerful Inconveniences

A whole set of behaviors, called inconvenience displays, simultaneously communicate humility, subordination, and politeness. Aspiring managers may scramble to see who

Positions of Power

Courtesy and good manners are a lost art. Want to subtly make an impression on others? Try these little body displays: Open doors for others, especially women. Pass the peas and fetch the fettuccini. Help people put on their sweaters and jackets. Politeness is irresistible. Providing for others is paradoxically powerful.

Body Talk

Here is a rule for powerful speaking. When making a strong, passionate public speech, use large gestures. Make sure the gesture is timed to coincide with the words you are emphasizing. This synchronized body language signals authority.

gets to open the door for the CEO, and a well-mannered host or hostess may bustle between the kitchen and dining room to make sure important guests are accommodated. It is customary for subordinates to rise in the presence of a judge, a king, or an honored guest.

While these behaviors have waned in recent years, things like opening a car door for another person, holding a door to let another person enter first, escorting another person home or to class, or carrying things for others are paradoxically powerful inconvenience displays. These are, on the one hand, submissive acts; but such polite, helpful behaviors, especially done by a powerful person, actually further empower them, since others now add civility and graciousness to the person's list of positive qualities.

Grand Gestures

Large and sweeping gestures have been shown in several studies to be perceived as powerful and important by observers. Gestures communicate confidence, especially when coordinated with vocal intonation.

Body positions that occupy space, such as the hands on the hips posture and spread legs, especially for men, communicate power. However, hands on hips, spread legs, and thumbs hooked in the belt may look too overtly bossy, and more subtle positions of power may work better.

Steepling, a gesture in which palms are touching and the fingers are vertically raised together in a symmetrical position, often accompanies a relaxed, laid-back posture. Research has shown that steepling is perceived as a powerful, confident, smug position associated with leaders and other high-status individuals.

As noted previously, pointing is an invasive, high-status gesture that is considered rude by many people and even obscene in some cultures. Research suggests that pointing is a powerful, intrusive form of body language that singles out a person or tells them where to go (literally, not figuratively).

Steepling is a power gesture used by leaders in professional settings.

(Image courtesy of Robert Avery)

Politicians, most notably John and Robert Kennedy, and more recently Bill Clinton, adopted a version of pointing by making a little child's fist and pointing with the thumb. This gesture is far less intrusive and offensive but still conveys powerful dynamism for a speaker.

The Least You Need to Know

◆ Tall people and positions still rule.

◆ Dominant speakers use more eye contact.

◆ Strong voices and good gesture communicate power.

◆ Relaxation is calmly powerful.

◆ Touch can strengthen or weaken relational control.

Chapter 12

Cues That Conceal and Reveal: Nonverbal Deception Detection

In This Chapter

- ◆ Can people detect deception with body language?
- ◆ How accurate are stereotypes about lying?
- ◆ Looking for a profile of deception
- ◆ Understanding body language leakage during deception
- ◆ Strategic management of deception cues

You like friends and colleagues who are truthful, right? And you are generally truthful and law abiding, too? Now think a bit more deeply. Have you even told a white lie about how much you love your wife's new outfit or husband's new tie? Exceeded the speed limit on the freeway? Called in sick and then gone golfing? Blew off a telemarketer by saying you were just leaving the house and went back to your favorite TV show? Put on makeup to cover a blemish? Told a beggar you had no money? Smiled at a co-worker you can't stand? Although we've all probably done one or more of these things, they are all deceptions; competent deceptions perhaps, but deceptions nonetheless.

And how much truth do you really want to hear from others? Do you want to know your boss's real attitude about your work? Whether a friend is glad about your promotion? If your kids think you are a perfect parent? Whether beauty contest judges would rate you attractive or not? Turns out that we all want the truth, more or less (and often less).

In this chapter, we will examine deception and discuss whether people are good deception detectives. We will look carefully at the research to determine whether or not you really can detect deception from body language.

Deceiving Ancestors?

When it comes to survival, people tell it like it ain't. Think about it. You're a teller at a bank and you see a masked man holding a gun coming your way. You press the silent alarm, and when he asks you whether you did, you tell say, "Why, yes, yes I did." *Not!* Let's rewind. "I didn't—I swear!" you say convincingly. We all like the truth, but when it comes to life and death, we lie and lie gladly. Similarly, when it comes to protecting someone we love, we lie and do it without remorse.

It turns out that we have been lying to protect ourselves and our loved ones for centuries. Boldar, the cave man sitting in his cave, having just stashed an entire mammoth safely underground, wasn't likely to tell a group of strangers where his family's precious winter food supply was hidden. Perhaps the strangers would get a scrap or two, but survival sometimes required guile. Few of us would criticize Boldar's behavior. Altruism stops where survival starts.

Animals probably don't think much about right and wrong, and I really doubt plants do, either. Yet they are naturally adapted for deception. Both plants and animals have been using deception for millions of years. Plants and animals employ illusory camouflage and protective coloration to fool enemies, trap prey, and enhance reproduction. Birds use calls that simulate Doppler effects to hide their true location from predators. Cats, like football running backs, fake one way and run the other.

So deception has ancient roots in the animal kingdom. But humans have an edge when it comes to deception—we can lie with our words! It's almost too easy to lie linguistically—just look somebody right in the eye and lie! In fact, some researchers believe that language is structured in such a way as to facilitate a little deceptive coloring or stretching of the truth.

Amazing research on chimpanzees suggests that both intelligence and language facilitate lying. Now, chimpanzees are pretty smart—they are a good rival for your two- or three-year-old in raw intelligence. Numerous published studies have reported that chimps engage in lying and concealing when it serves their own needs. When food is abundant, chimps will call other chimps to share in the abundance. But when food is scarce, chimps will not call other chimps and may even decoy them in the wrong direction! Chimps share food with trainers they like, but hide food from a trainer they dislike!

Moreover, when chimps were taught simple computer language, they used this new skill to lie about the presence or absence of their favorite foods. Indeed, when researchers asked the chimps for certain food items, they almost always produced the correct food, with one important exception. When researchers asked chimps for their favorite foods, like chocolate or oranges, the chimps would deny having any such food, even when they had it!

Like most people, I don't embrace or condone lying. Most of us try not to lie, and we really hate being lied to. But it's a bit more complicated than pure truth or falsehood. We often lie to protect another person from embarrassment, and certainly we would lie to protect our family. A nurse might not reveal a patient's condition is worsening if that knowledge could kill the patient. Without a doubt, we would support police who lied to a terrorist or kidnapper. These are altruistic lies, and most people don't find them that reprehensible even though we have a general belief that lying is wrong. We do not want to send or receive the whole truth and nothing but the truth, and we manipulate our body language as a cover.

In truth, it is self-serving lies that really get people bent out of shape—lies that start wars, bilk investors, unfairly win elections, or exploit personal relationships to gain sex, power, or money. We even forgive ourselves and others for those little white lies. But big, harmful lies are awful, and we would love to detect them if we could.

How Good Is Your Deception Detector?

Obviously, in many circumstances it would be nice to be able to detect deception. It would probably give us better brokers, more authentic politicians, and really upright salespeople if we had a reliable way of detecting falsehood.

Unfortunately, no such magic lie detector is available. Dozens of research studies have revealed that the ordinary person is slightly better than 50-50 at overall lie-detection. That's right, flipping a coin is just about as accurate as we are.

> **Nonverbally Speaking**
>
> Research shows that people do just a little better than 50 percent in distinguishing between lying and truth-telling. Despite the noteworthy failure of people to detect deception, most folks report extremely high levels of confidence in their detection ability.

> **Nonverbally Speaking**
>
> Sure, deception in strangers is hard to detect, but lying loved ones are easy to spot, right? Wrong. Studies show that because of our truth biases and lack of vigilance about loved ones' lies, we may actually be less accurate with them than with strangers. Plus, we might not want to know a loved one is deceiving us.

Most people operate with a truth bias, a belief that other people are generally telling the truth. To think otherwise would make us pretty cynical, bitter, and suspicious. In a number of experiments, people are just moderately accurate at detecting the truth; the numbers range above 60 percent, but that is partly because most of us have such a truth bias. When it comes to detecting lies, we are typically in the 40 percent range, because the truth bias causes more misses. Overall our hit rate is just above 50 percent.

Cues That Count: Stereotypes About Lying

Here is a set of 20 behaviors widely believed by the general public to be deception cues. Which of these do you think really are deception cues? Answers are in the Bodily Blunders box later in this section. So here goes: Check the cues that have generally been associated with deception:

❏ Defensive gestures

❏ Shakiness

❏ Unnatural gestures

❏ Excessive swallowing

❏ Adam's apple movement

❏ Increased eye contact

❏ Reduced eye contact

❏ Speech hesitations

❏ Increases in vocal pitch

❏ Speech errors

❏ Longer response time

❏ Postural shifts

❏ Pupil dilation

❏ Blinking

❏ Less smiling

❏ More smiling

❏ Head movements

❏ Hand shrugs

❏ Self-touching

❏ Fidgeting

Body Talk

In Shakespeare's play by the same name, Othello misreads Desdemona's distress over Cassio's death as evidence of her infidelity. The **Othello error** occurs when a truth-teller is falsely accused of lying based on body language cues such as anxiety or agitation.

Unfortunately, most of our stereotypes about deception are false. People can hide their lying eyes. Shifty eyes are not a good indicator of deception. In fact, people's stereotypes about deceptive body language bear only a slight resemblance to really deceptive body language.

Our BS detectors are tuned in to the unexpected. Unusual or weird-acting people are commonly thought to be deceptive even when they are completely truthful, suggesting it's a bit dangerous to be weird, even honestly weird.

Shifty-eyed people sure look deceptive, but there is no evidence to support the stereotype that eye behavior is a deception cue.

(Image courtesy of Robert Avery)

Suspicious people are most likely to read truthful body language as deceptive, an occurrence known as the *Othello error.* Moreover, Judee Burgoon and her colleagues at the University of Arizona have found that false accusations produce Othello errors, when the accused person's nervous body language appears to be deception.

Bodily Blunders

Here are the answers to the mini-quiz earlier in this section. Only the following seven cues are consistent indicators of deception:

- ◆ Speech hesitations
- ◆ Increases in vocal pitch
- ◆ Speech errors
- ◆ Pupil dilation
- ◆ Blinking
- ◆ Hand shrugs
- ◆ Self-touching

And don't forget that people manifest these body language behaviors for many reasons other than deception!

The Elusive Body Language Lie Detector

All right, in general, people are lousy lie detectors. Even body language experts rarely have hit rates above 70 percent.

Try as we might, we have never produced a totally valid deception profile. You cannot read a liar like a mystery novel, and there is no definite way to detect deception. The only way the following list of behaviors is useful at all is for comparing a set of allegedly deceptive behaviors to a normal or baseline set of truthful behaviors. This first list below discusses behaviors that are the best candidates for creating a body language profile of deception. But be sure to look for clusters of deception cues; one or two cues don't count for very much.

- ◆ **Speech errors and hesitations.** One fairly consistent finding is that liars tend to have more false speaking starts, mispronunciations, hesitations, and other speech errors than truth-tellers. These behaviors probably occur because deception is much more difficult than truth-telling.

- ◆ **Shorter speaking turns.** Because lying is harder than truth-telling, liars' answers tend to be shorter than those of truth-tellers. Remember, this cue is only valuable if you know how long a person normally speaks. Otherwise, you might wrongly accuse your reticent friend of deceptiveness.

- ◆ **Hand shrugs.** Hand shrugs are upward palm gestures that look like a person is unsure. Researchers disagree about whether hand shrugs are a deception cue. Early studies suggested these were deception cues; more recent ones are somewhat more equivocal. Hand shrugs may leak a lack of confidence in a liar's stories.

The hand shrug, a sign of uncertainty or equivocation, has been found in several studies to be a deception cue.

(Image courtesy of Robert Avery)

◆ **Vocal pitch.** A number of studies have found that during deception the pitch of liars' voices goes up. This is probably due to increased tension; one study suggests that more stressful acts of deception result in the greatest increases in pitch.

◆ **Pupil dilation.** Several studies suggest that liars' eyes dilate more than truth-tellers. This is an odd finding since, as we discussed in Chapter 4, pupil dilation is a sign of interest, arousal, or attraction. Pupil dilation during lying is probably a function of increased mental effort and arousal that occurs while lying.

◆ **Eye blinks.** Research suggests that more blinking is associated with deception. But be careful! More mental activity and greater intelligence are also associated with blinking.

◆ **Self-touches.** Self-touching behaviors, called adaptors, show significant increases during deception. These behaviors, like wringing one's hands or touching the face, are probably the result of increased tension and nervousness. However, one study found that highly deceptive individuals used fewer adaptors, probably because they are so practiced at controlling deceptive body language.

Self-touching behaviors, called adaptors, are a potential deception cue.

(Image courtesy of Robert Avery)

◆ **Bodily discrepancies.** Several studies have shown discrepancies between various nonverbal cues. For example, deceivers may show a confident face while displaying jittery hands. Some of the latest research suggests that *the* best way to detect deception is to look for inconsistent messages.

Research on the next set of behaviors is mixed or equivocal. Some evidence suggests the following behaviors are deception cues, but other evidence suggests they are not:

◆ **Frequency of smiling.** Some studies have shown less smiling during deception, and some studies have found no difference in smiling when comparing truth-tellers and liars, while other studies suggest increased smiling among liars.

◆ **Eye contact.** Popular wisdom holds that you can't hide your lying eyes, but research suggests otherwise. Early studies found decreases in eye gaze but recent studies suggest that most deceivers engage in *more* eye contact than truth-tellers. This may be a case of public adaptation to the "shifty eyed" stereotype, by over-compensating with more eye contact during deception.

◆ **Foot and hand movements.** Despite early research that showed jittery limbs and trembling accompanied deception, recent research suggests this is not a reliable deceptive cue. Excessive hand movements are often controlled by deceivers but some experts think that jittery feet are difficult to control.

◆ **Squirmy body language.** Fidgety, squirmy people might look deceptive, but there is little evidence that more of these behaviors occur during deception.

Positions of Power _____

To detect deceptive behavior, follow these steps:

◆ Obtain a baseline of a person's normal behavior and carefully record changes during an alleged deception.

◆ Look for clusters of cues. No one change in behavior is a reliable or valid indicator of deception.

The bottom line is that there is no single definitive sign that reveals that a person is lying.

The Leaky Liar

When we are deceptive, we leak emotional body language that may give us away. Ironically, unconscious leakage occurs for numerous reasons, which is one reason why no standard profile of lying has been developed with any high degree of accuracy. So what makes you leak body language during deception?

Falsification Anxiety

Lying can be pretty nerve-racking, especially when the stakes are high. It makes most people nervous to lie, and it is compounded by nervousness about getting caught. Feelings of guilt and shame may further augment the anxiety. Many of the deception cues we discussed are caused by anxiety, including self-touching behaviors, adaptors, blinking, speech errors including stuttering, and trembling.

But here is the rub. There is no deceptive body language, only anxious body language, and many things other than deception can cause anxiety. People can display anxious body language because they suffer from general anxiety, shyness, communication anxiety, or because they are stressed out from being accused of lying, have a lot of deadlines, are worried about a loved one's health, and a hundred other things. So once more, caution is advised.

Fabrication Stimulation

When you are about to lie to someone, you become physically stimulated and aroused. Even if you are not experiencing anxiety, your body is preparing for activity. As a result, your heart rate, blood pressure, and respiration increase; your skin becomes more sensitive; and you may begin to perspire slightly.

Many deception cues, such as self-touching behaviors, blinking, speech errors, increases in vocal pitch, and pupil dilation, may be associated with increases in arousal. Of course, like anxiety, arousal can be caused by a lot of different things including general activity, rooting for the home team, stress, or even sexual desire. And it's really a bummer to mistake passion for deception.

> **Nonverbally Speaking**
>
> Arousal is the basis for the polygraph test, which compares physiological responses during a baseline period, to arousal during potentially deceptive behavior when arousal should peak.

Dissembling Difficulty

Mentally, lying is hard work. First you must keep track of the truth, then you have to conjure up a good lie, and finally you have to perform it convincingly. At the same time, you need to monitor the receiver's reactions to see how you're doing, and adjust your behavior accordingly. In fact, lying is such a difficult mental activity that it can lead to an unconvincing performance, and a fake, stammering, or self-conscious body language.

Some deception cues, such as pupil dilation and speech errors like stuttering and hesitating, could be the byproduct of the mental overload during lying. In fact, research shows that if you give people very difficult mental tasks that don't involve lying, they manifest some of these same behaviors. You don't want to accuse somebody of lying when he or she is merely overloaded with information, do you?

Leaking Negative Emotions

To all but the pathological liar, deception feels lousy. Lying is often characterized by fear, shame, anger, guilt, embarrassment, or frustration. Plus, many of us feel remorse, guilt, and compassion for the person we are deceiving. Our body language could easily leak these negative emotions. Several studies have shown that liars send more negative and emotional body language than truth-tellers. Likewise, certain body language behaviors like blinking and self-touching could easily be a result of negative emotions.

But once again, these are not deception cues per se. Deception causes negative emotions, which in turn lead to negative expressions. However, lots of other stuff can cause these negative emotional displays, such as a hard day at work, low body cycles, or fatigue. Just because a person looks depressed or is engaging in self-touching behaviors doesn't mean that he or she is lying.

Duping Delight

Some liars really enjoy putting one over on others. Maybe they think fooling someone is fun, perhaps they are just evil, manipulative people, or it could be that they enjoy it so much because they think their target deserves it. Or maybe they are just enjoying the quality of their own performance, getting off on the danger of lying, or feel good because they are overconfident. The positive feeling some people experience during deception is called *duping delight*.

Deception cues associated with duping delight consist of all the immediacy cues we will discuss in Chapter 17, including more direct eye contact, smiling, or gleeful tones of voice. Happy people are not usually deceptive people, so duping delight is likely to seem like garden-variety happiness. Only when observed with other deceptive body language cues will it help you detect deception.

Strategic Deception Cues

Most liars think they're pretty smart, and some are. We are strategic and tactical creatures who plan, scheme, and plot when we are being deceptive. We might practice looking straight into the mirror with direct eye contact while speaking a lie. Likewise, if we know we fidget when we're nervous, we might try to suppress these nervous fidgets when we are lying. These strategies and tactics create a whole new set of behaviors, called strategic deception cues. Let's look at some of them.

Warming to the Occasion

Body language cues that communicate availability, warmth, and psychological closeness are called immediacy behaviors (more about these in Chapter 16). Sometimes liars think that warm, ingratiating behaviors will help conceal lying. But some receivers overcompensate by being a little too friendly and unctuous, thereby creating yet another deceptive profile. Of course, warmth and immediacy per se should not be treated as deceptive, but if they are accompanied by other deception cues and a suspicious situation, you have every reason to be concerned.

Coldness Cues

Coldness is even more common than warmth during deception. Let's face it, lying is distasteful to most people, and we usually emotionally distance ourselves from targets of our deception. A businesslike lie also makes it less likely to face probing that may occur during a longer, warmer interaction. Sometimes deceivers smile less, sit further away, cut interactions short, and in general communicate in a cool, nonimmediate style.

Positions of Power

Deception experts Judee Burgoon and David Buller have found that when motivation to deceive is high, deceivers display an overcontrolled appearance that appears unexpected and dishonest. To detect deception, they recommend looking for both leakage cues and strategic cues to find inconsistencies.

Calmness Cues

Recognizing that deception is highly arousing, deceivers sometimes seek to calm themselves down to avoid appearing agitated. Deceivers may restrain bodily activity so as not to appear nervous, overactive, or aroused. Masking is a very common approach in which a liar will go deadpan to suppress obvious emotional displays. As with other strategic deception cues, strategically calm liars may be outsmarting themselves. Excessively composed, deadpan expressions may actually be a new form of deceptive body language that tips off a receiver that deception is occurring.

Image Management

Deceivers are motivated to make a good impression, but some go a bit overboard. Research suggests that deceivers may be excessively polite and agreeable, and avoid interrupting their deceptive target, like Eddy Haskell on *Leave It to Beaver*. Some liars dress up to appear more credible and even do things like send flowers. This is a pretty lame strategy for husbands who rarely or never send flowers. Most wives would be pretty suspicious of such a gift and might actually treat it as an infidelity-gram.

Indistinctness Increases

Lots of liars try to create vague, indistinct, ambiguous messages that are hard to pin down. While this often involves the use of vague or equivocal language, it also is conveyed via body language. Hand shrugs, ignoring questions, looking confused, and playing dumb are common strategies.

If you combine all the types of leakage cues with strategic cues, you get at least 10 profiles of deceptive body language. Deceivers may manifest an entire set of body language cues associated with anxiety, arousal, mental difficulty, negative emotions, duping delight, warmness, coldness, calmness, image management, and ambiguity. And worse, a given profile can combine any combination of these cues, resulting in millions of possibilities. Small wonder there is no single set of reliable deception cues available through body language.

> **Nonverbally Speaking**
>
> Collaborative deceptions occur when somebody picks up deceptive body language but chooses to ignore it. Sometimes people don't want to know the truth, believing that "ignorance is bliss." Other times we accept lies to avoid the embarrassment and conflict associated with an accusation of deception. We do not always want the whole truth and nothing but the truth.

But all is not lost. When we are being deceived, we are often already suspicious and so interrogate the person whom we suspect of lying. This gives us a chance to keep a watch for deception cues. But always be careful, because you cannot read a person like a book, and you cannot read deception cues like a polygraph or a confession. They are suggestive, not conclusive. Compare deceptive body language to baseline behavior. And when reading deception, like all types of body language, look for sets of cues and patterns of behavior. No part of body language is meaningful in isolation.

The Least You Need to Know

◆ People are poor detectors of deception. Flipping a coin to determine truths and lies is almost as accurate.

◆ Despite the widespread prevalence of lying, our erroneous stereotypes and truth biases prevents us from accurately detecting lies.

◆ A major source of deception cues is body language leakage caused by anxiety, arousal, mental effort, negative emotions, and duping delight.

◆ Another source of deception cues is strategic manipulation of body language, which occurs as we try to be warm, cool, calm, confident, or ambiguous.

◆ When you suspect you're being deceived, look for deviations from baseline behaviors, clusters of body language behaviors, and inconsistencies.

Chapter **13**

Fleshing Out Feelings: Emotional Communication

In This Chapter

- ◆ The nature of our emotions
- ◆ Reading emotional body language profiles
- ◆ Reactions to jealousy
- ◆ The survival value of expression
- ◆ Emotional intelligence

One of the primary purposes of body language is emotional expression. Your body, face, hands, legs, and voice are rich channels of emotional communication.

Most people think emotions are just private feelings, but nothing could be further from the truth. In fact, emotions are designed to be expressed, and the primary mode of expression is through body language.

Your posture, voice, hands, body, and face are designed to convey emotions. In truth, you can't really shut down your expressive body language—you can only manage it intelligently. Your moving body postures are always revealing something. Your eyes continuously provide clues about how you feel. Even your best poker face looks bored, deceptive, sleepy, or depressed. And covering your face with your hands makes you look sad, scared, or shy. So get set for an emotional tour of your body and how you communicate your fabulous feelings.

Expressing Self-Conscious Emotions

Professors June Tangney of George Mason University and Kurt Fischer of Harvard University call a certain class of emotions *self-conscious emotions.* These emotions originate in our social interactions and are often quickly and automatically expressed though our body language in social situations. They include guilt, embarrassment, shame, pride, envy, and jealousy. Each such emotion has a special body language profile that is important to understand.

The Appearance of Guilt

Guilt arises out of recognizing that your actions hurt another person or group, especially if the people are close to you. The transgression you committed leaves you feeling responsible and remorseful. Guilt is a highly interpersonal emotion with a special body language profile. Guilty people look like the cat that ate the canary. My cats frequently look guilty and I've never even had a canary! You probably know the look. Guilty people sneak around and slink away. Their heads are lowered, and their eyes are often cast upward. While no single facial expression is associated with guilt, guilty people look sad, sorry, and apologetic. Guilty people are often silent because they don't know what to say. Guilty people don't look especially happy and rarely smile unless it is a stupid, sheepish smile that looks kind of fearful.

> **Bodily Blunders**
>
> Identifying the body language of self-conscious emotions is more like completing a jigsaw puzzle than reading a book. Look for a syndrome, patterns, or sets of symptoms to correctly spot emotions like guilt, shame, or embarrassment. You cannot read a person like a book.

Expressing Embarrassment

When you suffer temporary humiliation, lose face, find yourself in an awkward social situation, are conspicuously put on view, or receive excessive praise, you experience embarrassment. Giving a speech with your pants unzipped, using the wrong restroom, or putting a car in reverse rather than forward may cause some embarrassment, especially if others notice. The body language of embarrassment includes sheepish smiles, looking at witnesses then lowering the eyes, nervous half-hearted laughter, covering the mouth or face, and turning away from others. Embarrassment also often causes blushing, a totally involuntary form of body language.

The Shape of Shame

Shame is embarrassment on steroids. It is experienced when a person has lost face, feels like a complete failure, suffers from inferiority, and generally feels long-term negative feelings about him- or herself. Shame occurs publicly and is accompanied by feelings of humiliation and loss of pride. Shamed individuals show a pattern of body language characterized by the desire to disappear and make themselves invisible, which is a difficult form of body language to pull off. Unable to disappear, shamed people hide their faces, erroneously thinking that if they can't see others, others can't see them. They tend to deflate their postures. They try to shrink by stooping over, exhaling air, slouching, and avoiding eye contact.

Embarrassed people try to disappear or hide.

(Image courtesy of Robert Avery)

Prideful Posturing

You probably think of pride as a positive emotion, but it is also considered one of the seven deadly sins. Pride is a mixture of good and evil feelings. On the one hand, pride is a positive response to success, progress, and compliments. Pride builds self-esteem and self-confidence and is displayed publicly with prideful posturing. On the other hand, it is said that "pride comes before a fall!" Pride can also make you seem aloof, arrogant, or boastful, and often is a barrier in accepting help from other people. Proud body language includes standing taller and straighter, strutting, making yourself larger, and flexing your muscles. Pride is accompanied by confident smiles and can include celebration gestures like raised fists and high fives. But pride can induce a negative emotion in others, envy, another of the "seven deadly sins"!

Envious Expressions

Envy is a strong desire to be someone you are not or have what someone else has. Envy includes stuff like yearning for your neighbor's new Beemer, wanting a body that looks like Brad Pitt's or Nicole Kidman's, feeling desirous greed over your co-worker's promotion, wishing you were as witty as Robin Williams, or wanting to be as wealthy as Bill Gates. Envy can have positive consequences when it leads to self-improvement and motivation. But the dark side of envy can include a desire to steal what others have, an impulse to weaken or diminish another person, or harboring feelings of resentment and inadequacy.

Envious body language is a pattern of expressions that includes sneaky glances at the target of your envy or the possessions you covet, rapid breathing, and other negative, suspicious body language in the presence of the target of your bitterness. Envy often involves a combination of the body languages of anger, sadness, fear, resentment, and dislike. Envious people rarely smile and may be fixated on the object of their envy.

Jealousy, the Green-Eyed Monster

Jealousy is a cousin of both love and envy. We experience jealousy when a real or imagined rival threatens a close relationship, usually a romantic one. Jealousy usually involves a perceived love triangle composed of you, your partner, and a possible rival. Sociobiologists believe that jealous feelings and jealous behavior evolved as a form of mate protection. Jealousy has a long history. Shakespeare called it the "Green eyed monster, which doth mock." Upon experiencing jealousy many people report a "jealousy flash," a powerful burning feeling due to intense physical and psychological arousal. This passion can produce violence, and research suggests it is a leading cause of murder! Jealous feelings are combinations of hurt, fear, anger, and sadness.

My colleagues Laura Guerrero of Arizona State University and Brian Spitzberg of San Diego State University and I have done research on jealousy. Based on our findings, here are the top 10 body language reactions to jealousy. But be careful! Most of these responses are dysfunctional and destructive. Can you pick out the lone effective response?

10. **Surveillance.** You are feeling jealous and you can't resist the temptation to turn into James Bond or one of Charlie's Angels. You spy on your partner, follow them around, and search their wallet for a motel receipt or their car for someone else's clothing. You push the redial button on their phone, listen to their voice mail, and call them at unexpected times.

9. **Threats and violence.** Here you make relational, emotional, psychological, and physical threats against your partner and your rival. You throw things, feign punches, or storm around like a middle linebacker. This sort of brutal body language can only cause catastrophe!

8. **Relational enhancement.** Realizing a rival threatens your relationship, you immediately start a program of personal and relational improvement. You go to the gym twice a day and consider getting a face-lift. You perform sordid and humiliating services for your partner. You buy flowers or make their favorite foods. The psychology of this perverse strategy goes something like this: My philandering partner's infidelity is *my* fault, so I need to try harder.

7. **Negative body language.** When you catch your partner flirting with someone else, you resort to blatant body language: You put your arm around your partner while glaring at your adversary. You grab your partner and pull them away from your rival. You direct ice-cold looks at your partner.

6. **Jealous revenge.** "Okay, I'll show you for hanging out with that tramp!" says your body language. So you show up arm in arm with a gorgeous (but preferably trashy-looking) date who you parade around in front of your partner (who may actually be your ex because now you are *both* jealous).

5. **Playing it cool.** Here your body language says "nothing is the matter," "I'm not upset," "I am too strong to get distressed." Worse, however, your partner may not notice your passive-aggressiveness! Remember some people are clueless when it comes to reading body language, and "playing it cool" is a deliberately understated display.

4. **The blame game.** You start yelling, screaming, and crying in the midst of accusations about the legitimacy of your partner's birth or their resemblance to a female dog. It includes quarrelling as well rude and uncouth gestural behavior. And this is supposed to win your partner back?

3. **Interaction avoidance.** You give your partner the cold shoulder (rather than your warm front), use the silent treatment, storm out of the room (don't forget

to slam the door), withdraw into a cocoon, or shun your partner when you see them on the street. Two problems with this approach are that it makes relational repairs pretty tough and tends to hamper rational communication. Plus, you're acting like a five-year-old.

2. **Rational communication.** You sit down with your partner and express your concerns through both body language and talk. You describe your partner's behavior while using direct eye contact and a serious tone of voice. You may employ a touch of humor to defuse the tension during this discussion. A tear or two during this conversation never hurts, either!

Positions of Power

Research shows that both the experience and expression of jealousy is usually bad for a relationship. Though expressing jealousy can make your partner realize you love them, expressing your jealousy tends to make matters worse. However, rational dialog with direct eye contact and a serious facial expression can heal hurt feelings and restore relationships.

And the most common response to jealousy is …

1. **The negative emotional outburst!** Your body language expresses anger, depression, frustration, resentment, anxiety, hurt, insecurity, and fear. This is like a total temper tantrum or a one-person riot. It is not a pretty picture, but if you have been the recipient of this display I'm sure you got the picture.

With one exception, all of these displays send your relationship into a death spiral of negative thoughts and feelings. So which one of these jealous responses helps a person get beyond their jealous feelings and gets the relationship back on track? By itself, only rational communication mends jealous relationships and alleviates jealous feelings.

The Manifestation of Melancholy

Melancholy and other miserable emotions are usually caused by social forces such as the death of a loved one, a relationship breakup, a disability, or the disappearance of supportive friends (though totaling your Mercedes may induce melancholy, too). So get out your hankies for a tour of the melancholy emotions.

Sadness: The Look of Loss

We've all experienced sadness. Sad body language includes downcast eyes, a lowered head, sad facial expressions, slouching posture, frowning, moping, long silences, talking in a monotone, and sometimes crying or sobbing. In extreme cases sad people throw themselves on the ground, refuse to get up, and go limp.

Sadness can be communicated through many forms of body language.

(Image courtesy of Robert Avery)

Doing Depression

Depression is a chronically sad, unmotivated, and pessimistic emotional state. Depression has the same body language profile as sadness. In addition, depressed people may also sleep endlessly or have difficulty sleeping, have difficulty rising in the morning, maintain little or no eye contact, show no vocal animation, and gesture little or not at all.

Positions of Power _____

How do you best comfort a loved one who is sad or depressed? Not by saying you know how someone feels or trying to "fix" their problem, research by Professor Brant Burleson of Purdue University tells us. Real comfort occurs when you actively listen and use body language that facilitates your partner's reappraisals of their situation and helps them find their own solutions.

Feeling Good About Hedonism

In our hedonistic society, nothing feels better than feeling good. Generations ago, getting by and feeling well were probably enough; but today feeling good, even excellent, seems to be the goal for most of us. People think there are shortcuts for first-rate feelings, but most of these are temporary fixes. Health and good relationships are probably the leading way to joy and gratification.

The Language of Love

Love is the most profound of your emotions. Love typically occurs in the context of your closest relationships, though people also love God or nature. (I also love chocolate ice cream, but that's probably really more like fondness or infatuation than true love.) Love creates unique feelings of joy, connection, and bondedness that come from deep within our genes.

While the words "I love you" have special meaning, actions speak louder than words. The body language of love includes close distances, spending time together, and prolonged eye contact, which is pretty sickening if you are having dinner with a couple who has just fallen in love. Love includes blissful, delighted facial expressions, increased prolonged and intimate touch, pupil dilation, blushing, and increased smiling.

Sending Those Warm Fuzzy Feelings

Interpersonal warmth is characterized by feelings of intimacy, sharing, pleasantness, and contentment that we experience in our closest, most intimate relationships. Warm body language includes pleasant tones of voice, hugs, welcoming gestures, contented and happy facial expressions, affectionate glances, synchronous behaviors, and a mellow experience of time spent together for its own sake. Just thinking about interpersonal warmth makes me want share a good bottle of wine around the fireplace with close friends.

Glad to Be Happy

Probably your favorite emotion is happiness. When you feel delight, contentment, mellowness, satisfaction, and joy, you're experiencing happiness. Happiness can occur when you are alone, but it's pretty rare. As noted in Chapter 5, we tend to smile when we bowl a strike and cheer for a touchdown when others are around but rarely when we are alone. Happy body language is inherently communicative and includes increased laughing and giggling, a lighter gait, positive tones of voice, smiling, hugs, pupil dilation, and closer interpersonal distances.

If you smile at me I will understand because that is something everybody everywhere does in the same language.

(Image courtesy of Peter Andersen)

Sexual Signals

Sexual desire or sexual arousal is both a physical state and an emotion. It is characterized by sexual yearning, usually directed at a particular person. In contrast to the warmth of intimacy, sexual arousal is hot! Sexual arousal is generally a positive state, though undesired arousal can be uncomfortable, embarrassing, and unfulfilling. Sexually aroused body language includes heavy breathing; erections of the penis (in men), clitoris (in women), nipples and even hair follicles (in both men and women); sometimes audible and visible increases in heart rate; flushed skin; and passionate vocal behaviors. Frankly, if you have ever seen it, it's pretty hard to miss.

The Avoidant Emotions

Some emotions are warnings. They tell us to be aware, be cautious, or flee. We inherited these emotions from a long line of cautious ancestors who lived by sayings like "He who fights and runs away will live to fight another day," and "We have nothing to fear but lots of stuff." Good thing, too, or you wouldn't be around to read this.

Fearful Feelings

Fear is a fleeting emotion characterized by riveted attention, bodily readiness, and avoidance of dangerous stuff. Fearful body language warned your ancestors of impending threats without having a big conversation about it. Today, these fearful behaviors still include muscular tension, directing the body toward the threat, a fearful facial expression, increased limb movements, flinching or ducking, widened eyes, cowering, bodily protection, hiding, and outright flight.

Fear produces an automatic response, including a fearful facial expression.

(Image courtesy of Peter Andersen)

Bodily Blunders _____

More than 200 million Americans suffer from communication anxiety. Yup, that's most of us. When someone is nervous during interaction their body language includes shifty eyes, facial covering, fidgety hands, and a shaky voice—a profile that looks a lot like deception. So how do you distinguish between the two? Here is a clue: Anxious body language is worse in front of a large group and deceptive communication is not!

The Look of Disgust

Disgust is typified by feelings of repugnance and intense dislike. It all started when your ancestors tasted something rotten, spit it out, and said "yuck!" Clever creatures that we are, we have generalized disgust to disgusting people, movies, words, and situations. Disgust is often accompanied by mock gagging, a finger part way down one's throat, sticking out the tongue, turning away the head, and the disgust facial expression.

Dirty looks and irritated facial expressions communicate disgust and annoyance.

(Image courtesy of Peter Andersen)

Surprising Symptoms

Surprise is the most fleeting emotion; it rarely lasts for more than a second. Surprise wakes you up, orients you to a stimulus, and quickly blends into another emotion like fear, anger, or happiness. Surprised body language includes open eyes, a surprised facial expression, turning toward the stimulus, erect hair follicles, and startled yells or squeals.

Surprise is a fleeting emotion that quickly turns to another emotion such as fear, or in this case joy and delight.

(Images courtesy of Peter Andersen)

The Injured Emotions

When other people injure us, we usually experience hurt and anger. These feelings are almost uncontrollable and often lead to retaliation and escalation of conflict.

Hurtful Happenings

You experience emotional hurt when someone injures you, makes negative statements about your personality, spreads false rumors, or makes false accusations. Hurt body language includes pained expression, sad facial movements, crying, running away and hiding, or aggressive action. Many of these behaviors are directed toward the source of the hurt and may be intended to induce guilt or seek repair. Emotional hurt can be worse than physical pain.

Angry Actions

Anger typically occurs when you think you have been wrongly harmed or mistreated by another person. Although it can occur outside of social interaction, like when you hit your thumb with a hammer, anger is typically the result of an interpersonal transgression. Angry body language is easy to spot. It includes direct stares, fist shaking and possibly obscene gestures, slamming doors, clenching one's fists, giving someone the silent treatment, yelling or swearing, angry facial expressions, throwing objects, and sometimes physical aggression or revenge. It is a dramatic and frightening display.

Anger is a basic and universal facial expression.

(Image courtesy of Robert Avery)

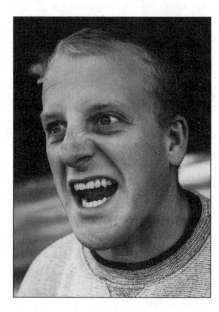

Feeling Like Your Ancestors

We don't think about it much but emotions helped our ancestors survive, and they continue to help us thrive today. How so?

First, our emotions motivate us to act. When we feel fear or anxiety, we are motivated to run away from whatever's scaring us or we get ready to defend ourselves. Unfortunately, the anxiety we feel in tense meetings or tough final exams also produce a flight or fight response. But in boardrooms and classrooms, it is inappropriate to run away, and we definitely should resist the temptation to punch out people in those situations. So what happens to our desire to flee or fight? Sometimes emotions get displaced—fidgeting is a common way of displacing emotional energy—or suppressed.

Emotions also help us to survive and thrive by sending important messages to our friends and family. Think of great-great-uncle Turok's face when a saber-tooth tiger strolled into the campsite. His fear expressions warned everyone of potential danger. We do the same thing today when danger is upon us.

Warning: Emotions Are Contagious

People share emotions with other people. In fact, emotions are more contagious than the common cold. Take happiness and excitement, for example. When you're at a party and your friends are happy and excited, it's hard to be sad and apathetic. And people living with a depressed person often become depressed themselves. Ever been with a group of paranoid people? Hard not to feel a little fear yourself. Because emotions are inherently expressive, we tend to feel what others feel.

Emotional Intelligence

It's so important to be smart about our body language, but it's not always easy. Nonverbal behavior is spontaneous, and we are not even aware of most of the things we do. But we can learn to better manage our expressions and be emotionally intelligent.

Emotional intelligence, a concept pioneered by Peter Salovey of Yale and Daniel Goleman of Harvard, has become a popular topic in academic laboratories and on airport bookstands. Emotions are information. If you tune in to

> ### Nonverbally Speaking
>
> Lots of studies support the facial feedback hypothesis, which suggests our nervous systems read our own body language. In other words, when we look angry, fearful, or happy, we tend to actually experience that emotion. So the old advice "put on a happy face" might be right on target.

your feelings, your own body language, and the body language of others, you will tap into a whole new source of knowledge. But don't let your emotions control you. In other words, increase your emotional IQ! Here are some tips for upping your emotional intelligence:

- Don't suppress your emotions; they exist for a reason.

- Tune in to your emotions and their expression. This is a learned skill.

- Think about your feelings. They contain vital information.

- Observe how you express your feelings. Read your own body language.

- Be open to others' emotions. It's great data!

- Be emotionally empathic. It will let you connect with others.

- Use emotional states to facilitate creativity and problem-solving.

- Manage your emotions: Expressing emotional body language intelligently and strategically is the key.

The Least You Need to Know

- Emotions are inherently expressive.

- Each emotion has a unique body language profile.

- Most reactions to jealousy are dysfunctional.

- Expressions have survival value.

- Emotions are contagious.

- Emotional intelligence is important to develop.

Part 4

Body Language in Everyday Life

Throughout our lives, wherever we go, our body language is ever present. However, as we grow and develop our social skills, our body language changes. In the following chapters, you'll learn how babies, toddlers, and teens use their bodies to communicate their needs and desires.

In addition, you'll find chapters on intimate interactions, dating and mating, communicating at work, political posturing, sporting behavior, and classroom cues. So sit back, relax, and have some fun while you learn how your body language impacts all aspects of your life.

Chapter 14

Childish Behaviors: Body Language in Infants and Toddlers

In This Chapter

- ◆ Understanding baby body language
- ◆ Avoiding stress and boredom for your baby
- ◆ Rewarding and punishing body language
- ◆ The importance of infant attachment
- ◆ Touching behaviors in infancy

Babies are great communicators, though poor talkers. Our dialog with an infant is conducted entirely via body language. For nearly their first year, and in some cases first two years, verbal dialog has little importance. From the time of a baby's birth it is essential to start an intimate two-way dialog with your baby via body language.

Communication is vital to an infant's survival. In Chapter 6, on touch, you learned that too little touch could damage and even kill an infant.

Competent, quality communication between infant and parent predicts subsequent learning, physical health, psychological adjustment, and life and relationship satisfaction.

Fortunately, most babies come fully equipped with expressive little faces, baby gestures, interactive eyes, and warm touches that make interacting with them rewarding.

Infantile Appeals: Understanding Baby Body Language

Unlike baby animals, who mature quickly, a child is totally dependent on its caregivers during its first years of life. Human babies must be held or carried, whereas young apes can cling. Being born with a small, undeveloped body is one price of a big brain and a large head. And any new mother is painfully aware that baby's biggest body part is the head.

Human babies cannot walk around, change their own clothes, talk, find food, or do dozens of things that we as adults take for granted. So how do babies tell us what they need? They do it through excellent body language—language that is often clearer than words. But as a parent or caregiver, you must listen, look, and feel. Perhaps the greatest parental skill is the ability to read baby body language, a skill possessed by most women and many men.

Babies do all sorts of vocalizing. They coo, cry, babble, blow bubbles and "raspberries," scream, yell, and giggle. And these behaviors are not random. Tune in and you will hear many familiar syllables as they babble. Such sounds are precursors of language and are an essential part of learning to talk. Interestingly, deaf babies also practice language, but they babble with their hands! Baby vocalizations also tell us how they are feeling—from contented cooing to fussy grumbling and angry screams.

> **Nonverbally Speaking**
>
> People from all around the world use baby talk, in languages as diverse as Arabic, Swedish, and Comanche.

And adults talk back in baby talk, a variation of high-pitched children's speech used mostly with infants and small children, though interestingly it is sometime used between lovers. Usually baby talk is nonsense, like "puttche puttche pooo," but usually is just really high-pitched speech: "yourrrr a little rascal."

One of the amusing activities you can play with your baby is the turn-taking game. You've all seen it. Mom (or Dad) sits baby in a high chair or swing and starts the game with exaggerated facial expressions, a high-pitched voice, and sometimes a little tickle in the ribs:

Mom: "You're a little sweeeeetie!"

Baby: Giggles a little and looks surprised.

Mom: "I said you're a little sweeeeetie!"

Baby: Laugh with a bigger smile.

Mom: "Mommy's gooonna getcha!"

Baby: Laughs again and smiles.

Babies take turns and use facial expressions and vocalizations to communicate with us.

(Image courtesy of Peter Andersen)

Babies never seem to tire of this game, and from a developmental standpoint nothing could be better. Baby is learning how to carry on a conversation; only this one is done mostly in body language. Except for some word-use by Mom, the conversation is entirely in body language using voice, face, and touch. By the way, nonsense syllables like "kittcheee kittchhee kooo," work just as well as real words, so the entire verbal part is unnecessary. Most likely, however, baby hears and learns some words if real language is used.

This proto-conversation helps babies develop concepts of facial expression, gesture, touch, and voice. They begin to understand sequences of conversation, connect with the caregiver, and develop emotional expression. They also begin to understand the rhythms of human interaction and practice synchronization, or matching, a vital skill in all human relationships. They also learn what cues are used in starting, maintaining, avoiding, and terminating interactions.

Adults almost always use exaggerated facial expressions—especially surprise and happiness—when interacting with infants. In this way parents get the child's attention and they make sure baby recognizes the expression. Parents also hold their expressions—especially smiles and frowns—for several extra seconds. Babies are great imitators and learn the nuances and contexts for their facial expressions during this kind of interaction.

> ### Nonverbally Speaking
>
> Parents rarely make much effort to make sense of baby and toddler gestures. So check them out. They are less random and more meaningful than you would have guessed.

> ### Nonverbally Speaking
>
> Crying and trembling are pretty good signs of overstimulation, but look for other ways that baby nonverbally shouts "stressed!" Look for eye avoidance, struggling, or turning away. In toddlers, look for crawling or running away and hiding as signs of overstimulation. Use calming tactics when you witness such displays.

During these interactions, parents gesture as they speak, although frequently the gestures are actually little touches or tickles. It is likely that these tactile, body-focused gestures are easier for a baby to understand because they are more familiar with touch than with gestures. Watch a baby closely during one of these conversations. A baby uses little gestures that look pretty random at first, but upon closer scrutiny several things will become apparent. The little haphazard baby gestures are not haphazard at all; they are closely synchronized with vocalizations much like adult gestures are synchronized with talking. Second, sometimes these gestures are little grasping attempts that fail to connect. Babies aren't too coordinated yet, but these gestures and reaches are precursors of adult conversational and tactile behaviors.

As a baby approaches his or her first year, her or his gestures become much more recognizable. Waving hello and good-bye, pointing at objects, pounding a tray, and reaching for things are highly communicative forms of body language. One of my daughter's first words was "up," always accompanied by an upward pointing gesture, usually at an airplane flying overhead.

Double Difficulties: Understimulation and Overstimulation

Babies are excellent regulators of stimulation, fussing when they are overexcited and underexcited. Moms and dads are often excellent at reading baby's body language and adjusting the arousal level accordingly, in a ritual played out in millions of homes.

Nonverbally Speaking

At the time my daughter was born, the work of two scholars had a major impact on both my research and my parenting. The first was Daniel Stern of Harvard University, whose book *The First Relationship* is still one of the best ever written on parent-infant interaction. The second was Joseph Cappella, one of the finest communication researchers in the world, now at the Annenberg School for Communication at the University of Pennsylvania. Their theories form the basis of much of my research in this area as well as the foundation of this chapter.

Stimulating the Stressed?

Your baby has been fed, changed, and had a nap, but he or she is still crying; what's going on?

When it comes to babies, most parents use a lot of trial-and-error. Rocking is a great idea, but it only works on a bored, understimulated baby, not a baby who is stressed-out. So start by putting yourself in baby's shoes (tight fit, eh?). Did baby just get passed from Grandpa Alex, to Grandma Mildred, to Uncle Mark, to Dad, and back to Mom? Cripes, this is the equivalent of a baby mosh pit! Has baby been on the go, playing with cousins and crawling around for one of the first times? Is baby looking scared and worried, or is he or she trembling? These are situations and signs that baby is stressed-out, overstimulated, and too aroused. Any parent looking at baby's body language has a good chance of observing overarousal when it occurs.

Remember to read baby's facial expressions and body language. As you learned in Chapter 5, facial expressions are innate, and baby has miniature versions of all the adult expressions: fear, joy, contentment, anger, and so on. If you think baby's body language is saying, "Mom, I am scared and overstimulated," calm him or her down. Gentle rocking, but not jostling or bouncing, will soothe and quiet baby. Holding baby close and covering her or his head also will reduce stimulation.

Nonverbally Speaking

Covering baby's head with a blanket is a tried-and-true soothing behavior, because it reduces visual stimulation, filters out light, and is a warm and comforting interaction. As adults, most of us still find cuddling and hugging to be comforting, but babies thrive on it.

Some parents relentlessly pursue a child whose body language is actively saying that he or she wants to be left alone. When an infant turns away from Mom or Dad, some parents will continue to make eye contact and to vocalize. When a child succeeds in breaking visual contact, many adults will move closer or touch baby with their face or hands. When baby is really panicked and claustrophobic he or she will perform a "pass through" by rapidly swinging their face right past the adult's face to the other side. This is annoyed, avoidant body language and should be recognized as such. Other warning signs of overstimulation are direct daydreaming, where baby looks right through you but doesn't "see" your face, and going completely limp. Both behaviors tend to be last-ditch efforts to avoid stimulation when all else fails.

Repeatedly pursuing an overstimulated baby can have dire consequences. To avoid overstimulation, babies will refuse to establish eye contact and turn away from adults. Such behavior has been shown lead to insecure attachment and has even been associated with autism and schizophrenia, although no cause-and-effect relationship has been established with these severe disorders.

Soothing Bored Babies?

The term "bored to tears" probably originated with infants who cry to get attention. Humans, even very young ones, are curious explorers and avidly social creatures. They need new stimulation. Stimulation and an active body language dialog are as basic drives in infants as thirst or hunger. And because learning is so vital to the survival of all human beings, babies are like sponges that soak up everything around them.

And young kids thrive on stimulation, up to a point. Amazingly, studies of babies who sleep with patterned sheets showed better adjustment and quicker mental development than babies with plain sheets. This isn't so amazing if you think about it. How would you like to lie face down staring at a white sheet? Sounds like a torture used on political prisoners. You flip babies onto their back and they stare at a white ceiling. Not very exciting! A great crib toy (and an equally great baby gift) is a wind-up mobile. Some babies laugh and smile as each object goes past, interested in what's above them yet comforted by the certainty of its path.

Positions of Power

A great interactive game that most parents know is peek-a-boo. The adult hides behind a door or couch or just covers her or his face and then pops out and says "peek-a-boo." Babies will laugh and giggle and then pause. This actually is the seed of an adult conversation. And the suspense of the missing parent, followed by her or his return, is both stimulating and comforting.

Some babies' cries for help are pleas for more attention and stimulation. Crying, along with pitiful, hurt facial expressions, seeking Mom or Dad, or looking around and reaching out for people are signs of stimulation seeking. When you appear, these behaviors stop or diminish and the facial expressions turn from sad and hurt to surprised or happy. Your baby is glad to see you and ready for some action.

The Consequences of Parental Incompetence

Overstimulating a stressed baby or calming a bored baby are the two biggest mistakes that parents make in the comforting process. Their inability to recognize baby body language and to respond appropriately means they will have to tolerate lots of frustrated crying.

For baby, incompetent responses on the part of the parent may lead to an insecure interaction style and relationship difficulties that can persist throughout life. It may also produce a dangerous response, called "learned helplessness," in which a person comes to believe they have no control of their environment and their actions are unrelated to particular outcomes. Learned helplessness leads to increasingly random behaviors, an inability to make good decisions, and even depression.

> **Nonverbally Speaking**
>
> Social scientists have been extensively studying sensation seekers, people who thrive on stimulation. For most of us a moderate amount of stimulation is perfect, but for sensation avoiders it is too much, and for sensation seekers it is too little. Be aware of these inborn differences in babies and kids. The same moderate stimulation may freak out an avoider and bore a seeker to death.

The Power of Attachment

The attachments between you and your infant are vitally important to your offspring's future. Literally thousands of studies of adult and infant attachment have been conducted in the past decade. This research shows that patterns of infant interaction determine adult attachment patterns and relationship quality. Children have an innate need for attachment. Failing to provide love and affection to a baby is neglect, and it's as harmful as outright physical abuse. Attachment to a parent keeps children physically and psychologically close to their parents to protect them from danger and to provide a secure base for exploring their world. Moreover, children begin to learn about closeness and intimacy in their close relationships with Mom, Dad, and other caregivers.

High-quality interaction between children and caregivers provides the foundation for later attachments by enabling baby to learn about self and others. Good interactions in the first two to three years of life create a positive model of the self that does not rely on continuous external validation. Similarly, infants and toddlers develop positive models of others. These early interactions result in four attachment styles that are persistent throughout life:

◆ **Secure attachment.** Children with secure attachment styles come from warm, responsive parents who provided an appropriate amount of stimulation. They have positive concepts of themselves and other people. They grow into self-sufficient, well-adjusted teens and adults. Their body language suggests openness to friendship and intimacy, but not a dependency on other people.

Securely attached children can share affection with other children.

(Image courtesy of Peter Andersen)

◆ **Dismissive attachment.** Children who grow up with inconsistent caregivers develop negative models of other people and lose their trust in others. Even though their basic needs are met, they come to believe they can't rely on other people. These kids develop a fairly positive self-concept but have low regard for others. They see relationships as unimportant and have great difficulty showing warmth, immediacy, and intimacy, and have trouble finding and maintaining intimate relationships.

◆ **Preoccupied attachment.** Infants who fail to get enough love and support from caregivers may develop a low self-concept and spend a lot of their life desperately seeking intimacy and being dependent on others. Their frantic, desperate body language is unappealing to others, which in turn adds to an even lower self-concept and makes them more desperate than ever for intimacy.

◆ **Fearful-avoidant attachment.** Rejected as infants and sometimes abused, these folks have negative models of both themselves and other people. These kids are full of anxiety, may not explore new environments, and fail to make many friends. They want approval from others but are fearful of intimacy. Their body language is withdrawn and they are not very emotionally available.

These interaction styles are often self-reinforcing, and so attachment styles become fairly stable over the lifespan. What is critical is that early experiences with caregivers set the stage for lifelong patterns, though later experience can produce change. Friends and siblings may compensate for an unavailable or inconsistent parent. Likewise, traumatic experiences as adults can have a negative effect on our attachment style.

Reward and Punishment

The most esteemed and well-supported principle of psychology is that of positive reinforcement. Any animal, from alley rats to rug rats, responds to the principles of reinforcement. Positive reinforcement occurs when a given behavior is followed by a satisfier or a reward, which increases the chances of the behavior being repeated. Thus, following a baby's smile with a happy parent facial expression or a spoon of their favorite spinach will increase the chance of future smiles. *Negative reinforcement* also increases the occurrence of a behavior by removing a painful stimulus. If a toddler gets his or her foot stuck and calls for help, freeing the foot is an example of negative reinforcement. Such an action should increase verbal calls for help in similar kinds of situations.

Body Talk _____

Negative reinforcement is probably the most widely misunderstood term in the social sciences. It is not the same as punishment, which decreases the likelihood of a behavior. Negative reinforcement is the removal of an aversive or painful stimulus that increased the occurrence of a behavior. Changing a wet, uncomfortable diaper when baby fusses is an example of negative reinforcement, which will increase the likelihood that baby will communicate via fussing when he or she needs this sort of attention in the future.

Punishment, on the other hand, is the application of an aversive or unpleasant action that diminishes the incidence of a behavior. While punishment does have its place in child-rearing, experts suggest six problems with its frequent use:

♦ Punishment fails to work at all with infants and young kids. It takes a toddler to begin to understand punishment and its meaning.

◆ For punishment to be effective the child must be carefully watched, since punishment must be applied immediately following the occurrence of a negative behavior. For instance, if a child only occasionally gets caught and punished for stealing cookies, the successful heists may actually be intermittently reinforcing them.

◆ Punishment may disrupt and damage parent-child relationships. As a parent you want to be respected, not resented or feared. If you are thought of primarily as a punisher, your relationship may suffer.

◆ Some types of physical punishment can cross the line to physical abuse. Spankings and beating are not the best tactics.

◆ Punishments must be punishing. Giving a child a time out in a room full of toys, a computer, a stereo, or a CD is not all that punishing.

◆ Once a punishment is promised it must be applied. Idle threats reduce a parent's credibility and teach the child nothing except learned helplessness.

Training Your Parents

Babies are born knowing how to be babies, but parents must learn to be parents. Of course, some parents are naturals, but others need help and some have no clue at all.

One can argue that the baby actually shapes the behavior of the parent rather than the reverse. The baby decides when Mom or Dad will get up for a feeding, when the diaper needs changing, and when to play and interact.

Babies tell you with their body language when you have it right and will correct you when you have it wrong. What is more rewarding than viewing your baby smile or giggle, or watching that almost drunk, happy, sleepy body language when their little tummies are filled with milk? And what is more reinforcing than when baby stops crying? Babies are parent-training machines that reinforce all the right behaviors.

When you have it wrong, it's punishment time. A stubborn, crabby, or colicky baby is telling you to change your behavior to something more comforting to them. A crying baby demands attention and usually gets it. Babies do most of the training and parents do most of the learning. It may just be baby body language, but it is very effective in communicating baby's needs. It takes many months and years, if ever, before Mom and Dad take control and start to be the trainers rather than the students.

The Therapeutic Touch

As we discussed in Chapter 6, touch is vital to an infant. The helplessness of infants makes touch an essential component of communicating love and affection. Even pre-natal touch has some benefit, and the advantages of breast-feeding for both mother and child are well documented. Studies demonstrate that touch is essential for emotional, relational, physical, and intellectual development.

Why is touch so essential? Your first sensory experiences were through touch. Your impression of the world before birth and during the first days of life is almost exclusively based on tactile experiences. Infants are insecure, dependent, highly vulnerable, and virtually helpless (I even know a few adults like this). As a result, infants are highly dependent on physical contact, especially from the mother, who baby knows so well and who is the ultimate source of nourishment, support, and comfort.

Rocking, swaddling, and holding baby close is the most comforting form of body language because it closely replicates the womb. The protective touch, reinforcing nourishment, and oral contact of breast-feeding is very pleasurable and reassuring to a baby. Little babies, like young primates of other species, thrive when touched and cuddled and wither physically and emotionally when they are not.

It is hard to touch a baby too much.

(Image courtesy of Peter Andersen)

CAUTION

Bodily Blunders

As your child matures, the almost constant touch of infancy recedes to intermittent touch in childhood. Tune in to your kids' body language. One minute they crave touch and the next minute they'll pull away. As your child matures, touching too much can smother; touching too little makes a child feel isolated and anxious.

So how much touch is right for your baby? Research suggests that it is nearly impossible to touch a baby too much. Touch stimulates growth, improves immune function, releases hormones like insulin, and decreases stress. Gradually, as children mature, they require less and less touch. Yet even older children and teens will seek a parent's or friend's touch in a crisis.

The benefits of early touch last a lifetime. Studies show that warm, loving parents are some of the most important predictors of good, stable marriages, happy friendships, an outgoing communication style, intellectual achievement, higher educational attainment, greater love of life, and more job satisfaction decades later. As we said in Chapter 6: Be happy, be haptic.

The Least You Need to Know

◆ Watch, listen, and feel your baby's body language.

◆ Avoiding overstimulation and understimulation is the key to a happy, well-adjusted infant.

◆ Securely attached infants are healthier and happier.

◆ Watch baby's body language if you want to learn how to parent.

◆ Infant touch is an essential connection.

Adolescent Actions: Interacting with Teens

- ◆ Teen change, independence, and self-absorption
- ◆ The "boomerang effect" of parental control
- ◆ The emotional rollercoaster of becoming an adult
- ◆ Signs of teen distress
- ◆ Communicating with your teen

Some days living with a teen is like living with a terrorist. You wonder how a crazy person moved into your house, or you feel like you're cohabitating with a living-room lawyer. Although we love our kids more than anything in the world, teens seem to test that love on an almost daily basis. Much of this "testing" is done with teen body language, including freaky hair, a sulky demeanor, and dirty looks. Teens experiment with every kind of body language display imaginable, and provide unlimited opportunities for parents to test their body language reading skills as well as their patience.

Under Construction!

Teens are like 3-year-olds going on 30. At times they're kids: insecure, dependent, emotional, and helpless. Other times they're grown-ups:

confident, independent, stoic, and competent. Watching the transition is magical. It's a human construction project that changes day by day.

Most teenagers feel that they are always onstage and that the world has nothing better to do than to evaluate their actions. This is true of both boys and girls, but more so for girls. Young kids often don't care about their appearance and are irritated if you make them take a bath or comb their hair. By the late preteen years, however, most young adults realize that body language, including appearance, really matters.

Between the fourth and sixth grades, kids go from being oblivious about body language to obsessing about it. From that point on, teens feel like they are in a fishbowl, and everyone is watching and evaluating them. The wrong outfit, a prominent pimple, the less than perfect hair day is a body language catastrophe.

Positions of Power

One secret to a happy family life is to think of your loved ones' quirky body language and unusual communication as endearing, even when it may be irritating or peculiar. So when that punky appearance or insensitive body language bugs you, try to appreciate it for what it is: a person under construction.

Making matters worse, teens often misinterpret other people's body language. The 15-year-old girl is convinced her date is staring at her pimple when he is really love-struck. In a scene right out of a sitcom, her date misinterprets her paranoid glances as annoyance at his behavior. As this example illustrates all too clearly, teens live in a completely egocentric world.

Teens also labor under the misconception that their experiences are unique. They often truly believe that nobody else has ever suffered as much as they are over a breakup, a bad hair day, a bad grade, or failing to make the team. They dramatically overreact to all such situations. All a parent can do is be there for them during these traumatic times. By the way, don't say you know how they feel; you don't, and it belittles their experience.

Nonverbally Speaking

Teens desperately want romantic relationships. Their changing bodies, peer pressure, and intense hormones propel them into relationships. Rarely is the partner they pick the partner you would pick for them. But back off. Unless their partner is a convicted felon or a hooker, it's best to let them decide who to date and who to dump. Plus, if you oppose a partner, that partner becomes even more attractive in the teen's eyes. Be there for your teen, guide when requested, and try not to be heavy-handed.

Independence Day

For a teenager every day is Independence Day. This is a natural and good thing, though it can be alarming and disorienting for a parent. A parent's primary goal during this stage of their child's life should be to help launch a young person who is completely independent and functional. A parent's goal should be to let out the teen's tether a little farther each year, until the young adult can function on his or her own.

Teens react badly to parents who don't let their kids become independent. Often, overprotective parents use body language around their teens that would be a more appropriate reaction to a 7-year-old than to a 16-year-old.

And do not be too pushy about hanging out with your teen. Egocentric teens rarely give a rodent's rump about fulfilling your emotional voids or supporting your social calendar. You are the grown-up, so get a life, and be grateful if your life and your teen's life actually intersect. Be involved with your teen, but don't go overboard. If you want to maintain a quality relationship with your young adult, don't treat them like a child. Teens hate to feel dorky, and your body language will aggravate and frustrate your teenagers if you attempt to do any of the following:

◆ Hug them or kiss them in public

◆ Look over their shoulder to check on their homework

◆ Wear outdated or "too cool" clothes in their presence

◆ Adjust their clothing or hair (YO! They just spent an hour making it look appropriately messy!)

◆ Invade their personal space

◆ "Helpfully" straighten up a teen's bedroom or bathroom

◆ Mock their body language

◆ Use belittling gestures that you would use with a young child

A major goal of almost all teenagers is to avoid being embarrassed by their parents. Most teens actually like having their parents around, but on their terms. However "cool" you are in your social circle, you are a middle-aged geek to them. Teens like parents who are subtle. Being too cool with them and their friends will definitely "boomerang."

The "Boomerang Effect"

Most direct attempts to control a teenager fail. In fact, many teens resist control by actually increasing a prohibited behavior, a process social scientists call the "reactance theory" but is probably best termed the "boomerang effect."

In essence, the boomerang effect says that many forms of persuasion and influence that we use on teens will have the complete opposite effect than we intended. Of course, this is true of some people who are not teens, but teens are the most likely to respond in this fashion. Why? Human beings are biologically and socially programmed to become independent. Throughout childhood, kids are often stubborn, but during the teen years they are actively establishing an identity apart from their parents. To assert that new, independent identity, they increasingly reject adult control and advice, even darned good advice, and especially parental advice.

 Bodily Blunders _____

Research on teen behavior suggests that if you attempt to directly restrict their dress, behavior, or body language, they will produce the following boomerang effects:

◆ Value that behavior even more.

◆ Resist this direct attempt at influence.

◆ Adopt another, even more outrageous, behavior.

◆ Manifest violent reactions to such restrictions.

Of Freaks, Greeks, and Geeks

Many forms of teenage body language can be explained by attempts to achieve their independence. Their behavior can be pretty alarming to parents, but it's more commonplace than you might suppose. Here are some common teen behaviors you might recognize:

◆ **Scary hair.** Punk, spiky, green, or pink hair might be the most visible form of scary body language. The fact that others react to it is exactly the point. It screams "I am an individual," even if all their friends look the same.

◆ **Body piercing.** These teen rituals petrify parents. Today, studs and piercings may penetrate ears, eyelids, bellybuttons, noses, tongues, and even nipples. The good news is that these body adornments are removable, and the piercing usually heals. Plus, body piercings are not a whole lot different than the time-honored pierced earlobes socially respectable women have worn for decades.

◆ **Body art.** Many kids use their skin as a canvas for self-expression. From tiny butterflies, to military tattoos, to the full-body tattoos, the youth culture seeks expression and individuality though body art. But help your kids to make good decisions. Facial or full-body tattoos are disfiguring and hard to reverse.

◆ **Outlandish attire.** You may really dislike your daughter's tight jeans or that exposed midriff that becomes more exposed each year. Your son's shorts make him look like a Barbary pirate, and he has never laced up his basketball shoes. There is no stopping them. Even putting them in school uniforms is no help; young women will roll their skirts until they are back to the desired length or wear them low so their belly shows.

You may have forgotten about your own leather jacket, full beard, pieced ears, micro miniskirt, love beads, elephant bells, bralessness, or hot pants. Chances are your attire was designed to stretch the boundaries of fashion as well as your parents' patience. This is what teens do!

Teens often wear distinctive fashions like this young man's punk hairstyle, earring, and shades.

(Image courtesy of Robert Avery)

Rebelling for the Sake of Acceptance

Even though teens want to be independent rebels, what they really want is to be accepted, especially by their peer groups. This is a paradox not easily resolved: How can I rebel and still be accepted by my peers? The solution is to rebel in groups, so that certain kinds of rebellious body language result in peer acceptance. From flappers in the twenties, to beatniks and greasers in the fifties, to mods and hippies in the sixties, to preps, punkers, goths, and jocks today, each group wants to rebel, but only with others.

Perhaps the ultimate in institutionalized acceptance is the sorority or fraternity. On a daily basis, sorority girls exhibit so much similarity on many campuses you can pick out the sorority girls from crowd. One sorority craze on some campuses is the so-called Juicy-suit, a very pricey but casual sweat suit that few sorority sisters ever use for an actual workout. Its message is clear: I am casual, I am in with the in crowd, and I am high in status. Similarly, when sorority sisters get dressed up for special events they are careful to announce the appropriate attire so they all have the proper "look." The right "look" is a powerful message that establishes solidarity and camaraderie in the group.

These sorority girls wear similar attire for special occasions to increase identification and solidarity.

(Image courtesy of Peter Andersen)

Sororities and fraternities aren't all that different from gangs or street corner culture. The differences are primarily of social class, but the desire to be part of the "group" transcends economic and ethnic boundaries. Sororities are to the university what the street gang is to the inner city, a chance for group acceptance and instant friendships.

These hard-core young men are rebelling together with similar gestures, attire, hats, and jewelry.

(Image courtesy of Robert Avery)

The Emotional Roller Coaster

Some adults forget the emotional roller coaster of their teen years. Today you have job stress, a house payment, kids to raise, traffic to battle, and a marriage to maintain. You're thinking, "What is so hard about being a teen?" The combination of rapid maturation, raging hormones, greater expectations for success, new social relationships, and emerging sexuality make adolescence a stressful time. You are probably also thinking that teens have less to be stressed about than ever before; after all, they have no Great Depression, no World War II, no Vietnam. But teens face challenges today that you never experienced, including incredibly increased time pressures and commitments, competition for college, maintaining an inflated standard of living, the perceived threat of terrorism, increased urban congestion and traffic jams, and more social isolation that comes from increased urbanization.

Any of the following body language might signal that a teen is stressed out and needs help:

◆ Prolonged sadness or a blank facial expression

◆ Irritability and anger with little provocation

◆ Low energy, lethargy, and sleeping more than 12 hours a day

◆ Persistent boredom or malaise

- No appetite or insatiable hunger

- Constant headaches or stomachaches

- Suicidal thoughts or behavior—assume these are real

Social anxiety, the fear of interacting with others and being judged negatively by them, has been described as the most prevalent handicap in America. It is certainly the most widespread phobia of Americans. You probably can recognize the socially anxious teen. The first symptom is a desire to withdraw and hide. Their body language says "leave me alone," and that is usually exactly what other teens do. Socially anxious teens stay away from social gatherings, sit alone at parties when they do attend them, and block their bodies by crossing their arms and legs and covering their face.

> **Body Talk**
>
> **Social anxiety,** the fear of interaction with and negative evaluation by others, results in a pattern of social avoidance, preoccupation with self, and reduced awareness of other people.

Teens are highly susceptible to social anxiety because of the bodily changes and new responsibilities of adolescence and young adulthood. Not only are teens most susceptible to anxiety, most victims of adult anxiety trace its roots to adolescence. Teens are more likely than any other age group to experience embarrassment and rejection, and for a teen that is the worst fate imaginable.

Socially anxious teens are likely to focus on themselves and not read the body language of other teens. Their extreme self-consciousness and failure to tune in to the body language of other kids makes them inept, awkward communicators who are on a different wavelength than other kids. Anxiety leads to incompetence, which in turn leads to social rejection, which leads to even more anxiety.

> **Body Talk**
>
> Research suggests that the most emotional body language and most negative emotions occur during the "six o'clock crash." This is when parents and teens return home from their separate lives and have to negotiate time and space, meals and homework, transportation and communication. Research suggests that being other-oriented and attentive to the body language of other family members can minimize family distress.

The worst thing to do with a shy, socially anxious teen is to force them to be the life of the party. That is like throwing the nonswimmer in the deep end of the pool or curing a fear of heights by forcing someone to go mountain climbing. The best thing is to find small supportive gatherings or a supportive friend and let your teen get his or her social feet wet slowly.

Is Communication Possible?

Communication is possible with your teenager. Teens just seem like they were beamed in from another planet, but they really are earthlings. Here are a few handy tips for communicating with your teen:

- **Seize the moment.** Teens are like cats; they want strokes when *they* want them, not when *you* want to give them. So look for their attempts to reach out to you and be there when they do. Keep the communication channels open. And what is the most important way you can communicate that you care? Time together! The rich connections with your increasingly independent and elusive teen come during car pools, at lunch hours and sporting events, while shooting hoops or playing catch, and amidst parent-teen bull sessions that always occur long after a grown-up's bedtime.

- **If it's not life-threatening, let it go.** Some behaviors such as drunk driving, unprotected sex, street racing, or drugs are life-threatening and must be addressed and prevented at all cost. Most teen behavior, including weird dress, scary hair, grumpy moods, or sassy mouths, is not worth turning into a federal case. Bodacious body language and an appalling appearance are part and parcel of teenage experimentation.

- **Reinforce the positive.** When a teenager behaves respectfully or dresses in a way that's acceptable to you, reward her or him! Rewards can be as simple as a smile or a positive mood, or as substantial as a gift or a monetary award. But be careful: Too much blatant parental approval can backfire on you (refer back to the section on the boomerang effect).

- **Remind yourself that this, too, shall pass.** Think of some of the weird, dangerous, or rebellious stuff you did as a teen. You survived, and I bet you moved beyond the phase rather quickly. Remind yourself that a surprising number of successful business people, professors, teachers, lawyers, and doctors had a phase in their life when they were bikers, beatniks, punks, goths, dupers, hippies, hoodlums, gangstas, greasers, Rastafarians, skaters, or hoods.

- **Use psychological jujitsu.** A central premise of jujitsu is to disable an opponent by using another person's energy against them. Rather than battling your teenager, who has more time and definitely more energy than you do, try redirecting their energy. Sports, for example, are a great alternative to gangs. If a teen is into cars and drag racing, buy them an old car to fix up or look for a program like "Race Legal," which is a university- and police-sponsored drag-racing event. Channeling energy elsewhere is better than a clash.

♦ **Give them liberty, not license.** Healthy parent-teen relationships mean more freedom and independence for the teen, but more responsibility as well. Effective parents monitor their teen's behavior and body language for chemical, emotional, scholastic, and relational problems but are not excessively controlling or intrusive. Warm, caring parenting that holds teens responsible for their actions while giving them more and more autonomy is the best prescription for a developing young adult.

The Least You Need to Know

♦ Teens are 3-year-olds going on 30. Their body language and behavior may be childish one moment and mature the next.

♦ Teens are the world's biggest nonconformists; ironically, they do this in groups.

♦ Controlling a teen may result in a "boomerang effect" in which the young person does exactly what you don't want them to do.

♦ Read the body language of your teen for signs of distress. They might not be able to get help without you.

♦ Most importantly, communicate with your teen; but do it wisely, strategically, and on their terms. They might not encourage communication with you, but they want and need it.

Chapter 16

Closeness Counts: Communicating Warmth

In This Chapter

- ◆ Understanding intimate, immediate body language
- ◆ The intimacy of eyes, time, space, and face
- ◆ Connecting through touch
- ◆ Identifying intimate voices
- ◆ Creating "good vibrations"

Our relationships with friends and loved ones are life's greatest treasures. Friendships are the foundation of happiness, psychological well-being, and emotional support. Reflect for a moment on your most intimate interactions, your most touching reunions, the caring communication of close friends. The brightest side of life's experiences are shared in intimate interactions with those we care for.

How do friends send these special signals that warm your heart and create your intimate connections? As relationships develop we signal closeness through intimate, friendly body language that draws us closer together. Think of someone lacking in close relationships. Chances are they don't communicate much warm, inviting body language.

Intimate Interactions

For several decades the heart of my research has focused on how we connect with significant others through the many dimensions of body language. Researchers call these connections immediacy behaviors; you call them getting together with friends, hanging out with buddies, partying, or friendly conversation. Any aspect of body language that does all of the following is an immediacy behavior:

♦ Signals availability, openness, and inclusion. When you engage in body language such as eye contact, open body positions, increased touch, more direct stances, and closer distance with fewer barriers, you are open to interaction.

♦ Communicates involvement and approach, as opposed to autonomy and avoidance, by smiling, touching, and moving closer. This type of body language creates connection.

♦ Increases sensory stimulation. Physiological measures such as brain activity and heart rate increase when people touch, move closer, smile, or make eye contact with you. You may feel the buzz of these arousal-increases that are stimulating and, up to a point, feel good.

♦ Communicates intimacy and warmth. The basis of friendship, intimacy, and love is established through immediate behaviors such as smiles, warm hugs, spending time, attentive listening, and positive head nods, to mention but a few.

Intimate positions, close distances, touching, and sharing, communicate warmth and immediacy.

(Image courtesy of Peter Andersen)

Nonverbally Speaking

For years we thought only women had truly intimate same-sex relationships. *Au contraire*, says recent research. The obvious intimacy of female relationships—complete with synchronized body language, connected conversations, lots of eye contact, touch, and close distances—has a male counterpart. Guys get close by watching the game, having a beer, fixing the car, going for a run, or shooting some hoops. This is intimate connection, too, in a "mannish" manner.

The Bonds of Body Language

The *only* way you can become closer and more intimate with others is via immediacy behaviors. Immediate body language is the means of sending messages of closeness, warmth, and friendship. When we engage in these actions, we communicate immediacy and warmth; when others reciprocate, we have a real relationship.

Intimate Eyes

Gaze is so central to human body language that it is hard to imagine an intimate connection between two people that doesn't involve eye contact. That is, unless the lights are out—then other forms of body language take over! We have talked a lot about ocular body language in Chapter 4, but its importance in intimate interactions cannot be overemphasized.

In any relationship at any age, connection and intimacy are signaled through eye contact.

(Image courtesy of Peter Andersen)

In any relationship, eye contact signals availability for communication and enables you to tune in to your partner's body language. But in close relationships, it does much more than that. Hundreds of studies have shown that eye contact is an essential component of close relationships and warm and intimate interactions. Eye contact has been linked with friendship, intimacy, attachment, trust, believability, sincerity, connection, trustworthiness, immediacy, liking, closeness, romantic interest, infatuation, understanding, receptivity, politeness, enthusiasm, relational strength, and marital stability. Whew! Why does anyone look away?

In romantic relationships, researchers have found that eye contact is most important in the early and intermediate stages. Flirting with a guy is not all that complicated. Recent studies of flirtation suggest that good use of eye contact by a woman better predicts a guy's interest in her than does her physical attractiveness. Studies also show that dating partners have the highest levels of mutual gaze. Like some other forms of body language, eye contact diminishes in long-term relationships including marriages and committed gay relationships. Why would this be? First off, in stable, long-term relationships, like marriages, partners don't need the constant reassurance that body language behaviors, like intense eye contact, provide. Second, other signs of connectedness, like wedding rings or a house full of kids, are definite relational reminders. Third, we are less preoccupied with inspecting our partner for little signals of attraction or rejection. The dark side of this decline in affectionate body language, however, is that we may take our partner for granted. While we could all do better body language with our long-term partner, research suggests that some decline in visual, or tactile, intimacy is neither unusual nor detrimental.

Positions of Power

Want to spice up an old relationship? After years, or even decades, with a partner, you might be a bit relationally complacent. To reconnect, try using increased eye contact during a conversation. At worst your partner will find you connected, courteous, and compassionate. At best you may rekindle the old flame that attracted both of you in the first place.

Thwarting the Time Thieves

If there is one factor that most Americans have in common, it's the stress of pressure-packed lives. Life has gotten too busy! In fact, it's amazing that you have made it this far in the book given how busy you are! Americans work far more hours than a generation ago, and today it's likely that both partners in a household work. The time-crunch of each day is burdensome. Start with getting up, cleaning up, applying make-up, and hoping you don't mess up. Move to mail, e-mail, and voice mail—sometimes from multiple mailboxes. On to the all-important homework, housework, car-work, yardwork, and workouts. Then on to little league, piano lesson, basketball practice, and the math tutor. Finish with cooking, cleaning, paying, praying, and lying down. And maybe cap it off with some web surfing and TV. Been quite a day! And tomorrow may be worse. In the words of philosopher Kenneth Gergen, you are experiencing "The Saturated Self."

So far we've barely touched on the demands of other people. We might interact with more people in a single day than our grandparents did in an entire month! And everyone wants a piece of you, a friendly ear, just a few minutes. While each interaction is important, we can't be best friends with a thousand people. For many of us, time is our scarcest commodity. Something has to give. We devote less time to church, politics, and volunteering than people did a generation ago. We become disengaged from our communities and, even worse, we become disengaged from friends and family. Some studies reveal that working parents, especially fathers, may spend less than 10 minutes of quality time with their kids each day.

Actions speak louder than words. Spending quality time with your kids is truly the body language of love.

(Image courtesy of Peter Andersen)

Actions do speak louder than words! We can tell our friends and family we love them every day but if we don't spend much time with them, our body language is more lucid than language. Research that my colleagues and I conducted at San Diego State University indicates that the biggest predictor of relationship satisfaction is spending time together. Think of who is really important to you: your friends, your folks, your kids, your spouse? Americans need to jettison some of the frenzy and spend time with the people who really count. Spending time with a loved one is the clearest message of their importance that we can send.

Sharing Living Space and Breathing Space

Sharing space is among the most intimate message we send through body language. The closest spatial zones, called intimate space and personal space (see Chapter 10), are reserved for our closest friends. Look carefully at people's body language. Close distances typically equal close relationships.

The people you find most rewarding are the ones you allow to become physically close to you. They get close enough to touch and often do. They are welcome in your home, for minutes or months. You share your private spaces with them, such as basement family rooms, the kitchen table, or your bedroom. Acquaintances remain at more respectful distances and enemies and adversaries are advised to "keep their distance."

> ### Nonverbally Speaking
>
> We have all been visited by alien space invaders, such as neighbors, people we met in a bar, co-workers, or distant relatives we haven't seen since high school, who look us up, drop in, and hang out. These people act as though we are really good friends. It feels really weird! We want to be nice to these lost souls looking to connect, but our closest spaces and private places are for close connections, not random acquaintances. And worse, some of them come and stay! Like unrefrigerated fish, this gets pretty old after a couple of days!

Face-to-face communication is intimate body language. Just think about the language we use to describe body language. When you are trying to blow somebody off, you give him the "cold shoulder," not a nice warm front. When somebody denies your friendship or help, they "turn their back" on you instead of "giving you face time." We like to meet "face-to-face" to discuss important issues rather than using the phone, which is less personal, or e-mail, which is the least personal.

When somebody faces you, her or his body language sends messages of intimacy and involvement. Real conversations, in which the connections are deep, occur face-to-face. Facing the television or turning away from someone will effectively prevent an intimate interaction from occurring. Research suggests that face-to-face positions increase understanding and communicates closeness.

Leaning forward also increases the intimacy and the involvement in a conversation. This is exactly why we lean in during a romantic dinner with someone special and "keep our distance" during a disagreement. On the other hand, forward leans during a conflict interaction signify "getting in somebody's face," an intimidating behavior that can provoke greater conflict and even physical aggression. Leaning in during an affectionate conversation allows for quieter, more intimate tones of voice and sends the message that your interaction partner is somebody special. It also increases the personal quality and privacy of an interaction, as it excludes others and makes the conversation less public.

Face-to-face and eye-to-eye signal intimacy and involvement.

(Image courtesy of Peter Andersen)

Leveling the Playing Field

During interaction some people tower over others. Many conversations take place standing, where any height differences are at their maximum. Tall men loom head and shoulders above short women. Grown-ups seemingly soar into the stratosphere over kids. Standing people loom high above people in wheelchairs. Think about it for a second. When is the last time you interacted with someone twice your height? But that's exactly what people in wheelchairs and young kids experience all the time. These height discrepancies signal that you are not on the same level in more ways that just height.

As a man who's 6'3", it's pretty common for me to have standing interactions with women who are a foot or more shorter than me. This is particularly problematic at receptions, meet and greets, cocktail parties, and intermissions. It's worse in a crowded room when the shorter person has to crane their neck to make eye contact or read facial body language. If the room is noisy, this height discrepancy can make it nearly impossible to hear. Something needs to be done!

A shorter person cannot make herself or himself taller, so one solution is for the taller person to make himself or herself shorter. My personal favorite tactic is to half sit on the back of a couch or chair, which can reduce your height by more than a foot and really communicates closeness and connectedness. Plus, after a lot of standing, taking a load off your feet can feel pretty good. Another solution is to suggest having a seat, if one is available. Suddenly you are both on the same plane and the connection is palpable. Your interaction becomes more private, too, given that you are "below the fracas."

Positions of Power

When talking to someone in a wheelchair, sit down. This creates more opportunities for a real connection.

When I used to tutor in a second grade classroom, my miniature students were barely half my height. As soon as I sat down on one of their tiny chairs (which was quite a maneuver), interaction would improve in both quality and quantity. When you get down on the floor with kids of any age, your body language establishes an instant connection. It says "I am entering your world."

Touching Relationships

Like close distances, warm, tactile contact is reserved for close friends, family, and loved ones. Aside from social and professional touches like handshakes or pats on the back, most touch occurs in the contact of our closest relationships.

Touch is inherently intimate. In positive relationships, where it is appropriate, touch is a real indicator of warmth, intimacy, caring, sharing, closeness, and connection (and we are not even talking about sexual touch). In studies of photographed relationships and videotaped interactions, viewers attributed far more intimacy and closeness to people who were touching than those who were not. Most researchers in communication and psychology put touch at the head of list of behaviors that communicate warmth and intimacy.

Why is touch special in communicating closeness?

First, touch stimulates the tactile cortex, a very large and important part of your brain. Touch sensations resonate through the brain and produce opiate-like substances that make us feel good. Second, touch is your closest space zone. If very close physical distances are intimate, then touch is even more intimate, for it is closer than the closest distances. Third, since touch has the potential to hurt or violate, when we let someone touch us it means that we trust them. When touch is friendly and not hurtful, it can lead to even more trust and closeness. Finally, humans are great rationalizers. If I am touching someone, he or she must be a close friend, because only close friends touch.

Embracing and kissing communicate high levels of closeness and intimacy and signify the type of relationship. What sort of relationship do these people have?

(Image courtesy of Peter Andersen)

What ordinary sorts of touches convey intimacy and connect friends? Many kinds of touch are valuable in close relationships with friends, romantic partners, or relatives. Stanley Jones, a communication professor at the University of Colorado, compiled some of this research on these types of touch. He found that the following touches bond people together, sustain closeness, and maintain our finest relationships:

- **Affectionate greetings.** Touch is expected with friends and loved ones during meetings and greetings. If you picked up your relational partner at the airport and didn't hug her or him, something would be missing. In bonded relationships, greeting hugs are expected and necessary to sustain closeness.

- **Simple touches.** Sometimes the simplest touches are the most meaningful. A parent washing your hair, a date helping you on with your coat, a squeeze of the arm are all simple touches that have special meaning.

- **Tactile thanks.** Touches that say "thanks" are appreciated in any relationship, but they sustain relational bonds in close relationships. A pat on the back for a favor, a peck on the cheek for help with the housework, or a hug to a friend who has provided comfort and soothed hurt feelings are underused and undervalued forms of touch.

- **Support strokes.** Friends who provide support and comfort are sort of like free "shrinks," who get us through tough times. Rather than providing gratuitous advice, holding a distressed friend, hugging someone who's sad, or just placing your hand on their hand or arm, provides more comfort than words.

- **Togetherness touches.** Also called tie signs, these behaviors such as walking arm-in-arm, holding hands, or putting an arm around each other's waist say "We're a couple."

◆ **Affectionate touches.** Unlike touches that say thanks or provide comfort, these warm exchanges are "just because" touches. It's important that these kisses, squeezes, high-fives, or hugs occur spontaneously, not as thank-yous, sexual invitations, or support behaviors. Humans are amateur social scientists, who try to figure out why things happen. So when you receive a touch "out of the blue," for no apparent reason, you believe it is about the relationship.

◆ **Touch sequences.** In close relationships single touches are never enough. Repeated or continued touch such as a couple holding hands while sitting together watching TV or cuddling while they sleep, comforting a sick child with touch, or repeated high fives by friends during a football game are instances of repeated touch that strengthens a relationship.

◆ **Secret touches.** You don't have to be in a sorority or fraternity to have secret handshakes. Many friends and couples have their own secret touches that include attention-getting little kicks under the table, subtle flirtations, and even secret "turn-ons." To one couple, three quick taps means "I love you."

◆ **Departing touches.** It is more than mere ritual to touch intensely during relational farewells. We are likely to remember the last thing that happened, so during the days or years apart, you and your partner will likely assess your closeness based on your last tactile interaction.

Warm tactile greetings are a universal expression of warmth regardless of age or culture.

(Image courtesy of Laura Guerrero)

Like eye contact, touch sometimes declines in long-term relationships. In a series of studies, Professor Laura Guerrero of Arizona State University and I found that public touch starts in new romances, peaks in steady and engaged relationships, and declines again in marital relationships. In new relationships, public presentations of touch are a bit risky because such displays may signal that two people are a couple, for everyone else to see, including potential partners. For newly committed couples, like those who are engaged, public presentations of their togetherness are desirable, while for long-term marriages such public displays may be not be necessary to signal bondedness, but they sure do enhance the relationship.

> **Nonverbally Speaking**
>
> My colleague, Dr. Ed McDaniel, and a team of students observed hundreds of departure touches at Los Angeles Airport's international terminal. They were amazed and moved by these intense and poignant tactile farewells.

A true sign of intimacy and connection is mutual touch. If your partner of many years touches you when you touch him or her, that is a good sign. Failure to reciprocate touch is a potential warning sign between any couple, but especially in long-term marriages.

> **Nonverbally Speaking**
>
> The finding that touch is highest in intermediate relational stages has also been confirmed for private touch, so something else is going on besides the public nature of these presentations.

The Face of Intimacy

Your face is the bulletin board of your body. In Chapter 5, I described the face in some detail; here I'll focus on facial messages of warmth and intimacy. At the top of the list of warm behaviors is the smile. Smiles send good feelings, invite interaction, create positive moods, and signal affection. Some couples are all smiley with friends but forget to smile for each other. It is said "You always hurt the one you love." It's little unkind actions like forgetting to show warm expressions when your partner returns from work that can be really hurtful. Remember, little things count!

Facial expressions are particularly important during intimate conversations. It is especially important to look interested and to respond with appropriate expressions when you're listening. Nobody likes a deadpan listener; you wonder if they are listening at all or if they really care.

The Voice of Connection

When we talk, we use more than language—we use vocal body language. When you say yes to another person, you can say it about 20 different ways: A warm "yes," a reluctant "yes," a sexy "yes," a confused "yes," or a confident "yes." In the dictionary all these yes's mean the same thing, but in real life they mean totally different things. We use vocal body language, technically called paralanguage or vocalics, to vary the pitch, amplitude, and rate of our speech, thereby sending messages that reinforce, contradict, or modify our language.

Another kind of vocal body language serves as a linguistic shortcut: words like *uh-huh* or *mm-hmm* to signal agreement or *unh-ah* to signal disagreement. Using these vocal listener responses such as *hmmm* or *uh-huh* while someone is talking lets your partner know you are listening and signals a more intimate connection.

Three special kinds of vocal body language are baby talk, lovers' talk, and elder talk. Adults talk crazy to babies. They say stuff like *kitchee kitchee koo* in high-pitched voices. Even when we say normal things to a baby, like "you're a little darlin'," we say it in these ridiculous high-pitched voices. The theory here is that high pitch is less frightening to babies, and there is some research to support that. Interestingly, lovers frequently speak baby talk to each other at sexually intimate times. This is used to communicate intense intimacy and bondedness, and may be a throwback to the extreme intimacy of infancy.

Baby talk may also be used with the elderly to convey warmth and intimacy. But be careful; it may also seem condescending. "Elder speak" may also involve speaking very loud and overpronouncing each word. That may be okay for the very hard-of-hearing, but many elderly people find it patronizing.

Matched Sets: Convergence and Synchrony

Increasingly, communication researchers have realized that an essential part of intimacy is moving together, doing the dance!

Intuitively you already understand that synchronous body language is the core of connection. When people are connected intimately, we say they are "in sync" with each other or "on the same wavelength." In the dance of intimate interaction, we avoid "stepping on each other's toes" because we want to feel "good vibes" as opposed to "giving someone static." You want to be "in touch" and not "rub someone the wrong way." This is real language you use every day to describe synchronous body language that sends "those good, good, good vibrations."

Watch two really close friends talking about something they love—the synchronicity is astounding. Talk, smiles, gestures, laughs, touches, and more are totally coordinated down to the microsecond! Research by communication professor Judee Burgoon and her colleagues at the University of Arizona shows that adaptation to another person's rhythms leads to similarity or convergence. This is what you would call being "in step" or "in sync" with one another. When convergence occurs, people feel greater attraction, intimacy, and affiliation with their interaction partner. And the partner is viewed as more competent, friendly, and attractive. When people admire or feel connected to other people, they often use identical body language, a process called *mirroring*.

Did you ever notice how people begin to gesture the same or talk the same when they spend time together? Communication professors Howard Giles of the University of California, Santa Barbara, and Rick Street of Texas Tech University have shown that people do indeed adapt to one another. Most people naturally adjust their communication style to their partner through a process called accommodation or convergence. The most competent communicators adjust their body language by becoming increasingly similar to their interaction partners. For example, you might speak slower with a person who speaks very slowly, touch less with a person who touches very little, and use more eye contact with someone who uses a lot of eye contact. Research shows convergence produces greater rapport, more persuasive power, and greater intimacy.

> **Body Talk**
>
> **Mirroring** occurs when people adopt the same postures such as crossing the same leg in the same way, or both resting their chins on the same hand. It is related to greater rapport, similarity, immediacy, and liking, whether mirroring occurs intentionally or unintentionally.

Closeness Counts: The Importance of Intimacy

It is hard to overstate the importance of intimacy. Close friends, family, loved ones, and romantic partners are the cornerstone of our lives. Intimate feelings are healing and mood-altering. You release happy chemicals into your bloodstream when you have warm, intimate relationships. Intimacy is a buffer against stress. People with intimate relationships live longer and enjoy better health. Intimacy is the essence of friendship, and may be our greatest human achievement.

Intimacy does not mean smothering another person with immediacy behaviors and affection. In intimate relationships, people have warm interchanges when they are together and are satisfied and confident during separations. As a matter of fact, some breathing space actually increases intimacy.

> **Nonverbally Speaking**
>
> In the famous book of philosophy *The Prophet*, Kailil Gibran offers this profound advice about intimacy: "Stand together, yet not too near together: For the pillars of the temple stand apart. And the oak tree and cypress grow not in each other's shadow."

The Least You Need to Know

◆ Immediacy behaviors signal availability and increase intimacy.

◆ Throughout life, intimate touch is essential.

◆ The most important immediacy behaviors are eye contact, smiling, and sharing time and space.

◆ "Good vibrations" come from body synchrony.

◆ Immediacy behaviors are *the* way intimacy occurs.

Chapter 17

Courtship Cues: Flirtation and Romance

◆ Physical appearance and initial attraction

◆ Flirtatious body language

◆ Intensifying romance with body language

◆ Deactivating flirtation

◆ How to leave your love

Think about the beginning of your most recent romantic relationship—even if it was back when Carter or Ford was president. If your courtship was like most, it had a lot of wonderful highs as well as some painful and uncertain lows. As you recall the past, ask yourself these questions: What was my partner's body language saying? Did I have a chance with this person? Did he or she like me? What did that smile mean? Was I escalating the relationship too quickly or too slowly?

Navigating a course through the minefields of new relationships is thrilling but dangerous; they can blow up in your face and leave you hurt and swimming without a lifeboat. But building a new relational beachhead can be exciting. Plotting a course to a new relationship is a learned ability, and I bet you won't be surprised when I tell you that body language is a vital navigational skill.

Initial Attraction

You already know how important first impressions are, and how important body language and physical appearance are in creating that impression.

In any prospective romantic relationship, physical appearance is the most important initial quality, especially for men, who are often attracted and sometimes aroused by a pretty face, a nice body, or a revealing outfit. Of course, women are not immune to the allure of broad shoulders, a handsome face, and a strong trim body, though looks don't completely dominate most women's agendas.

An hourglass figure is the traditional ideal feminine frame.
(Images courtesy of Peter Andersen)

Nonverbally Speaking

Relationship research reveals that in the mating game we reject people with undesirable qualities, including those who appear to be desperate, are rude, or are physically unattractive. We use our first impressions of people to screen out those we don't find attractive in the first seconds of an interaction.

But physical attraction isn't just about high cheekbones, broad shoulders, or an hourglass figure. Some of the most attractive, charismatic people have a glow, are energetic, or communicate a quiet confidence that makes them highly attractive. Self-confident nonverbal cues and beaming body language make anyone look their best.

Physical attraction is nature's shortcut in the dating and mating game. As humans evolved, they began to use physical appearance as a sign of a healthy mate. Although it's important to be physically attracted to a possible mate, it's also important to look past beauty to other qualities of the person that may be more important in the long run.

> **⚠ CAUTION**
>
> **Bodily Blunders** _____
>
> In our postmodern era, what you see in your first encounter might not be the real deal. The pseudo body, including wigs, toupees, and hair dye, give many folks a youthful, transformative makeover. And let's face it, makeup, false eyelashes, contact lenses, facelifts, collagen lip enhancement, and nose jobs can transform a beast into a beauty. Add liposuction, breast enhancement, and tummy tucks, and you can make yourself virtually a new person. Can the cyborg partner be far off? (See Chapter 28 to find out.)

Flirtation: The Dating Dance

Rather than just a trivial topic for romance magazines, flirtation is an essential element of courtship and romantic relationships. Flirting is a negotiation process that tells us whether to begin a courtship that could lead to a long-term relationship.

Flirting has a biological basis. Our ancestors needed a quick and dirty way of ascertaining mutual sexual or romantic interest. When a connection takes place via prolonged eye contact and body language, for example, it's a green light to move forward and try to develop a romantic relationship. Like peacocks, humans strut their stuff at bars, gyms, school, or the office, all the while reading the body language of potential partners. Here are some of our most common flirtation behaviors:

- **Eye contact.** This is *the* classic flirtation behavior. Particularly when combined with positive facial expressions, prolonged or frequent eye gaze is the most powerful flirtation cue. Likewise, repeated gazes suggest that you passed initial screening. Longer mutual gazes are a sign of shared interest. However, the last person to look away signals more interest and must wait for a return gaze to confirm mutual interest.

- **Smiling.** Combined with eye contact, the smile is very friendly and often a flirtatious gesture. Smiles can transform the face, changing its shape and making it look more attractive and approachable.

- **Raised eyebrows.** In any context, raised eyebrows convey surprise, interest, and recognition. The quick eyebrow flash is a sign of acknowledgment and greeting. Prolonged upward eyebrows signal unmistakable interest. When combined with eye contact and a smile, raised eyebrows are clearly flirtatious. Many women use eyebrow pencil to accentuate and even raise their eyebrows into a permanent interest expression.

Direct eye contact and raised eyebrows are an unmistakable flirtation cue.

(Image courtesy of Peter Andersen)

- **Preening behavior.** Adjusting your tie, tucking in your blouse, picking lint off your coat, and smoothing your clothes are all examples of what social scientists call preening behaviors. Such activities do much more than make us tidy; research has shown that in humans and other mammals preening is a courtship cue, and we're more likely to do them in the presence of people we are attracted to.

- **Self-touching.** Touching the face, neck, breasts, or thighs sends powerful courtship cues.

- **Hair flips.** If you're a woman, running your hand through your hair and letting it fall back into place (a real California cue) or touching your hair as it hangs above the shoulder are both flirtatious actions. Men also use their hair to flirt, although it's usually a rough and tough touch that conveys their masculinity.

- **Exposed neck.** When women lean their head back and expose the front of their neck, it's often a flirtatious maneuver—and a surefire attention-getter. Languidly stroking the exposed neck turns a flirtation cue into a really suggestive signal.

- **Laughing and giggling.** Laughing is so unabashedly cheery and positive that it is bound to be attractive. Especially combined with other cues like self-touching or hair flips, laughing is unmistakably flirtatious body language.

This young woman's smile, hair touching, and raised eyebrows send a flirtatious message.

(Image courtesy of Robert Avery)

◆ **Accidental touches.** Sometimes accidental touches aren't that accidental. Touching someone's hand while handing them a drink or brushing by someone's body can be forms of flirtation. This is particularly true when combined with other cues like eye contact or a smile.

◆ **Beguiling walks.** Walking tall for men or with a hip swing for women sends cues that are sure to create some interest if the walker is attractive.

◆ **Chest thrusts.** Barrel-chested men and big-breasted women often flaunt their stuff as part of flirtation rituals. Women often enact this cue subtly while reaching behind themselves or putting on a coat. Men try to stand tall and pull in their paunch in the presence of an attractive woman.

◆ **Holding court.** Surrounded by admirers, who are often younger or less powerful, dominant men or women often sit in a central or powerful position and tell stories, spin yarns, and entertain. This is a compelling courtship cue, reminiscent of tribal chieftains, that signals power and strength.

◆ **The lip lick.** Not too subtle, but unmistakably provocative, licking the lips, especially combined with other courtship cues, is unmistakably flirtatious. However, its very blatancy can make this gesture seem brazen and vulgar.

◆ **The lookover.** Males are most likely to check out a woman from head to toe. They are notorious for doing this as a blatant "sidewalk sport" when in groups. One-on-one, men are likely to do this quickly to avoid appearing rude.

Groups of men are notorious for checking out women.

(Image courtesy of Robert Avery)

Once two people have established initial mutual interest, they often escalate the interaction by behaving even more flirtatiously:

◆ **Blowing a kiss.** If your target seems charmed or flattered by this blatant flirtation cue, the green light is on. But if he or she makes a negative expression or turns away, you've just been rejected.

◆ **Buying a drink.** This is another none-too-subtle flirtation cue. Accepting the drink suggests some interest, though your target may just be thirsty or like free drinks. Rejecting the drink is a definite stop sign.

◆ **Back rubs.** Walking up behind someone and massaging his or her shoulders is a bold move that either will be greeted with warm, accepting body language or revulsion. Pulling back, moving away, or swatting or removing your hands are definite stop signs.

◆ **Footsie.** Touching a target's foot with your foot is an age-old courtship cue that will seem creepy or cute depending on the target's attitude. Smiles and return touches are definitely a go sign.

Intensifying Dating Relationships

Once you are dating, the rules of engagement and escalation change. Communication investigator Jim Tolhuizen found that people use numerous strategies to turn casual dating relationships into more serious relationships. Based on his findings and those of others, here is a top-10 list of ways that people intensify dating relationships with body language:

10. **Nonverbal expressions of affection.** Partners try to increase intimacy with prolonged eye contact, head-to-head contact, handholding, and other types of affectionate body language.

9. **Suggestive actions.** Flirting, hinting, and playing hard-to-get are nonverbal actions designed to up the ante in a relationship.

What forms of suggestive body language are indicated by this barroom behavior?

(Image courtesy of Peter Andersen)

8. **Expressions of affection.** Although primarily verbal, this intensification strategy involves talk about falling in love and how much you care. The authenticity and consistency of your body language must back up the talk for it to be effective. Engaging in clusters of immediacy behaviors, as discussed in Chapter 16, is the key to genuine expressions of affection.

7. **Personalized communication.** Talk or body language designed to personalize the communication intensify a couple's connection. Listening with interest and sharing private revelations are behaviors that make a connection seem special. Because of the openness of the body language, public displays of affection suggest an intimate and exclusive relationship.

6. **Tokens of affection.** Cards, flowers, and gifts can be used to move the relationship the next level.

5. **Relationship redefinition.** Going steady, getting pinned, or becoming engaged all serve to intensify relationships. Letterman's jackets, lavalieres, and rings that accompany relationship redefinitions are powerful body language bonds.

Intimate, open, and recipro-cal touch sends powerful cou-ple cues to your partner and to the public.

(Image courtesy of Robert Avery)

4. **Relationship rewards.** Doing favors or running errands for your partner, pick-ing them up at work or school, cleaning up after them, offering compliments when they look good, and helping them with their studies or work all serve to increase closeness.

3. **Social support and comfort.** Being there when your partner needs you is a potent form of body language. Often it just involves non-evaluative listening, holding or other soothing forms of touch, and just "being there" for your partner.

2. **Relationship renegotiation.** Although this is a mostly verbal strategy in which a couple sits down and talks about the relationship, body language plays an important part in communicating attentiveness, sincerity, and support.

1. **Increased contact.** And finally, the most important way to escalate the intensity of a relationship is to spend more time with your partner. There is no substitute for quality time with a partner. And when you can't be with your partner, phone calls, cards, letters, and e-mails communicate their importance over space and time. This is increasingly challenging as the pace of life continues to accelerate, but is essential to developing a serious relationship. No form of body language says more about your seriousness than sharing space and time.

It might seem obvious, but relationships always involve two people. Life is splendid when you and your partner are both ready for more commitment. But alas, couples don't always see eye-to-eye on the direction they think their relationship should take. If partners are on different relational trajectories, intensified body language may seem pushy and claustrophobic. Unless you want to chase away your partner by moving too fast, ascertain your partner's readiness for a more intense relationship before escalating it.

> **Bodily Blunders** _____
>
> Body language that escalates a relationship pleases partners who have the urge to merge. Sending more intense and intimate messages to a partner who isn't ready for the next step is like catching a cat. Dating partners, like cats, love increased intimacy when—and only when—they are ready. Your partner's body language and words will communicate his or her readiness for intimacy.

Cooling the Courtship

Now you know more about attraction, flirtation, and intensification, all stuff that increases intimacy and gets folks together. But what if you want to cool down an overheated relationship?

Flirtation Deactivation

What do you do when flirting gets too intense and you want to slow things down? As the traditional gatekeepers of sexual escalation, most women are experts at cooling a hot interaction. Some women will cut back eye contact to an occasional glance, being careful not to get caught looking. If mutual eye contact occurs, the first person to break the gaze is showing less interest and thereby slowing the pace of the flirtation. Similarly, body barriers—using hands to cover the face or folding the arms in front of the body—can be used to send frosty cues that douse the flames of an intense flirtation. Flirting with someone else will send the message that nothing was all that special about the original flirtation, although it will make you appear to be temperamentally flirtatious. Yawns during eye contact also tend to undercut flirtatious body signals.

If you really want to raise an obstacle to ongoing flirtation, shake your head from side to side, avoid eye contact, and, of course, move away. Taking your leave unobtrusively—whether it's from a party, a bar, or anywhere else—is the ultimate avoidance cue.

Flirtatious Finales

A courtship getting too heavy? In his song "Fifty Ways to Leave Your Lover," Paul Simon proposed you "make a new plan, Stan" or "set yourself free, Lee." But does research back up Simon's suggestions? Here are the top nine strategies for using body language to end a relationship:

◆ **Slip out the back, Jack.** Complete avoidance is the most common relationship breakup strategy; yet, it's neither kind nor effective. Avoidance creates rampant uncertainty, hope for reconciliation, and considerable distress on the other person's part. Slipping out the back makes for good song lyrics, but your ex deserves better.

◆ **Relational alternatives, a.k.a. cheating.** If your partner starts showing up with a new girlfriend or boyfriend they've never told you about, you are experiencing the age-old relational alternative breakup strategy. This is a cruel blow and an ambiguous one because it is unclear if your partner is just playing the field, trying to make you jealous, or signaling that you've just been dumped.

◆ **The cold shoulder.** During many breakups, body language that was formerly warm and inviting becomes cold and distant. In thriving relationships, partners touch, make constant eye contact, and look upon each other with warm, positive expressions. An absence of warm body language may signal problems and an impending breakup. The only problem is this: How does your partner know if it's a breakup or just a rough spot? You should probably tell them.

◆ **The repulsion ruse.** One pretty lame strategy used by a surprisingly large minority of people is the repulsion ruse. This involves some pretty hideous stuff like discontinuing bathing, chain-smoking in your nonsmoking partner's apartment, coming in drunk, and making yourself as unattractive as possible. Not only is this strategy often pretty transparent, it's demeaning to both you and your partner. Plus, it could be the real you coming out—scary!

◆ **Cost escalation.** Some people use a similar, ugly, manipulative strategy called cost escalation. Here the person who wants to break up is deliberately messy, obnoxious, rude, argumentative, and fails to contribute anything to the relationship. This is really "great" for your reputation and self-concept, as people may believe that being a butt comes naturally to you. The sad thing is that it just might work; though the price is your self-respect and the erasure of any fond memories your partner may have retained.

◆ **Fading away.** Some folks just stop calling and returning phone calls. I briefly dated a young woman who, according to her roommate, was always in the shower! She was certainly a clean young woman, though she didn't come clean with me. Some folks just disappear and never again call, leaving you wondering if they have been kidnapped by terrorists, moved to Tibet, or just lost interest.

◆ **The fake break.** Sometimes a relational partner disingenuously recommends "taking a little break" from the relationship. This looks a lot like a temporary de-escalation but is really a cover for a partner's complete exit. Like fading away, this disengagement tactic is rampant with ambiguity and uncertainty. Research shows that less than 10 percent of the dumpees get the message that the relationship is really over.

◆ **The direct dump.** This one-way strategy employs consistent verbal messages and body language that the relationship is really over. The direct dump is a clear, but not a really kind, strategy because no explanation or conversation is provided for the demise of the once blissful relationship. This strategy provides no chance for conversation or negotiation.

Uniting Language and Body Language

In reality, using only body language to break up is a bad idea. Although body language plays an important role in any splitup, direct honest communication is the best policy. Be kind, but certain. Nobody likes to be abused during a breakup, left twisting in the wind and feeling uncertain about whether the relationship is really over. The best strategies make it clear that the relationship is over, but also make it clear that you have no regrets about the time spent in the relationship and you harbor no hard feelings. Appeals to fatalism may work well, such as "God just didn't mean this to be." Or you might use a fairness approach and say stuff like, "It isn't fair for me to fake it. I don't love you as much as you love me." The keys to a tasteful breakup are kindness, clarity, and consistency.

Though this book is about body language, talk must be used in conjunction with body language for your communication to be effective. Although our pathologically talkative culture is far too blind to body language, overcompensating by avoiding talk is equally myopic. Communication is a system; language and body language should compliment each other to provide a complete, competent message.

The Least You Need to Know

- Initial attraction based on appearance and body language is a powerful shortcut in the dating and mating game.

- Flirtation, an age-old method of mate selection, takes many forms that require competent sending and reading of body language.

- Intensification strategies escalate and strengthen a good relationship

- Body language plays an essential role in deactivating flirtation.

- Though body language plays a key role in relationship termination, it is best used in conjunction with talk.

Chapter 18

Sexual Signals: The Presentation of Passion

In This Chapter

- ◆ The sequence of sexual escalation
- ◆ Sex talk: Moving beyond body language
- ◆ Understanding male and female sexual body language
- ◆ Aroused and orgasmic body language
- ◆ Safe sex body behaviors

Lots of body language is pretty sexy. Now admit it, at least several times a day, you check out someone sexually. More like several times an hour, or several times a minute, if you are young and/or male. Bodies—particularly bodies in motion—automatically send sexual cues.

Americans have a love-hate relationship with sex. Most people spend a lot of time thinking about sex, but not much time talking about it. Sex brings out a lot of emotions in people, including desire, love, lust, and intimacy as well as embarrassment, guilt, disgust, and jealousy.

This chapter presents a candid discussion about sex as it relates to body language. It is intended for mature teens and adults. If you are uncomfortable tackling this topic, skip to Chapter 19.

Why Are We Sexual Beings?

Sex isn't just about making babies. During human evolution sexual desire was important for survival for three reasons:

- ◆ **Procreating.** This is the part about making babies. If your ancestors hadn't had sex, you wouldn't be here! Think about this amazing fact: Every one of your ancestors was sexually active and sexually successful. Small wonder sex is important to most of us.

- ◆ **Recreating.** For many people sex is simply fun. Sex is pleasurable so we don't forget to do it. In contemporary society sex is the basis of many of our dating, mating, and recreational activities.

- ◆ **Relating.** Sexuality bonds us to a mate. Most people, even men, would rather have a single good partner than any other sexual setup. The fact the women are sexually receptive all year—even when they aren't fertile—suggests that sex is more about bonding than about reproduction.

Steps to Erotic Escalation

Most sexual escalation in relationships follows a fairly fixed behavioral sequence. Getting involved sexually usually involves a step-by-step process of greater sexual intimacy. Anthropologist Desmond Morris calls this the "sexual sequence," and I will "flesh out" some of the details here:

1. **Eye to body.** Although ogling somebody's body is normally taboo, this is often the initial cue that instigates a sexual relationship. For males, and most females as well, the visual cues of an attractive sexual partner are certainly sexually arousing. Interestingly, getting caught looking at your partner's body is, in itself, an important body language cue communicating romantic or sexual interest.

2. **Eye to eye.** Eye contact, especially when it lasts more than a few seconds, is a meaningful moment for most couples. Prolonged eye contact is a real connection and likely to lead to more interaction.

The eye contact and the open body position of this partier is an early step toward more sexual involvement.

(Image courtesy of Peter Andersen)

3. **Voice to voice.** Research suggests that for many couples, intimate talk is an important step in moving toward greater sexual intimacy. There's another reason—besides intimacy—to talk about sex: the necessity for any sexual encounter to be consensual.

4. **Hand to hand.** Handholding is a major tie sign and a public pronouncement that you are a couple. When couples start holding hands, it's an important turning point in their relationship.

5. **Arm to shoulder.** Especially for young people, putting one's arm around a date's shoulder can be a major turning point in the relationship.

The arm to shoulder and the arm to waist are intermediate steps in sexual escalation.

(Image courtesy of Peter Andersen)

6. **Arm to waist.** With this move, a man's hand shifts to a more sensitive region, below the breasts and above the buttocks and genitals. Clearly this is an escalation in intimacy.

7. **Mouth to mouth.** A couple's first kiss is a real turning point, particularly if it's a long or a deep kiss.

8. **Hand to head.** Caressing a partner's head, or pulling their head closer during a long kiss, intensifies an embrace. Caressing the face and head while engaged in eye contact is another way to increase intimacy.

9. **Hand to body.** This is serious stuff, especially when the hands touch the breasts or buttocks. Often, this sequence will progress to sexual intercourse.

10. **Mouth to breast.** Although couples often skip this sequence, it typically occurs before hand to genitals and after hand to breast. This is an erotic and intimate behavior that is likely to be a turn-on for both partners.

11. **Hand to genitals.** Whether as a prelude to sex or as an end in itself, this is a definite turn-on for both men and women.

12. **Genitals to genitals.** Sexual intercourse is about as involved as a couple can be, and having sex usually is a major turning point for a couple.

> **Bodily Blunders**
>
> Despite the beauty and mystery of body language, its Achilles heel is how ambiguous it can be. Nowhere is bodily ambiguity more potentially dangerous than in sexual situations, where real resistance is often interpreted as token resistance, where a person says no but might mean yes. Date rape and sexual assault sometimes occur from bad body language and erroneous assumptions. That's why it's always important to communicate your sexual desires with your body as well as your voice.

Beguiling Body Language

Perverts and prudes aside, normal people are, well, usually into sex. Most people think about sex at least once an hour, and some normal people think about sex more than once a minute. Males and females are both sexual creatures, but sexual psychology and body language differs somewhat for males and females.

Stimulating Sights: Male Sexual Arousal

Sexual sights are arousing for both men and women, but men are much more visually stimulated than women. Most men will check out women, including complete strangers, friends, work associates, and romantic partners, with sex on their brain. Maybe they never intend to initiate sexual contact, but they think about it. Men are far more likely to attribute any sign of warm, friendly behavior as being sexual behavior, and are more primed to interpret body language as sexual.

The greater visual sexual stimulation for men is a major gender difference between men and women. Men consume the majority of sexually explicit photographs in magazines, on the Internet, or anywhere else they are available. Men also place more importance on a pretty face or great body than do women. For men, a trophy wife doesn't mean a woman with a good job or who is a good conversationalist, though these are important qualities in a mate. For most men, the leading criterion in a date or a mate is good looks.

Positions of Power

Undressing a woman or watching a woman undress is a major turn-on for most men. And take your time; a slow strip is the most sensual and sexual. In *The Complete Idiot's Guide to Amazing Sex*, Sari Locker provides lovers with a detailed guide to successful stripping, one of the most provocative forms of body language.

Cleavage is a universal attractor and erotic cue for most men.

(Image courtesy of Robert Avery)

While visual stimulation is at the top of the list for men, lots of other forms of body language turn them on, too. Touch is a biggie. Although men tend to be more stimulated by genital touch with little or no foreplay, men like many kinds of touch. Blowing in his ear, touching his leg, kissing, stroking his chest, or rubbing your body against his are all amazingly arousing forms of tactile body language.

Don't forget the other senses. Smells can be erotic; the pheromones we discussed in Chapter 9 can be highly arousing. Whether they emanate from a lover's own body or a partner's perfume, most men are turned on by smell. Olfactory remembrances can even create a nostalgic note; the smell of a lover's body or her perfume may rekindle passionate sentiments. The sounds of love, such as sighs or heavy breathing, also trigger arousal.

Nonverbally Speaking

It has been said that for women, good love leads to good sex; for men, good sex leads to good love. Perhaps that's why good relationships represent a slow body language dance, with affection and love escalating at the same rate as sexual involvement. This is a recipe that works for both men and women.

Bodily Blunders

Even though women say they want gentle, sensitive mates, that isn't always who they select. Many normal, even conservative, women select alpha males, bad boys who tend to walk on the wild side. Biologists believe that selecting males with bad, bold body language may be programmed into women to keep strength and survivability in the gene pool. Or maybe women just want a walk on the wild side.

Sexy Situations: The Feminine Face of Sex

Sex for most women is all about context: the right man, the right relationship, the right place, and all the small touches. As you will learn in Chapter 26, women are the guardians of the relationship. So for women sex always has been, and probably always will be, more about relationships than anything.

Studies reveal that when women look for a permanent sexual partner, they are seeking resources, especially status and wealth. Women are more likely to be exploited for their looks and sexuality; men are more likely to be exploited for wealth, power, and status. From Bangladesh to Brazil, from Berlin to Boston, women appear to be material girls who are turned on by resources. Of course, women also want their men to be emotionally loyal, to be good partners, and to put the relationship first. Near the top of most women's lists are men who are sensitive to their body language: Women want a man who senses her moods, especially her emotional and sexual moods.

Whereas most men like to get down to good old-fashion sex without much delay, women are aroused more slowly. So when you're making love to woman, foreplay is the body language of love. Women are more likely to love contextual factors like music, gentle lighting, candles, incense, flowers, the right fabric, the right sheets, and a beautiful room.

Like men, women are aroused by touch. Unlike most men, who are more genitally focused, women's entire bodies can turn them on. Women (and of course, some men) are aroused by all kinds of touch, including kissing, nibbling, breast stimulation, touching the hair, ears, and neck, all-over body massages, tracing fingers over virtually any part of their body, back rubs, facial touching, as well as genital stimulation.

Nonverbally Speaking

Men are fairly predictable—most guys peg their interest in sex between 60 and 80 on a 100-point interest scale. Women are far less sexually predictable, and their interest varies between 0 and 100. Social scientists refer to this wide range in sexual interest as *sexual variability* or *erotic plasticity*. Women range from completely and contentedly celibate to multi-orgasmic. It's just another way in which women are mighty mysterious.

Orgasmic Enchantment

No doubt about it, an orgasm is the ultimate sexual experience.

A male orgasm is hard to fake. First, it is accompanied by ejaculation, a sure sign that orgasm has occurred. Second, after an orgasm, males enter a period where sexual desire diminishes, and an erection is usually lost. Third, most males are not sensitive enough to fake an orgasm, so their partner feels like a success.

Not so for women. Most women report faking an orgasm at least once, and some women are darn good actors. A fake orgasm doesn't mean that a woman didn't enjoy herself; it just means that she could have gotten off even more. She does this to save her partner's face and pride, so he thinks he is the great lover, which he may not be. On the other hand, many women can have multiple orgasms and blissfully skim from one to the next with no significant decline in sexual arousal like males. This is the ultimate in sexual prowess.

The body language of a real female orgasm is pretty distinctive. Her back arches, her vaginal muscles repeatedly contract, her muscles tense, she may vocalize loudly, or moan uncontrollably. Many women get a red flush over their face and chest. It's pretty powerful body language.

The male orgasm is accompanied by feelings of inevitability, an even stronger erection, a desire to thrust deeply, and, of course, ejaculation. Males often groan, moan, vocalize, and have contorted facial expressions that make them look like they're in pain; but they are in no pain. Unlike women, after orgasm men enter a phase where sexual desire diminishes or disappears. Young, healthy, or passionate men may spend only moments in this phase before they are ready again, unlike women who are potentially ready immediately after an orgasm.

> **Bodily Blunders**
>
> Orgasm should not be an obsessive goal; it should be the culmination of great sex. In fact, for both sexes, but especially for women, trying too hard to have an orgasm may make it more elusive. Most women take more time to reach an orgasm than most men, so men need to monitor their partners and slow down if their own orgasm is impending. This, of course, leads to a whole new meaning for the expression "nice guys finish last." While a mutual orgasm is special, it shouldn't always be a goal.

After the Ball

Body language after sex is crucial. Spending time with your partner is a real statement of intimacy and commitment. For many couples, this is a time of great closeness and bonding. Free of the tension, urgency, and energy expended during sex, a couple can relax, engage in prolonged eye contact or gentle touching, or quietly drift off into an amazing and deep sleep.

> **Bodily Blunders**
>
> Sex is a wonderful thing, but if you catch an STD, especially an incurable or a fatal one, your life will take a terrible turn for the worse. Lots of safe sex activities employ erotic body language. Instead of intercourse, try stripping, mutual masturbation, and cybersex. If you still want to have sex, use a condom, and enjoy putting it on as part of the turn-on.

Some couples engage in "pillow talk," "baby talk" or talk about their most intimate feelings after sex. This can be a special time of sharing when, literally, all barriers are down. Sometimes couples talk about their great sex, their relationship, laugh, share mischievous feelings, or tell each other about their love for each other. For other couples, body language such as tender touch, nudity, eye contact, shared space, and sweet dreams says it all.

For some people, the moments after sex or the next morning are a time of reflection and reconsideration. Having sexual intercourse is a turning point in any relationship, one that can lead to greater closeness or "buyer's remorse." Although sex can bond, it can also create uncertainty.

The Least You Need to Know

- Erotic escalation proceeds through distinct steps, each with their own unique body language display.

- Males and females have their own unique set of body language cues that produce sexual arousal. Males are most aroused by physical appearance and visual cues such as nudity and genital touch. Females are aroused by a close relationship, the right setting, and virtually any type of touch.

- Good sexual communication requires talk as well as body language.

- Sexual arousal and orgasm have their own unique displays of erotic body language.

Chapter 19

Interviewing Intelligently: The Role of Body Language

In This Chapter

- ◆ Dressing for successful interviews
- ◆ Employing body language
- ◆ Using enthusiasm
- ◆ Avoiding interview *faux pas*
- ◆ Interacting with health-care professionals

You've seen them on TV: Bad interviews! Bad questions! Bad answers! The widow of a man shot in a local post office is asked, "Ma'am how are you feeling right now?" DUHH! And how about this one? Reporter: "Coach, what's the key to the game?" Coach: "Well, we got to put more points on the board than they do and tighten up our defense." Double DUHH!

And insipid interviews are not confined to dumb dialog; they are also bedeviled by bad body language. You may have seen employment interviews where the applicant looks like he stopped by for a chat on the way from the beach. And you've seen jocks bouncing up and down, never looking at the camera, and saying stuff such as "Like, you know, man, we, ah, were, you know, like, tough, man, on like, defense, umm, dig it." They are nearly impossible to watch. You feel so embarrassed, and you're just an observer!

Fortunately, researchers have learned a lot about dynamic dialogs and intelligent interviews. While you're not likely to be interviewed at the Superbowl, you will probably participate in a number of interviews and watch scores of others. By tuning in to body language you can conduct great interviews and be an inspiring interviewee. This chapter will focus on two of important interview situations, employment interviews and medical interviews.

Telling a Book by Its Cover

In employment interviews, first impressions really count. In fact, the whole interview is basically a first impression. And you know the old cliché about never having a second chance to make a first impression. You walk in, and before you utter a word dozens of impressions have been formed. Some of these you can't do too much about; it's hard to change your sex, race, or height. But you can do a lot to make the most of your appearance. So go for it and have fun! Though people know you can't tell a book by its cover, the cover—and maybe the introduction—is all you get to read in an interview. To maximize your opportunities, here are five dress rules to follow:

- ◆ **Rule 1: Dress for success.** Dress like you already have the job, even a tad nicer. Teachers should dress like teachers, stockbrokers like stockbrokers, and coaches like coaches. Not only does the body language communicated by your attire say you are professional and competent, subconsciously you want the interviewer to think you already have this position. Conservative and appropriate dress is the safest route.

> **Nonverbally Speaking**
>
> Attractive people are more likely to get good jobs. That fact is frustrating to people who would like to be more handsome or have a different body shape. Here is the good news: Literally hundreds of studies show that warm, expressive people are more attractive and more employable. And you can do something about that!

- ◆ **Rule 2: Dress to impress.** If your friends don't say, "wow, where are you going?" you're underdressed for an interview. Lots more people fail by underdressing for interviews than by overdressing. Unless you are interviewing for a job as a lifeguard or soccer coach, wear your best suit.

- ◆ **Rule 3: Don't dress for excess.** Women in particular should wear achievement attire, especially if they are interviewing in a traditionally male occupation or organization. While sexy clothing with high hemlines and plunging necklines is certainly attention-getting, it might attract the wrong kind of attention. Negative attributions about the morality, trustworthiness, intensions, or reliability of sketchy-looking people abound. Nothing impedes like excess.

This fellow is dressed for success. His polished interview attire and his body language communicate professionalism and competence.

(Image courtesy of Robert Avery)

Likewise, avoid outdated fashions, wild and weird color schemes, and mixing and matching of different clothing styles. If your body is pierced in a lot of places you might want to temporarily remove some of the hardware. Clothing should cover tattoos. Long hair can also create negative impressions. If you are a woman with long hair, consider wearing it up. If you are a man with long hair, a ponytail beats long flowing locks.

♦ **Rule 4: Don't dress like a mess.** Clothes that are spotted or wrinkled generate awful impressions. After you get dressed for an interview, take a look at yourself in the mirror. Don't be afraid to do some spot cleaning, use a lint brush, get out the

Positions of Power

Not sure how to dress for that job interview? Talk to an employee or call the human resources department and ask for the dress code and how much it is followed. And be careful of informal Fridays. Even on Fridays you should dress for success, but don't look like a stuffed shirt in your pin stripes when everyone else is wearing jeans.

iron, or change clothes, even if this is your favorite outfit. Consider wearing a shirt or blouse that has been professionally cleaned and has a bit of starch in it. Clothes from the cleaner look neater, more professional, and say that you are already a successful person.

◆ **Rule 5: Put your best feet forward.** Don't forget about the shoes. Shoes should be neatly polished and go with the outfit. I once interviewed a young man in a nice suit and running shoes. I, too, am a runner, and I like the comfort of running shoes; but only dress shoes should be worn with a suit. Avoid sandals and old tennis shoes; they're too casual for interviews. If you're a woman and you wear nylons, make sure they don't have any runs in them. The socks you wear should be dressy, since there may not be a desk between you and the interviewer.

Employing Body Language

Dress is not the only type of body language that can create positive or negative first impressions in the employment interview. A job interview is first and foremost about selling yourself, getting information, and asking good questions. So don't forget interviews are a two-way street, where both parties are using body language to form impressions and make important career decisions.

Here are the top-10 body language fouls when meeting someone for the first time, ripped from the literature of interviewing research.

10. **Maiming your manners.** Be sure to think a bit about etiquette. Let your interviewer enter a room before you, and don't sit down first unless they indicate you should sit. Shake hands with everyone you meet. Do not wipe your nose on your sleeve. Yes, this is an etiquette test!

9. **The face plant (tripping or falling).** Normally used by skiers and snowboarders and Chevy Chase on the original *Saturday Night Live*, this is an attention getter that gets the wrong kind of attention. When this happens, please apologize and hope the interviewer has sympathy for klutzes.

8. **The yawning listener.** It's hard to listen to an oral audit of the company books by Chuck the Comptroller from Hell. But don't yawn. If you do, you might as well just say, "Boy, this is a boring interview."

7. **The space invasion.** Nobody likes to interview an applicant from 10 inches away. Don't try to ingratiate yourself with instant intimacy. Save this for your spouse or kids.

6. **The Alice Cooper look (and other preparedness penalties).** You can say you came from rehearsal with your punk band, but it is pretty clear your mascara ran in the rain. And guys, please remove the bloody Kleenex you applied after shaving. It's always a good idea to make a quick trip to the restroom before the interview to make sure you are not wearing your breakfast or your shirttail isn't hanging out of your fly.

5. **The not-on-time crime.** Even if you are the most consistently late person you know, even if you were late for your own wedding, be on time for your interview. Tardiness slays!

4. **The dead-fish handshake.** Talk about an excuse to write you off from the start. Try a firm (not crushing) handshake, which says you have at least a pittance of passion for this job.

3. **The silent answer.** It is *not okay* to pass on a question. Sure you have a nice smile, but the interviewer was expecting you to at least have a clue!

2. **Flirting with your interviewer.** This makes you look very desperate. Heck, you probably don't even know if the person is married.

1. **Body odor.** Talk about a negative first impression! In Chapter 9, we discussed American aromaphobia. In the job world, if you reek, don't seek.

Avoiding an Energy Crisis

Dozens of studies have shown that enthusiasm impresses. People like energetic people, especially energetic employees. Weak, lackadaisical, halfhearted body language creates poor impressions in an employment interview. This lazy, unenthusiastic body language says to the interviewer that you will be a lazy, unenthusiastic employee.

If this were a piano recital, a basketball game, or a golf tournament, you would have practiced for weeks, months, or even years. Yet, most people go into a job interview cold, without a single practice session. Doing some practice interviews with a volunteer trainer, like your spouse or roommate, is essential. I even suggest to my students that they interview for some random jobs, just for practice.

> **Nonverbally Speaking**
>
> Turn-taking is an incredibly important conversational skill, and it's particularly vital in interviews. Body cues that signal potential turn switches include an audible and visible exhalation, direct eye contact, terminating gestures, and a pause. If you see any of these, it's your turn to talk.

When you practice, be sure to get some good feedback from someone who will tell you the negative stuff as well as the positive. Focus on what you do well and keep doing it. Work on what you are doing poorly and try alternatives until you and your coach see improvement. Suppose, for example, one of the things you are doing poorly is failing to gesture. Experiment with some gestures. Some will look fake, and some will look real. Some will be too big, or too small, or out of sync with the rest of your body language. Keep working on them until you feel comfortable and your trainer likes what you're doing. On the big day, you will be much more confident as a result of the practice and you'll be ready to call up some bubbly body language.

To communicate energy and enthusiasm, start with the face. Many people, in an effort to stay calm and to suppress fear and anxiety, use the blank face. But remember, there is no such thing as a blank face. The so-called blank or expressionless face looks tired, lazy, apathetic, arrogant, stupid, and unprepared. Show some emotions like happiness, surprise, interest, and warmth. It wouldn't hurt to spend some time with a mirror seeing if you can display these emotions.

Next, give yourself a body examination. Poor posture like slumping or slouching sends negative messages of disrespect, laziness, weakness, and disinterest. We describe people with good posture as upright; decent, straight, and honest; not slouches at their work; and people who would never shrink from an important task. Conversely, slouchers are crooked, in a slump, crash and burn, collapse in the face of adversity, and duck responsibility. Perceptions of posture are hardwired into judgments of character and competence.

Remember, the voice carries more than words. How you answer is as important as the content of the answer. Here are a few vocal body language tips:

- **Speak up.** Interview answers only count if they can be heard.

- **Enunciate (EE NUN SEE ATE).** Sloppy speaking creates terrible impressions.

- **Exercise speed control.** Fast talking is okay, but don't lapse into inarticulateness or rambling.

Bodily Blunders

People often fail in interviews because they are too aroused and anxious, resulting in nervous body language and poor performance. If your heart is racing and your palms are sweating before an interview, find a quiet room and do some stretching, deep breathing, or meditation. You want to be psyched up but not psyched out.

Positions of Power

It's an irony that your body language is invisible to yourself. We can't see our own face and we have a poor view of our own body! Rehearsing in front of a full-length mirror can help. Or you can do what professional communication coaches do: Videotape yourself so you can see and improve your own body language.

- ◆ **Squelch soporific speech.** Really slow speech is sleep inducing! Which may be a good thing, since slow speech is often associated with being slow-witted.

- ◆ **Reject regionalisms.** Come on now. Bostonians, you can turn off the "Hahvohd Yohd" speaking style if you concentrate and ya'll from Bama can cool it with the dialect a tad. Regional accents only work with others that have the same accent.

Dynamic Dialogues: The Two-Way Interview

Hey interviewees, you get to ask questions, too. In fact, some studies show that well-prepared questions by the applicant are the key to a job offer. Here you get to show off that you have researched the company and can ask good questions. Plus, it gets you off the hot seat for a while. Moreover, isn't there stuff you really want to know, like future company plans, those rumors about mergers, profit-sharing, starting salary, and such?

Most importantly, from a body language perspective, interrogators have the power. The mere role of questioning the interviewer switches the power role and leaves an impression in the interviewer's mind that you are an influential, take-charge person with leadership potential.

Confidence Counts

Confidence is compelling. In an employment interview, the employer has just a short time to determine whether you can do the job. The person with self-assured, secure, positive body language communicates competence and confidence. Employment interviewers believe, correctly or incorrectly, that unconfident, self-doubting people are insecure, incompetent, ignorant, and unskilled. Not the qualities of somebody I'd hire.

Confidence starts with the eyes. Steady eye contact, particularly when speaking, exudes confidence and credibility. This also takes practice, so in your mock interviews, spend time answering while looking the interviewer right in the eyes. As you learned in Chapter 9, reduced eye contact is not necessarily associated with lying, but people think low levels of eye contact or shifty eyes is a sign a lying.

Lack of eye contact in an interview leads to other negative attributes besides lying. Research suggests that eye avoiders are thought to be shy, secretive, threatened by other people, sneaky, and aloof. These incompetent and suspicious-looking cues often motivate an interviewer to probe further into negative territory to find out what is going on.

A big strong voice is also a major confidence communicator. Say things like you mean them. Be sure to breathe and use enough air that your voice doesn't sound shaky. Women can have big voices, too. Use plenty of air, speak a bit lower, and above all ditch the Minnie Mouse voice—it is not the voice of authority.

Confidence is also a function of posture. Round shoulders, postural collapse, slouching, sagging, and slumping communicate apathy, low energy, and insecurity. Avoid nervous fidgeting as well. This makes you appear jittery and unsure of yourself. Keep your feet still and rest your hands on your lap or the arm of the chair when not gesturing meaningfully.

> **CAUTION**
>
> ### Bodily Blunders
>
> Most people are at least a little nervous in an interview. When you're frightened, Stone Age emotions passed down by your ancestors click in. Suddenly your legs are saying: Flee! Run for your life! Get the heck outta here! Of course you can't do that, not if you want the job. But the flight response can't be completely suppressed, and it usually shows up in lively legs and fidgety feet. Rein in those doggies. Put your feet flat on the floor and convert that energy to face and voice.

Healthy Interviews

At some time in our lives we all see doctors, dentists, psychologists, chiropractors, or optometrists. Some of them are good interviewers and some are not. If you want a quality interaction, it's essential that you do a great job of interviewing them. Your life could depend on it.

Interviewing Your Doctor

Half a century ago, doctors ranked somewhere between gods and angels. Carrying their black bags, they arrived at our homes to heal and their advice was rarely questioned. For many people doctors are still deities, and their word is law. For others, doctors are arrogant money-grubbers who don't give us the attention we deserve.

Going to the doctor is really about communication. Doctors need to know about your symptoms and feelings, and you need to know about courses of treatment, their effectiveness and side effects, and your prognosis given various courses of action.

> **Nonverbally Speaking**
>
> Burnout in any job is bad, but a burned-out doctor can be fatal. Look for these signs of physician burn-out: grumpy, bored, or negative facial expressions; negative vocal cues when talking to staff; rushed body language; and poor bedside manner.

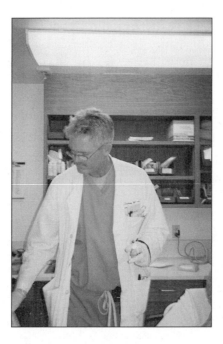

We need to be able to estab-lish a rapport with our doctors.

(Image courtesy of Peter Andersen)

When you meet with your doctor for the first time, you should think of her or him as auditioning to be your doctor. Here are a few things to look for:

- **Does your doctor listen with her or his whole body or do they seem far away, disconnected, or preoccupied?** When doctors listen, they should do all the right stuff: look at you, nod appropriately, show empathy, be warm, and be on your wavelength.

- **Is your doctor capable of being tough?** Nobody likes an autocrat, but some-times a doctor needs to use a little tough love and serious body language when getting you to quit smoking, lose weight, or take your medication. Don't pick a pushover.

- **Is your doctor warm and friendly?** If you can't connect with your doctor because her or his body language is a turn-off, you're not going to have a good relationship. You won't feel like you can openly talk to her or him, and you may even avoid going to your doctor altogether. Connection counts!

- **Is this a collaborative relationship?** Your doctor's body language should be respectful and collaborative. Arrogance stinks. Do the vibes say that this is col-laboration, or does your doctor's body language say "my way or the highway"?

- **Will your doctor hear you out?** Or like so many doctors today, do you only get your 10 minutes of care? Not every problem can be pigeonholed into a time slot. And you shouldn't feel anxious or guilty about taking your doctor's time. It's not your job to balance your HMO's books by jeopardizing your health. You deserve someone who will give you the time you need.

If your answer is no to one or more of these questions, you might consider firing your doctor. The doctor-patient relationship is far too important for bad vibes and negative feelings to cloud your interactions.

Be sure to ask your doctor questions. Today's doctors are swamped and might forget to mention everything that is important to your health, so you must take the initiative.

> **CAUTION**
>
> **Bodily Blunders**
>
> Cleanliness counts at the doctor's office. Studies show that better-dressed people get better care at the office. And take a bath! Nobody, not even a doctor, wants to examine a putrid patient. Now that is a body blunder.

Remember that in a doctor's office, quality interaction requires quality body language. First, let's talk about *your* body language.

Position yourself so you can make eye contact with the physician. Make sure the doctor knows that you are concerned about your health—you can signal your concern with your tone of voice and your facial expressions. In addition, interact with confidence. Unfortunately, some doctors are pretty aloof, so you need to come across as competent about your health and capable of taking action. Doctors are much more inclined to help people who help themselves.

Shrinking Together

Too few people in America seek counseling. Get a little bit of the stomach flu and off you go to the doctor. But people can suffer from severe anxiety or debilitating depression and never see a shrink. Receiving counseling isn't a stigma; in fact, visits to a counselor are confidential, so nobody has to know. Moreover, in places like California and New York it's pretty trendy to have a shrink. It's right up there with personal trainers, gardeners, and performance coaches on the status hierarchy.

Sometimes we all need help, and a trained counselor can guide you back to a centered space. It will not break your budget. Many counselors will adjust their fees to your income, and your insurance will probably cover most of the costs.

Now here is the *Complete Idiot's Guide* to not being an idiot in counseling. First, ignore virtually everything in this book when you go to your counselor. You don't have to be other-oriented; this is about you! You don't have to dress for success—this is about the real you, not your corporate image or false face. Do not control your emotions. This is the time to express anger, joy, guilt, shame, hurt, fear, sadness, or whatever! In fact, half the benefit of going to counseling comes from getting all the pent-up emotions off your chest.

Don't be alarmed if you do most of the communicating while your counselor nods, listens, and asks only an occasional question. Most therapists agree that real change has to come from within the client and can't be imposed by the therapist. Good therapists set up the situation so you can understand your own issues and solutions by providing the right environment and body language so you are comfortable with that process.

Just like selecting your doctor, use good intuition in selecting a counselor. Tons of research shows that warm, supportive counselors are keys to good dialog and successful outcomes. This same research shows that body language is the key to a therapist being warm, immediate, and supportive. Tune in to the vibes during the session with your counselor and let your intuition be your guide. If you are on the same wavelength, chances are you'll have a positive experience.

The Least You Need to Know

- ◆ Dress for success, not to excess, when going to an interview.
- ◆ Avoid bodily blunders: First impressions count.
- ◆ Warmth and enthusiasm are employable skills.
- ◆ Confidence counts.
- ◆ Interview your doctors.

Chapter 20

Silent Messages in the Workplace

In This Chapter

- ◆ The suit is trump
- ◆ Does size matter in the organization?
- ◆ The importance of location
- ◆ The body language of the ubiquitous meeting
- ◆ Tactile trepidations in the workplace

The workplace is a treasure chest of body language. Status symbols, power moves, territorial markers, courtships cues, gender indicators, command views, tactile connections and rejections, and positions of power are everywhere.

Since many Americans now spend a majority of their waking hours at work, corporate communication and workplace body language are more important than ever. So before you rush off to work, catch a section or two of this chapter, which should help you understand silent messages in the workplace.

Dressed for Success

The most visible body language cue is your attire. Clothes may not make the man (or woman), but they communicate your status, stylishness, gender, social class, wealth, conformity, traditionalism, and attitudes. All this body language forms powerful impressions long before you open your mouth to speak.

The Suit Is Trump

Formal apparel, like the business suit, increases your power and status. Dark blue suits are the organizational standard because black suits, according to Paul Malloy, author of *Dress for Success*, have funereal overtones. Of course, for women, wearing a bright blouse eliminates any "grave" perceptions, as does a brightly colored tie for men. Malloy also claims that pinstripes and wool are the gold standards for both men and women as they have been for decades.

Suits should be contemporary or classic: Nehru jackets, polyester leisure suits, and liberty bell-bottoms don't get the job done.

Suits are the uniform of the international business community

(Image courtesy of Peter Andersen)

Workplace dress codes have relaxed in many organizations to the point where a sport coat or a contemporary suit of virtually any color will work just fine. Some organizations still have informal, if not formal, dress codes, so it's always best to err on the side of being overdressed. Proper dress may also serve as a corporate uniform that says you are a part of the team, a member of the organizational culture. Of course, in some organizations actual uniforms are required.

Uniformly Excellent

No kind of attire is a clearer form of body language than the uniform. Uniforms both empower and subordinate. On one hand, the uniforms worn by police, soldiers, fire-fighters, nurses, doctors, and construction workers give them authority, power, and territorial access that other people lack. On the other hand, a uniform also restrains and restricts. It necessitates professional conduct, proscribes one's role, conceals individuality, and establishes one's rank.

Uniforms strip away individuality but afford status and power.

(Images courtesy of Peter Andersen)

The power of the uniform is substantial. Uniforms enable their wearers to stop cars, enter buildings, or probe the human body. On the other hand, food service workers, custodians, garbage collectors, and many other uniformed workers suffer lowered status from the subservience communicated by their attire.

Likewise, uniforms conceal and reveal power. School uniforms suppress individuality, create conformity, and cover over income differences. They also create a community and exclude nonmembers. Interestingly, both opponents and proponents of school uniforms agree that they curtail self-determination and individuality, for better or worse, depending on one's view. Even team uniforms empower and disempower. It may convey exceedingly high status and group solidarity to wear a Trojan football uniform or a Yankees baseball uniform, but at the cost of diminished individuality and uniformity.

Bodily Blunders _____

Stanley Milgram of Yale University explored the darkest side of power and authority. Dressed in the authoritative white lab coat, he asked ordinary people to administer shocks to other ordinary people in a learning experiment. They didn't really receive shocks, but the shock administrators did not know this, and the shock recipient was a trained actor who feigned pain and pleaded with the people to stop the shocks.

In the presence of uniformed authority at one of the nation's prestigious universities, the vast majority of people gave other people what they thought were nearly lethal doses of electric shocks. Despite pitiful pleas and beseeching body language, most people administered shock after shock and followed the commands of uniformed authority! Lest we think Stalin or Hitler were anomalies and that Americans could never be convinced to follow authority blindly, remember these were ordinary Americans in Milgram's experiments.

Looking Like a Professional

Unless you own the company, you should look and dress like the professional you are. In view of the fact that owners and CEOs spend a lot of time with clients, suppliers, and the media, they should dress for success as well. The very wealthy and powerful, from Howard Hughes to Bill Gates, from Cher to Madonna, from Osoma bin Laden to Tom Cruise, transcend fashion and convention. Michael Korda, in his novel *The Immortals*, speaks of Marilyn Monroe's attire in these same terms: "She was wearing a tight black dress of some shimmering material, which seemed two sizes too small for her, a white fox stole, and a cheap black patent leather handbag. The whole outfit looked like it might have been purchased at a thrift shop. Not that it mattered—Marilyn was beyond good taste, or bad."

In addition to the traditional business suit, expensive-looking, neatly polished shoes are still the look of status. For men heavy, noisy-sounding shoes have powerful connotations.

Though orthopedically outlandish, high heels are still the professional footwear for the corporate woman. Unfortunately, women's business attire is still governed more by tradition and fashion than by comfort or functionality. Nonconformists, while respected for their individuality, also pay the price for their eccentric ways.

Dark, polished shoes are an important part of business body language for men.

(Image courtesy of Robert Avery)

High heels are uncomfortable and difficult to walk in. Nonetheless, they are the gold standard of femininity and an important part of many women's business attire.

(Image courtesy of Robert Avery)

Other aspects of body language can create positive or negative impressions in the workplace. Appropriate, well-coordinated jewelry can be a plus, especially for women, but research suggests that excessive or ostentatious jewelry sends negative signals. Likewise, lots of body-piercing jewelry should be avoided unless you're working for a punk band or a tattoo shop. In aromaphobic America, some cologne or perfume is okay, but avoid overdoing it. Studies show that excessive perfume is obnoxious and sends the signal that you are low-class, cheap, and uneducated.

> ⚠ CAUTION
>
> **Bodily Blunders**
>
> Your hands are highly conspicuous in organization environments—you use them to pass papers, gesture, and shake other hands. Dirty hands constitute uncouth body language. Men should also avoid long or dirty nails. Women should have manicured nails, but nails that look like painted claws are considered unbusinesslike. Save the claws for the raptors.

Size Matters: Status Symbols

If you won the lottery today, would you still show up at work tomorrow? If your answer is yes, you have a really, really great job.

Americans work mostly to put food on the table, a roof over their heads, and gasoline in their cars so they can get to work. Once we make enough to satisfy the necessities, most of us still work for material possessions and social status. Let's face it, the car you drive and the house you live in are status symbols. Likewise, Americans love perks and seek status at work. These material possessions constitute the body language of success.

A large, attractive office is a status symbol and an indication of power.

(Image courtesy of Robert Avery)

Perhaps the biggest status symbol at work is your office. Frankly, just having an office is a bit of a status symbol. Chances are your grandparents didn't have one, probably just a field, or a counter, or a machine. And in the world of offices, size matters!

> ### Nonverbally Speaking
>
> Americans have an edifice complex. The most ostentatious forms of body language are the large buildings and stadiums that represent corporate images. These structures are to corporate Americans what the pyramids were to the Pharaohs.

Large offices are a sign of power and success. Look at the size of the office in your organization and you are viewing the organizational chart in action. In contrast to a work bay or a desk separated by partitions, a large office is pretty impressive and sends nonverbal messages about the important person the occupant has become.

But size isn't all that matters; quality counts, too. The best offices have lots of windows with commanding views of mountains, lakes, oceans, parks, and, of course, other buildings with commanding views. Corners are coolest, because you have a view in several directions; of course, what really rocks is a whole floor with a spectacular view. Any client would have to be impressed. Quality offices exude power and make other executives want to close the deal or settle the suit, because status speaks. Monarchs and royalty have always commanded the high ground, and castles were erected on the hilltop, not just for defense, not just for the view, but so all the peasants in the fields could see the symbol of status and know who the boss really was.

If you are not the CEO, the next best thing is to be her or his right-hand person. Thus, the offices next to the boss are powerful places. Being in the executive suite or even on the same floor as the bigwigs is a position of power. The powerful people who inhabit the executive suite are shielded from the riff-raff by layers of gate-keepers. If you can get to an executive without an okay from at least three secretaries or guards, they're not a powerful poobah. You can't even reach real mucky-mucks on the phone without talking to at least one or two receptionists.

> ### Nonverbally Speaking
>
> Receptionists really communicate an outdated form of organizational body language, because caller ID and voice mail make layers of receptionists a bit obsolete. But even the big technology firms still employ the low-tech, high-status secretary rather than the latest technology.

Executives fill their offices with all the latest gadgets: the cell phone, the palm pilot, the power fax, the photocopier, the color laser printer, the laptop with the wireless modem, all the cool stuff. Of course, few executives know how to operate all these things, which is akin to a full employment program for secretaries and IT guys.

Offices aren't the only organization status symbols. Executive parking spaces, a company car, elegant office appointments, and new furniture are signs of success. Executive bathrooms with private showers and heated towel racks, office putting greens, and heliports, actually seal the deal for executive recruiters who convince top managers that they have every possible perk.

Lofty positions, protected from the organization by layers of gatekeepers, have some big drawbacks. It can get lonely at the top. What happened to those great interactions at the coffee machine or those intriguing office flirtations with Darrin or Katlyn? To stay connected, head honchos might take an occasional stroll through subordinates' space, but this is likely to alarm employees who quickly pretend to be really busy and clam up because they think they're being evaluated or reprimanded.

The barricades also cause another problem, executive isolation. Management consultants are always amazed at how little some executives know what is really happening in their organization. The real index of organizational success and effectiveness is best monitored on the assembly line, in the sales force, or in the secretarial pool.

Professional body language should invite organizational interaction, not inhibit it. The best organizations have tried to open doors, take some of the stuffing out of the stuffed shirts, reward good ideas, and encourage face time. In this century, the nimble organization that breaks barriers and reinvents communication will be the one that prevails.

Beasts of Burden

One symbol of status or subservience is what you carry around. Real power brokers can't look like beasts of burden. Instead, they have their subordinates deliver projectors, carry computers, schlep file boxes, and carry large briefcases.

> **Nonverbally Speaking**
>
> Space and territory are not the only nonverbal status markers; time communicates, too. Superiors can keep subordinates waiting but not the reverse. In America, time is money. It's wrong to keep anybody waiting, but it's a major office penalty to make your boss wait.

This is an arena of body language where, indeed, size matters, but big is bad. At one time, bulky briefcases were a sign of a person moving quickly up the organizational ladder. Today, bulky briefcases are the body language of the pack mule. Real movers and shakers carry a very thin briefcase or a super-slim laptop. After all, the top cats only need to carry contracts, and you don't need a suitcase for those. Indeed, top consultants and managers don't need to carry anything at all. This hands-free body language says that all the important stuff is in their head.

People are always joking about the size of my 1990's laptop and cell phone. Bring these five-year-old devices to a meeting and they'll be scrutinized and discussed like archaeologists analyzing the first metal tools. "Remember these from the Bronze Age." "Gosh, my dad told me about mobile phones like this." "Look at the size of that computer, people must have been strong back in the '90s." Forget that my prototype cell phone pulls in calls other phones can't. It's all about the body language where thin is in. Petite palm pilots, miniature mobile phones, slim laptops, and sleek secretaries are the signs of the clean, lean, mean, executive machine.

Meeting Makers and Breakers

In today's business world, the meeting is omnipresent. If you are not reading e-mail, chances are you're in a meeting. While many of you are suffering from meeting burnout, meetings remain a centerpiece of business.

Meetings are usually held around a large rectangular or oval table. If all the chairs are facing forward, you're not in a meeting—you're in a speech or a lecture. Meetings are multi-person discussions, and the room arrangements can make or break a meeting. Real meetings should be designed to facilitate interaction.

Distinguished Chairs

Nowhere are positions of power more evident or important than at meetings. The head of the table is the traditional power position, but there's more to it than that: It's where body language can be easily sent and received. Unlike the side of the table, where people have difficulty observing those next to them, from the head of the table every person at the meeting can be monitored. Likewise, every person can observe the person at the head of the table.

Psychologically, when the leader is alone at the head of the table, he or she is "set apart" from the group. The traditional rectangular table facilitates these power discrepancies, where like oarsmen on a Roman galley, junior executives are all oriented toward the boss. In fact, it is uncommon for subordinates to select seats next to the leader until all the other seats are filled. Affording more space to a leader is one of the basic ABC's of body language.

Leaders intuitively know that the head sits at the head. Jury foremen have been shown in studies to occupy the head of the table. The person at the head of the table can do more talking and thus exert more influence. The most subordinate positions are at the corners of the table, or not at the table at all. Sitting away from the table or in a gallery is a distinctly subordinate position.

It is illuminating to watch the process of who selects what seats at a meeting. The highest-power, highest-interaction seats are at the head and in the middle of each side. Leaders pick prominent positions. The shy and introverted are no fools, either; they select low-interaction seats where communication is improbable if not impossible.

> **CAUTION** **Bodily Blunders**
>
> Feeling out of touch with your colleagues? Maybe you communicate the wrong kind of body language. Is your back to the door? Are you barricaded behind desks and tables? Is your door always closed? Such body barriers discourage other communicators and obstruct interaction.

Communication Locations

For decades, researchers in group dynamics and nonverbal communication have recognized the importance of seating position and meeting arrangements. Without a doubt, oval and circular meeting tables facilitate interaction. Throughout *The Complete*

Idiot's Guide to Body Language we have emphasized that people interact best when they're face-to-face and eye-to-eye. When a room arrangement or meeting table facilitates face-to-face communication and enables eye contact, communication will occur.

Face-to-face and eye-to-eye is the key to good meeting interaction.

(Image courtesy of Robert Avery)

Positions of Power

Want to enhance your own productivity and that of your employees? Turn down the thermostat. You will notice sudden changes in people's body language. A whole series of studies show that at near 70° productivity increases, workers become more task-oriented, and look and act less lethargic.

If you want to facilitate interaction, circular or oval tables work best. The key question is this: Can every participant clearly and continuously see and hear the other participants? Remember, almost all workplace body language is visual and oral. If the arrangement facilitates viewing and hearing, it is good meeting milieu.

On the other hand, if you are making a speech or giving information, and you don't want a dialog, all the seats should face the front. Remember, as a rule people only communicate when facing each other. When people are looking at the back of co-workers' heads, they are less likely to communicate.

Corporate Characters

For better or worse, much of our organizational time is spent in meetings. Your colleagues can become known for their bizarre body language. Perhaps some of these characters are familiar, though hopefully not personally familiar.

Peter Powerful radiates self-confidence and certainty. His direct eye contact, booming, resolute voice, and serious facial expressions exude conviction and confidence, despite the drastic and unacceptable nature of many of his proposals.

Rachael Responder is the emotional captain of the team. She supports everyone by smiling and nodding incessantly regardless of the merits of the proposal.

Sam Skeptical's body language expresses doubt, anxiety, and angst. He never met a plan that made him comfortable, and his perplexed, unconvinced facial expressions clearly convey concern.

Diane Distracted tunes out the meeting and uses this as an opportunity to do the week's correspondence or billing. Occasionally she looks up and utters a feeble "uh-huh" to seem engaged, as if anyone buys that!

William the Chronicler writes down every utterance at the meeting. He never looks up so the chance of him processing even bare-naked bodily language is nil.

Ballistic Bob is the poster child for angry expressions. His red and menacing face, anxious voice, and threatening gestures makes you hope he doesn't go postal at a meeting.

Charles Comatose has been at every meeting but has never participated. If Charlie kicked off would anyone know, or care?

Tactile Trepidations

You already know that touch communicates closeness and strengthens group solidarity. As you will learn in Chapter 22, in sports touch generates and sustains team solidarity. In many organizations, hugs and high fives, pats on the back, and hearty handshakes work as organizational glue to sustain closeness and transform teams.

More than two decades ago, long before the Internet, John Naisbett in his classic, *Megatrends*, suggested we are entering the era of "high tech/high touch." He maintained that for every new technology that alienates and separates, a counterbalancing human force, "high touch," must be introduced. High touch is a metaphor for the body language of face-to-face encounters but it is also a literal call for genuine tactile warmth.

Positions of Power

Even in the starkest corporate setting, clever employees personalize their offices. Family photos, books, and objects of art do more than decorate, they communicate to others about your values and relationships.

The spiritual and human needs of the workplace are not satisfied by new technology. Real human contact comforts, builds unity, and nourishes spirit. Hugging a bereaved co-worker, giving your overworked secretary a back rub, providing a subordinate a literal and figurative pat on the back, giving high fives to your team for landing that new contract; this is the stuff of personal expansion and interpersonal connection.

However, touch can compel or repel. Just as touch can create connection, so too can touch intimidate, harass, and assault. Tactile excesses have created touch paranoia in the contemporary organization. Many human resource manuals recommend against any form of touch. Others recommend only the most perfunctory handshakes. In many ways this is sound advice in a litigious and paranoid society; a company has to think of its own survival first.

> **Body Talk**
>
> Men and women often unconsciously send playfully flirtatious messages that get confused with real flirtation. While these displays breathe some life into dull encounters, receivers of such messages need to read between the lines to understand these are not serious invitations.

The touch-free environment of the new technological organization is exactly the opposite of what Naisbett recommended. And recommendations from human resource departments go beyond touch and warn us against eye contact, close distances, and friendly smiles. The touch-free corporate environment may be bulletproof from harassment grievances and hostile environment lawsuits, but they advocate a cold corporate climate where alienation, turnover, absenteeism, and disaffection reign.

Common sense should rule your organizational behavior. Here are the top 10 handy dandy tips for touch in the high-tech workplace.

10. Relationships rule! If you have a close friendship with a co-worker, some touch is okay, but keep it light.

9. Read your co-worker's body language. If a person startles or cringes when you touch them, back off. They may not appreciate your pats on the back.

8. Use language as well as body language. If someone's touch or other body language is intrusive or creepy, tell them to stop. If they don't stop after the second time, talk to your supervisor.

7. Since nine out of ten harassment complaints are against men, guys should be especially careful about unwanted touch and other intimate body language.

6. Women, watch what you do; there is no such thing as casual flirting. Men need little encouragement. If you want to be purely professional, then be purely professional!

5. Location matters. Touches on the shoulder and upper arm are usually okay. Other areas should be avoided.

4. Different types of touch are not equivalent. Light touches or pats are the safest. Strokes and kisses are risky.

3. Recognize individual differences. A recent study found one third of respondents strongly agreed that facial touches were sexually harassing while another one third strongly disagreed.

2. All body language should be warm, not hot. Your company is not a dating service; go to a gym or a bar.

1. When in doubt, don't touch. Better to be considered cold than to be out in the cold.

The Least You Need to Know

- Suits are the high-status uniform of the corporation.

- In the office, the higher-ups are higher up.

- Size matters: For offices big is better; in technology big is bad.

- Leaders are the head and sit at the head.

- Touch compels and repels in organizations. Use it wisely.

Chapter 21

Political Postures: Communicating Candidacy

- ◆ The compelling power of candidate image
- ◆ The body language of political competence
- ◆ Cultivating the friendly "good ol' boy" image
- ◆ Body language and media bias

The high regard we had for politicians in the past lies shipwrecked among the shoals of political scandals, unpopular wars, and personal failings. It has been further devoured by cynical media sharks who like nothing better than the scent of a scandal and the feeding frenzy that follows. They may be an endangered species, but there are many honest, dedicated politicians running for office—your job is to find them in an era in which image is confused with reality.

In an era of media politics, image is everything, and image is dictated by body language. Political critics and scholars have lamented that image so often trumps issues in American politics. Policy papers and issue statements hold a lot less sway with most voters than candidates' image and body language. It's your role as a citizen not to be duped by manipulated images and staged body language.

The Image of Authority

In the Lincoln-Douglas debates of 1858, most voters actually saw and heard the candidates in person. They could assess firsthand the candidates' images and positions on issues. Today, the vast majority of voters have never met any political candidate, let alone a presidential candidate. Voters get the majority of their political information from television, and most of that information deals not with issues, but images.

One of the most popular presidents in recent memory, Ronald Reagan, was a triumph of image over issue. Reagan, "the great communicator," was a master of body language and always struck a pose as a confident leader while maintaining a friendly, warm, good ol' boy image. Voters elected Reagan by huge majorities, despite the fact that most of them disagreed with his stands on many issues.

> **CAUTION**
>
> **Bodily Blunders**
>
> Recent surveys show that many, perhaps most, voters get their information from late-night TV. From Chevy Chase's imitations of President Ford to satires of Howard Dean's growl, late-night comedy has been the downfall of many candidates.

Studies of Reagan's body language reveal that he connected emotionally with the American people. When Reagan smiled, voters felt happy; when he looked downtrodden, voters felt sad. Reagan's expressive body language directly affected voter emotions, providing a powerful mechanism that influenced voter attitudes and voting behavior.

> **Positions of Power**
>
> Although women have captured some senate seats and governorships, a political glass ceiling exists for women seeking national office. Only one woman, Geraldine Ferraro, has ever run for vice president, and no woman has been elected to the second-highest office in the land. The campaigns of female presidential candidates like Patricia Schroeder, Elizabeth Dole, or Shirley Chisholm barely got off the ground, and none of them won a single presidential primary. Unless former first lady Hillary Clinton makes a run for the White House, it's doubtful that presidential elections of the near future will be anything other than all-male contests. Unlike voters in Britain, Norway, India, Pakistan, and Israel, all of whom have elected female leaders, male body language is still the image of authority in the United States.

Command Presence

Neither President Bill Clinton nor President George W. Bush ever saw military combat, but as commanders in chief they frequently appeared with troops in flight jackets and military uniforms. President Bush landed on the deck of the Aircraft Carrier *Abraham Lincoln* in full flight gear, and later flew to Iraq to share Thanksgiving dinner with the troops not because these events had any military significance but because they gave him opportunities to demonstrate his command presence and support for the troops.

An image of a president supporting the troops, saluting the flag, or dressed in military garb communicates patriotism and exudes leadership. Unlike debate rhetoric or policy speeches, patriotic body language communicates directly to the part of the voter's brain (the right hemisphere) that uncritically processes and stores the image.

Presidents use images of themselves standing by the American flag to communicate their patriotism.

(Image courtesy of National Archives and Records Administration Digital Archives)

So what's the big deal, you might be wondering? So what if presidents and presidential candidates use images to convey their messages? Unfortunately, body language isn't subjected to the same critical analysis that governs logic and language—it has an automatic validity that is virtually irrefutable. Social psychologist Robert Cialdini calls this "our heart of hearts"—our "true" feelings before we rationalize, analyze, and intellectualize a message.

The great image manipulators like presidential image advisors James Carville, Roger Ailes, Michael Dever, and Karl Rove have been packaging presidential winners for decades. These publicity geniuses understand that packaging a president is all about image. Fix a positive or negative image in a voter's mind, and all the oratory and issues pale by comparison. In 1964, the campaign of President Lyndon B. Johnson produced the famous daisy commercial that portrayed a little girl picking daisies, while the voice-over warned of candidate Barry Goldwater's extremism. The commercial ended with an image of a nuclear explosion in the background. Words were unnecessary—the relationship between Goldwater and nuclear war was visually etched in the minds of the American voters.

Nonverbally Speaking

Perhaps the ultimate image-maker and political strategist, Roger Ailes was the man who remade the tricky image of Richard Nixon and helped put him in the White House. He crafted the body language of Ronald Reagan and George H. W. Bush in their successful presidential campaigns in the 1980's, made Rush Limbaugh a media celebrity, and now manages Fox News. Ailes is an important force behind the resurgence of conservatism and is a major image-maker for the American right.

The Allure of Attraction

Human beings love a good leader. Deep inside we desire to follow authority, for someone to lead us, protect us from enemies, and watch over us and our families. Yet, we don't want just any old leader. Instead, we want our leaders to be competent, charismatic individuals who are friendly and a lot like we are.

Let's look at each of the qualities we desire in our leaders more closely.

Physical Attraction

Research on male political candidates shows that physical appearance is an especially important quality. Arguably, in every presidential election in your lifetime, the more handsome candidate prevailed (although neither Richard Nixon nor his democratic opponent in 1972, George McGovern, would have won many beauty contests). Certainly the image of the composed, suntanned, handsome JFK, next to the homely, swarthy, sweating Nixon in 1960 during the first televised presidential debate helped turn the tide in favor of the lesser-known Kennedy.

Positions of Power

In the last 80 years, in all but two presidential races, the taller candidate won (Nixon in 1972 and Carter in 1976). As I said in Chapter 8, greater height for men means more power, authority, and status, and this is clearly the case in presidential elections.

Because there have been so few female candidates for high political offices, researchers are less certain of what traits win votes for women. Initially, several experimental studies showed that less attractive female candidates are preferred to their more attractive counterparts. Other, more recent studies show that physical attractiveness benefits both male and female candidates. Few very attractive women have emerged domestically or internationally as high-level political leaders, though Christie Todd Whitman, Barbara Boxer, Hillary Clinton, and Patricia Schroeder are certainly above average in physical attraction. Certainly, Golda Meir and Margaret Thatcher would never be mistaken for runway models, though former Pakistani Prime Minister Benazir Bhutto was quite beautiful. One can only hope that our society is ready for female leaders regardless of their physical attractiveness.

Social Attraction

Research on political communication demonstrates that social attraction is one of the most vital components of electability. Voters don't support "eggheads" like Adlai Stevenson, Newt Gingrich, or George McGovern, or "bureaucrats" like Gray Davis, Dick Cheney, or Michael Dukakis.

Voters like candidates they think are plain-talking, friendly, good ol' boys. My research on candidate image suggests that voters like candidates they think they could have a friendly chat with over a pitcher of beer or just hang out with. In short, candidates should look and act like the voters' friends.

Candidates like Ronald Reagan, Bill Clinton, and Arnold Schwartzenegger were able to portray themselves as good ol' boys that you could easily meet at a picnic, barber shop, or little league game. Forget that Reagan was a Hollywood star and California governor, that Clinton was an Ivy League–educated governor, or that Schwartzenegger is a millionaire media celebrity. These politicians display the body language of ordinary guys, buddies down the block.

In addition to being ordinary Joes, we want our candidates to exhibit traits of power and leadership. In other words, successful candidates must have ordinary body language but supernatural competencies. This is a tough row to hoe. Candidate Bill Clinton's advisors were never sure whether Clinton's folksy, warm, press-the flesh, compassionate image could be perceived as a country bumpkin, a character in "Billy-Bob and the Clampetts go to Washington," or a man just a bit too eager to press the flesh with women. President George W. Bush's handlers were never sure if casual body language and low-brow, joking style would be perceived as a friendly man of the people, an ordinary Joe, or as an immature party-boy. Bush was regarded by many as so immature and lacking in substance that many in the media believed he selected Dick Cheney as vice president so that the Republicans would have at least one grown-up on the ticket.

It's difficult to simultaneously be an ordinary, "regular guy" who seems just like the average voter and yet to have the extraordinary qualities needed to lead the country. Politicians must have body language that communicates both down-to-earth qualities and those of a charismatic leader—somebody you could have a beer with but trust their hand on the nuclear trigger.

Competence

Voters want somebody who can get things done. Think about the leaders who have made it to the White House. Despite their many flaws, Americans love leaders who offer a vision, a plan, and can get the job done. It is important to be perceived as someone who has a vision and can do the job, and body language plays a key role in such perceptions. All three incumbent presidents defeated during the last 30 years had body language that failed to communicate competence. Ford often seemed bumbling and unsure. Carter failed to provide a clear, decisive image that radiated competence, and George H. W. Bush was perceived as weak and unsure if he even wanted to be re-elected. By contrast, the two-term presidents Reagan and Clinton radiated vision and competence. Studies in political science and political communication show that communicating confident, competent body language is a key to presidential success.

Similarity Rules

One of the most crucial aspects of voter preference is attitude similarity. In short, voters like candidates who believe the same things they do. In today's world, voters don't often take the time to carefully consider the nuances of American policy in Afghanistan or the details of a prescription drug plan for the elderly. So candidates have a tough time communicating with voters about issues.

Instead candidates cynically, but often effectively, manipulate their body language to suggest a certain stand on the issues. President George W. Bush, who according to environmental organizations has one of the weakest environmental records of any president in history, never misses a photo-op in a National Park. Many critics have suggested that President Clinton's appearance in a flight jacket and his attacks on terrorist camps were well-timed attempts to deflect attention away from his own lack of a military record and his philandering in the White House. This is body language designed to convey the *appearance* of support for a policy while actually *doing* just the opposite.

Of course, such attempts can fail. It is hard to forget the ridiculous body language of presidential candidate Michael Dukakis peering out from beneath an oversized helmet in a giant tank. That incongruous picture of the shrinking Dukakis as commander in chief defined his image and was a critical turning point in his losing campaign.

Candidates also strive to make voters believe they share similar backgrounds, a much easier task when the vast majority of qualified voters were of European ancestry and mostly white. In an increasingly diverse country, it's more difficult than ever to appeal to similarity on racial or ethnic grounds. Instead, candidates surround themselves with ethnically diverse staffs and make sure they are photographed shaking hands with middle-class people of all races. This is the body language of inclusion, and while it's just a part of image-making, it has actually helped make the United States a more diverse and inclusive country.

Character and Trust

According to Tom Hollihan, a professor at the Annenberg School for Communication at the University of Southern California, the advertised images of political candidates emphasize humble origins, strength of character, and the self-made man. To watch a documentary on Edward Kennedy, Al Gore, or George W. Bush, you would think they grew up in ordinary families and made it completely on their own, when in reality, they come from some of America's most wealthy and well-connected political families.

Certainly, voters have been deceived too often to hold much trust in politicians. During Watergate, Nixon engaged in numerous illegal acts against his opponents, then lied about them. Reagan secretly and illegally sold arms to Iran and used the profits to support an illegal and covert war in Nicaragua. Clinton claimed he never had sex with Monica Lewinsky and lied about it. Some people believe that George W. Bush's justification for the war in Iraq involved weapons of mass deception, not mass destruction.

Part of the reason political participation and trust are declining in the United States is that candidates are marketed like beer or cars, only maybe even more cleverly. Voters say they hate campaign commercials, but research shows that voters get most of their information from paid political ads. Yet, both issues and images are manipulated in commercial spots, including the candidates' body language. Live speeches, news conferences, and debates are real ways to judge the content of candidates' speeches and to assess their more spontaneous body language.

Candidate character is an important quality that can attract voters. The rapid emergence of relatively unknown—at least on the national scene—Governor Howard Dean as presidential contender is mostly due to his tell-it-like-it-is image. His no-frills body language suggests an honest, unmanipulated image—an image that is difficult to maintain as a candidate enters the national media spotlight. Dean's reputation for flying off the handle was reinforced by an overly exuberant pep talk following a loss in the Iowa caucus—an incident that severely harmed his image.

There is precedent for the success of candidates with little or no image manipulation, such as Harry Truman, Gerald Ford, and Jimmy Carter, whom nobody could accuse of being too slick. A longer list of good candidates with unrefined images would include John McCain, Robert Dole, Michael Dukakis, George McGovern, and Walter Mondale; but each of these candidates lost to a political foe with a slicker, more cultivated media image. Based on their voting behavior, Americans seem to prefer the refined, manipulated image to more homespun, unmanipulated people.

As we discussed in Chapter 12, there is no surefire way to detect deception, but tuning in to both the issues and the body language of candidates is still the best avenue to making good voting decisions. Some research suggests that voters assess body language in two phases—first to assess trust and character, and then to evaluate a candidate's competence and effectiveness.

Although voters assess numerous aspects of a candidate's image, research suggests that many constituents are particularly concerned about character and honesty in politics. Interestingly, voters who get most of their information from television are more likely to make voting judgments based on image and body language, whereas voters who get most of their information from newspapers seem to be more issue-oriented. The fact that young people don't frequently read newspapers may suggest that American voters in the future will rely more on image and body language and less on policy issues.

Covering the Candidates

News coverage is rarely totally objective in the American media. In fact, stations that purport to be "fair and balanced" might actually be the least objective, consistent with an emerging trend in politics and the media of saying one thing and doing another. Media bias is often subtly conveyed through body language.

Studies of national newscasters show that they leak their voting preferences nonverbally. These studies also show that viewers tend to vote for the candidate favored by their preferred newscaster. For example, Peter Jennings showed much more positive body language toward Reagan than Mondale in the 1984 presidential campaign. Not surprisingly, ABC and Jennings had significantly more Reagan supporters than other stations. It's hard to know if Jennings's biased body language attracted more Reagan voters, or if his nonverbal cues subtly influenced ABC viewers to vote for Reagan. Regardless, it shows a strong relationship between voting behavior and biased media body language.

> **Nonverbally Speaking**
>
> During the Carter-Ford presidential race, national news anchors Walter Cronkhite, Harry Reasoner, and David Brinkley showed more positive body language when reporting about Jimmy Carter. Conversely, Barbara Walters and John Chancellor showed more positive body language toward Ford than Carter.

Democracy is an imperfect form of government. But as Winston Churchill once said, "democracy is the worst form of government, except for all those other forms that have been tried from time to time." Democracy cannot work without the participation of a huge number of citizens. It is important not to become cynical or alienated, to keep participating, and—most important—not to be fooled by the image-makers and fraudulent candidate body language.

The Least You Need to Know

- Images are compelling: Body language doesn't get the same critical and logical analysis that governs logic and language.

- Political handlers and image-makers manipulate candidates' body language and sell candidates like beer or cars.

- Voters like candidates whose body language communicates a friendly image that reminds them of their own friends.

- Character and trust, vital qualities in a candidate, are best assessed by using logic and carefully watching body language.

- Media partiality is often subtle and is communicated through biased body language.

Chapter 22

Sporting Behavior: Athletic Actions

In This Chapter

- ◆ Sports as modern-day combat rituals
- ◆ Intimidation and symbolic killing in sports
- ◆ The culture wars and excessive celebration
- ◆ Faking out your opponent with body language
- ◆ Are teams with black uniforms really bad boys?

No human activity celebrates the human body like sports.

Sport puts people in action and provides an arena for wonderfully expressive body language. Watching Serena Williams play tennis, Lance Armstrong ride a bicycle, or Marshall Faulk play football is like watching poetry in motion. Sports are competitive ballets, with beauty, speed, and violence that attract millions of live and television viewers from around the world. Some people think sport is the highest of human achievements, a form of civilized combat and coordinated action, and just pure fun. Others consider sports to be a form of commercial exploitation and a big waste of time.

Today many people are more than spectators—we also participate in sports like never before. Americans run, swim, lift, jump, kick, climb, step, walk, and pedal, all in an effort to feel and look better. Sport is all about bodies and body language. So let's take a tour of bodies in motion and what it all means.

The Rite of Sport

Why are so many people so preoccupied with sports? Playing them, watching them, discussing them, and even betting on them. Many anthropologists believe that sports are modern-day versions of primal hunting or combat rituals. They see sports as mimicking the life-and-death struggles of our ancestors. These early survival behaviors, embedded deep within our genes, form the basis of our desire to play games that mimic them.

Think about it. The goal of most sports is territorial. Penetrate the opponents' territory: the end zone, the goal, the basket, the finish line, or home plate. And we defend the end zone, home plate, the basket, and the goal with the zeal of homeowners protecting their property. Lots of sports are controlled violence, though some sports like American football, rugby, and boxing are almost real combat. Even so-called noncontact sports get somewhat violent: taking a charge in basketball, taking out a second baseman with a slide in baseball, and the "slide tackle" in soccer are legal forms of body contact.

So although some people think sports are meaningless mayhem, I believe that sports represent a positive evolution in how we control and display our aggression. Most of us have learned to channel our competitive energies that were once used for territorial invasion and defending the campsite into less deadly activities.

The Trappings of Triumph

Sports are about competing and doing your best, but sports are also about winning and losing. And an athlete's body language can set the stage for victory long before the contest starts.

The Art of Intimidation

In the 1960s, Muhammad Ali was the ultimate champion. His speed, agility, and strength dazzled opponents. His good looks, loquacious lip, and bold body language set him apart from others. Perhaps his most famous body language was the Ali Stare. The stare consisted of unflinching eye contact, a bold and angry facial expression, with occasional menacing gestures and feigned punches. Many analysts believe that opponents were already psychologically defeated by Ali's intimidating body language at the weigh-in. Ali would say nothing, which was unusual for a man known as the Louisville Lip, but his body language said it all.

Not until the early '70s did anyone really challenge Ali's body language, when boxer Joe Frazier and Ali had their famous stare down. Frazier wasn't intimidated by Ali, and their three fights culminating in the "Thrilla in Manila" were among the best fights ever.

During their six basketball championships, the Chicago Bulls often beat their opponents in a five-minute episode during which, in the words of coach Phil Jackson, he would "unleash the Dobermans," a defensive press by Michael Jordan, Scottie Pippin, and their teammates. It was designed to steal the ball and score on fast breaks, but more importantly, it was meant to psychologically defeat their opponents with its intimidating style.

Intimidation is not unique to Muhammad Ali or the Chicago Bulls. The mere sight of a New York Yankees uniform in the 1950s, a Green Bay Packers or Boston Celtics uniform in the 1960s, an Oakland Raiders uniform of the 1970s or 1980s, or a Chicago Bulls uniform in the 1990s provided instant intimidation. It was certainly due to the winning tradition, but the body language of these teams carried over to the very uniforms they wore. All over America and the world, teens and young adults sported these uniforms as signs of power and prowess.

Symbolic Killing

Watch an athlete's body language when they score a point or win a game. Victorious fighters raise their hand in victory and tower over defeated opponents. Basketball players "get in the face" of their opponent after a slam-dunk. Baseball pitchers have been known to blow on a phantom pistol or make the death sign across their throat following a strikeout. Blitzing linebackers throw mock punches after sacking the quarterback.

The victory face isn't usually a face of joy, but a face of anger and hostility. Boxers after a knockout and basketball players after a dunk display a furious face with an open mouth more reminiscent of a predator than a person. This body language communicates the symbolic slaughter of an opponent.

Victorious gestures by athletes rarely include the civilized V for victory sign. They usually take the form of violent body language like Junior Seau's contemptuous knock-out punch after sacking a quarterback or Ali's pseudo-swing over the body of a fallen opponent. Gestures may point up to God or make the sign of the cross.

The victory face is the face of a prevailing predator.

(Image courtesy of Robert Avery)

Of course, in some sports symbolic killing gets too real. Soccer fans, in particular, seem to step over this line too often, where celebration of victory on the field turns into homicides on the street.

A traditional triumphant victorious gesture as displayed by this marathon runner after finishing the race.

(Image courtesy of Peter Andersen)

Excessive Celebration

In the past two decades, celebrations in sporting events have become increasingly demonstrative. Who could forget Brandy Chastain ripping off her jersey after the U.S. women won soccer's World Cup? Though not particularly risqué, this victory gesture was praised by some as liberating and spontaneous, while others criticized it as unladylike and calculated, since she revealed a Nike sports bra and Nike just happened to be her sponsor. Similarly, after breaking a world record in the 400-meter relay in the 2000 Olympics, the U.S. team consisting of Jon Drummond, Brian Lewis, Bernard Williams, and Maurice Greene stripped to the waist, struck muscular poses, and wrapped themselves in American flags.

Several sports have banned "excessive celebration" to speed up games and protect the alleged dignity of sports. The very idea that excessive celebration is punishable with a technical foul or a 15-yard penalty is offensive to some folks who think that celebrations are merely freedom of expression, a revered American birthright. Who can forget Ickey Woods's "Ickey Shuffle," Jamal Anderson's "dirty bird," or the muscle poses of Terrell Owens? Others critics believe that restricting this proud celebratory style, which is often characteristic of African American body language, is downright racist. Whether restricting certain types of celebrations restores dignity to sports or is just a thinly veiled form of racism that attempts to reign in powerful black men, body language is front and center in this controversy. Watch some football or basketball games, and you be the judge.

High fives, slaps on the back, and common uniforms are the body language of connection among teammates.

(Image courtesy of Peter Andersen)

Bodily Blunders _____

Excessive celebrations and extreme intimidation aren't limited to the field or the court; they are also out of control in the stands. And this is most unseemly at youth sporting events. Don't be a militant mom or a dangerous dad by being overly critical of referees, coaches, or players. Sure a lot of them suck, but get over it! Be supportive and avoid angry outbursts.

Fakes on the Field

Sometimes faking out your opponent is more important than being a better athlete. The motto of the Olympics is "higher, faster, and stronger." Given the importance of deception in sports, it should probably be "trickier, shiftier, and wilier."

Baseball

Baseball is a perfect example of a sport that uses body language designed to deceive. In fact, baseball is often more body language than action, a fact that diehard fans appreciate. For either the hard-core or casual fans, here are some types of body language to look for that could fake you out:

- **The fake pickoff.** A pitcher can really irritate a runner by faking a throw to the base. This usually causes a runner to dive back to the base flat on his face.

- **The fake steal.** Here the runner on first, second, or third base takes off like he is going to steal then stops dead in his tracks. A fake steal can be used to draw an error by forcing the pitcher to throw a wild pitch or an errant pickoff throw; or it could be used to lull the opposition into complacency for a real steal coming on a later pitch.

Nonverbally Speaking

One of the great baseball ruses is the hidden-ball trick. With a man on first base, the first baseman goes to the mound and talks to the pitcher. The pitcher sneaks the ball to the first baseman, which he hides in his glove and returns to his position. For this to work, nobody's body language can tip off the runner. The catcher gives a sign, the pitcher gets ready to pitch, the runner leads off first and is promptly tagged out by the devious first baseman.

- **The fake throw.** On a delayed double steal, the catcher fakes a throw to second base and throws to third base, hoping to trap the late-breaking runner from third.

- **The catcher's con.** Catchers will often move their glove quickly toward the plate in an effort to influence a slow-reacting umpire into calling a strike.

- **The cutoff play.** On a throw from the outfield, usually to third base or home plate, an infielder cuts off the ball, conceding third base or home to the lead runner. Meanwhile the infielder tries to throw out the inattentive batter, who thought the throw was to third or home.

- **The fake bunt.** A batter shortens up on the bat in the bunting position, causing the third baseman, pitcher, and sometimes the first baseman to charge the plate. The batter then takes a full swing at the ball and tries to drive it though the drawn-in infield. Scares the heck out of the third baseman!

Football

Football is a game of deception. On every offensive play, the quarterback and the offense attempt to fake the defense into committing the wrong moves. Likewise, the defense, before and during the play, tries to disguise itself and cause an offensive error. Here are but a few football fakes:

- **The fake handoff.** Also called a play action pass, the quarterback fakes a hand-off to a running back, drawing away the defense, and then passes the ball down field.

- **The option play.** This is a whole series of fakes. The quarterback runs to the outside escorted by one, two, or three running backs. If the quarterback is in the open, he will run upfield, but if he is about to be tackled, he will pitch to one of the running backs. The defense never knows for sure who will eventually get the ball.

- **The fake kick.** The offense lines up like they are going to punt or kick a field goal, then, lo and behold, they run or pass the ball instead. This is a real gamble that often results in a turnover, but when it works, it's a victory for deceptive body language and fake formations.

- **The bootleg.** The quarterback fakes a handoff, puts the ball on his hip, and rolls out. He can either run around the tight end for a gain or throw a pass downfield. Like the bootleggers during prohibition, the quarterback is in possession of something he shouldn't have.

- **The screen play.** Offensive linemen throw a token block and let the defensive linemen go after the quarterback. Just before the defenders arrive, the quarterback throws a short pass to a running back who heads downfield escorted by the same offensive linemen.

- **The fumblerooski.** This is perhaps the epitome of deceptive football body language. Here, the quarterback takes the snap from the center and lays the ball on the ground while faking that he has the ball and dropping back to pass. The guard or the center, who almost never carries the ball, picks up the ball and heads downfield.

Basketball

Like other sports, basketball has its share of trickery; though the game moves so fast that fakery in basketball takes place on the fly. Ball handlers or dribblers try to fake one way and go another; sometimes called a "shake and bake," this has nothing to do with home cooking. A pump fake communicates all the body language of a shot, but the shooter never leaves the ground. The idea is to get a defender airborne and draw a foul or blow right by them. The fake pass similarly uses body language that sends a defender one way, while you dribble or pass another way.

Body Talk _____

Deke originated in Canada and is short for "decoy." Now used universally in the world of ice hockey, this deceptive form of body language is designed to make a defensive player think you are going to pass or move in one direction when you are really moving, passing, or shooting in another direction.

Hockey

Hockey is also full of fakes, only in ice hockey they're called *dekes*. There are head dekes, skate dekes, and stick dekes, all designed to make an opponent think you are doing one thing when you are really doing another.

Staying in front of the player and reacting to a real move rather than a deke is key to defensive hockey. The hips are the hardest part of the body to deke, so some coaches suggest reading a player's hips rather than his head, his skates, or the puck.

Uniformly Excellent

Psychologists Mark Frank and Thomas Gilovich have studied the black uniform and its relationship to aggression in professional sports. Are black uniforms like the

Oakland Raiders' really more intimidating than uniforms of other colors? Do they cause more aggression? Their research demonstrates that …

♦ Fans think black-clad teams are more malevolent.

♦ When teams switch to black uniforms, their penalties increase. When teams switch away from black uniforms, their penalties decrease.

♦ Both fans and referees perceive black-clad teams as more aggressive and illegal—whether or not they really are.

♦ Aggressive individuals are more likely to select black uniforms.

So teams like the Oakland Raiders and Chicago Blackhawks may really be the bad boys of the league. In the case of the Raiders, their black-clad fans have become a virtual cult. These fans, who flock to their stadium known as the black hole, are called the Raider Nation, and are some of the most bizarre in a sport with a lot of weird fans. Oakland (or not so long ago, Los Angeles) Raider fans come decked out in body armor, black jerseys, blade runner outfits, Alice Cooper makeup, Darth Vader masks, and motorcycle jackets in what is a cross between a religious cult, a punk-rock concert, a soccer match and a Halloween ball. You have to see it in person, because television barely captures the full magnitude of this freak show and their bizarre body language.

The Least You Need to Know

♦ Sports are modern-day hunting and combat rituals.

♦ Body language is used to intimidate opponents and symbolically kill defeated adversaries.

♦ Excessive celebration is penalized in some sports.

♦ Fakes and dekes are a central aspect of sports.

♦ Teams and fans with black uniforms really are bad boys.

Chapter 23

Classroom Cues: Body Language in Education

In This Chapter

- ◆ The power of body language in the classroom
- ◆ The effect of affect: Feelings count in class
- ◆ Dynamic body language for students
- ◆ Controlling classroom behavior nonverbally
- ◆ The body language of PowerPoint

The classroom is a laboratory of body language. You probably have vivid memories of teachers and their body language, good or bad. To a remarkable degree, studies show that teaching effectiveness is due to body language, which can communicate enthusiasm and compassion, or boredom and rigidity. As any fifth grader has probably figured out by now, a teacher with a comatose communication style doesn't facilitate learning.

Likewise, students' body language sends thousands of messages to one another, as well as to the teacher. Good teachers, of course, try to understand student body language, and good students try to communicate effectively in all ways, including with their body language.

Warm Teachers and Immediate Results

New teachers have been warned for many years, "Never smile until Christmas." This is based on the assumption that friendly, warm, expressive teachers are push-overs whereas as stern, demanding teachers get results. Research suggests that the "no smile rule" is misinformed and can actually do far more harm than good. Dozens of studies show that teachers with pleasant, warm body language are far more effective. Positive demeanor and positive attitudes create positive outcomes!

Recent research has also rejected the corollary myth "nice guys finish last," which may be true in the bedroom (see Chapter 18), but provides little support for this rule in the classroom or, for that matter, the boardroom or the courtroom. Think about it: Nice teachers, managers, doctors, and lawyers are motivational and get much better results from their students, employees, patients, and clients than those who are cold, impersonal, or mean.

Positions of Power

Warmth and power are not opposites. The best teachers, parents, lawyers, doctors, and managers are *both* warm and strong. Tough, cold teachers are perceived as mean dictators. Weak, warm teachers are perceived as doormats. Weak, cold teachers may not make it though the first year. The best advice? Go with strength and warmth.

In the preschool classroom, getting down on the students' level and making direct eye contact make instruction more involving and intimate.

(Image courtesy of Peter Andersen)

The Effect of Affect

Students like learning from teachers with immediate body language. Immediacy behaviors are warm, enthusiastic, approachable forms of body language, such as eye contact, smiling, and pleasant vocal tones. From kindergarten through college, studies show that warmth, affection, and friendliness result in higher student satisfaction, better teacher-student relationships, and higher student evaluations of teaching effectiveness.

Teachers should do more than teach facts and convey information; they should create positive attitudes about learning. This is called *affective learning* and, arguably, it provides more long-term learning than short-term gains in information or cognitive learning. When students walk out of the classroom, you hope you have helped create lifelong learners. I don't know about you, but I want my mechanic, my lawyer, and my doctor to continue to seek information throughout their lives. It is affective or attitudinal learning that produces lifelong learners. Any teacher can force students to read Shakespeare; the real test is if the student reads Shakespeare 10, 20, or 50 years later. A teacher's body language plays a large part in affective learning.

Body Talk

Affective learning deals with emotional reactions, attitudes, and psychological aspects of learning. Successful students have positive attitudes toward education, their instructor, and the subject matter.

Approach, Not Avoidance

Although there is some truth to the admonition "no pain, no gain," there is a lot more validity to the notion that "you catch more bees with honey than vinegar." Think about it. Most of us would rather do stuff we like than stuff we dislike. The most revered rule of behavioral psychology is that people do things that are rewarding! Research suggests that students continue to approach learning if their teachers have communicated warmth and enthusiasm about the material.

Nonverbally Speaking

Teachers with warmer, more enthusiastic body language have been found to motivate students to ...

- Read more about the subject voluntarily.
- Select majors taught by warm teachers.
- Sign up for more courses in that subject.
- Practice lifetime learning in that subject area.

Such is the case in the classroom. Starting with a classic study by Janis Andersen, a communication professor at San Diego State University, dozens of studies have found that motivation, sometimes called behavioral learning, is dramatically facilitated by teachers with warm, immediate body language.

Relaxed positions, facial animation, and expressive gestures lead to more attention and positive attitudes in the classroom.

(Image courtesy of Peter Andersen)

Teacher Influence

Teachers with pleasant, warm body language are far more persuasive than cold, inaccessible teachers. Studies demonstrate that warm body language motivates students to do homework more regularly and to actually engage in behaviors recommended by the teacher. Although warmth is not the only form of effective communication; warm, immediate teachers can actually use more forceful communication in the classroom and get away with it.

Warm body language produces more classroom interaction, more visits to the teacher's or professor's office for help, and more involvement in the class. A positive teacher-student relationship can help teachers to persuade students to avoid risk and adopt positive behaviors. From sunscreen to condoms, from avoiding drugs to avoiding teen pregnancy, teachers with warm body language are more persuasive with students than their colder, less approachable counterparts.

Knowledge Gain

Research suggests that students learn more from teachers with warm positive body language. Moreover, students report that they learned a lot more from teachers with warm body language than cold teachers. Just smiling and increasing eye contact will often do the trick. Students also report that the knowledge is more useful and applicable when the information comes from immediate teachers.

Positions of Power

Warm teachers get more warmth from their students, producing better relationships with students, which results in heightened teacher satisfaction. In a career that frequently involves low pay and high burnout, liking your job is no small benefit.

Passionate Presentations

Whether you are a teacher, a trainer, a seminar leader, or are just giving a presentation, here are some of things you can do to increase your passion, warmth, immediacy, and enthusiasm:

- **Visual vitality.** Looking at your class is rule number one for teachers and trainers. It is impossible to establish any connection or show any enthusiasm without connecting with your audience visually. Plus, without eye contact, you can't read any of the audience's body language.

- **Move around.** Don't just stand behind a desk or podium. Movement enhances interest and indirectly involves students in the class. But don't pace like a caged tiger; people in the first row might get dizzy.

- **Gesture.** In Chapter 7, I described the gestures one can use while speaking. Using your hands and body to reinforce what you're saying increases warmth, promotes enthusiasm, and creates interest.

- **Vary your voice.** It's okay to use a lot of vocal variation, to speak dramatically, enthusiastically, and solemnly. It's fine to laugh, shout for emphasis, or even do imitations if you can pull it off. People like enthusiastic speakers, and animation holds their attention. The voice communicates far more than content; it conveys contagious feelings and empowering energy.

- **Face up to it.** Facial expressions convey plenty of energy, passion, and involvement. Show joy, seriousness, concern, and all the other emotions you can send with your expressive face. The deadpan face just doesn't get it done in the classroom, especially when students are forced to endure drab presentations day in and day out.

◆ **Spend time.** Arriving late, leaving in haste, and blowing people off is not the way to create connection and communicate immediacy. Time talks, and spending time with students, trainees, or clients says that you care.

◆ **Approachable attire.** Teaching a freshman class in an $800 suit does not create connection, nor does showing up in wrinkled, sloppy clothes for a corporate seminar. Dress for success, but don't dress to excess.

◆ **Touch appropriately.** Handshakes and pats on the shoulder can increase warmth and immediacy. Be careful with more intimate touch; a classroom is a professional environment, not a personal one.

◆ **Move closer.** Warmer, friendlier distances are closer distances. But don't trespass into the personal space of your audience.

> **Bodily Blunders**
>
> Teachers, trainers, and professors are the appointed leaders in the classroom and have status. A major blunder is to exaggerate your status as a teacher by being standoffish or displaying aloof, arrogant, overdressed, and self-inflated body language. Remember, as a status figure, it's more important to break down barriers and create connections than to power-trip when you already have authority.

In Synch with Your Prof

Warm, enthusiastic teachers are important, but what about students? Given that you're reading this book, chances are you spent a decade or two in the classroom on the other side of the desk. If my crystal ball is clear, chances are you will be back in the classroom once or twice more regardless of your age.

Student body language is vital in the classroom. Unfortunately, way back in the first or second grade, we learned to sit still and be quiet in class. We learned to lay low, because in many classrooms, students are like nails: the ones that stick out get hammered. So we learned to be passive and respectful and not to communicate.

Interactive classrooms are the best learning environments. They are more relevant to individual student learning needs, they are way more interesting, and amazingly, students actually learn from each other in such environments. The responsibility for an interesting, educational class lies with the student as well as the teacher. So here are a few things you can do with your body language to make the class more interesting:

◆ **Use positive body language.** In some classrooms the students look cadaverous. Students, how about some positive facial expressions and head nods when the teacher makes a good point? How about at least a smirk when your prof uses humor? The best communication is interactive, and the classroom is no exception.

◆ **Put up your hand.** Many students refuse to use this simple cue to ask a question or make a comment because they believe that teachers don't want questions or comments. Obviously, most of these students have never taught. The majority of teachers actually like interaction!

◆ **Laugh!** When a teacher tells a joke or does something funny, laugh! The poor instructor is dying up there! The emotional tone of a classroom is reciprocal. Sure the teacher can make the classroom a more happy and interesting environment, but so can the student.

◆ **Give feedback.** It's really nice to know if the students are getting it. So when you understand or agree, nod and smile! When you don't get it, give the teacher that confused look and shake your head a little from side to side. Experienced teachers love and appreciate that kind of feedback. Expressions are wonderful signals that tell the teacher to speed up, slow down, or try again.

Reading the Student

First-rate teachers all have one thing in common: They look at their class. Of course, eye contact is vital for sending messages of confidence, competence, warmth, and connection. Eye contact for a teacher is like radar for an airline pilot—without it, you are flying blind. But what can a teacher see out there in the classroom? The answer is plenty. Eye contact will enable a teacher to perform the following important classroom functions:

◆ **Defeating disruptions.** Anarchy in the classroom never facilitates learning. A teacher's first responsibility is to make sure that the classroom is an attentive and safe environment. Sticking your nose in a book or your head in the sand is no way to monitor your class. Look and listen for students harassing other students, loud and irrelevant comments, and side conversations. Observing and curtailing disruptive behavior is key to a quality classroom environment.

◆ **Clearing up classroom confusion.** Students seldom provide honest feedback, even when they are completely lost. To admit you are confused and clueless takes a lot of guts. Students risk embarrassment, damage to their self-esteem, and criticism from other students (and in some classes, the teacher), when they admit they don't understand. Look for the confused facial expression, panicky looks at other students' notes, and the zone out, where students who are completely clueless stop paying attention.

◆ **Promoting participation.** It is oh-so-frustrating to put your hand up in class 20 times and never get called on. Try to intermittently call on every student in the classroom who wants to participate. But you can only see raised hands if you look for them.

◆ **Defeating cheating.** It's unfair to let students cheat on a test or an assignment. You are reinforcing swindlers and teaching your students that rule-breaking pays. Proctoring a test might make you feel like you're a kindergarten cop, but it's your job to enforce the rules so grades reflect actual knowledge and effort, not deviousness and deception.

◆ **Deterring distress.** Teachers are in a great position to observe the emotions of their students. Especially in the early grades where students haven't learned emotional control, teachers can read student feelings easily if they watch them. Look for signs of fear, anger, hurt, or sadness, which might indicate that a child is being abused, harassed, suffering from sexual assault, or has severe health problems. Signs of emotional distress might also indicate that a student is ill, lost and panicked, or simply has a negative attitude. Monitoring the dark side of emotional body language is a vital skill for teachers.

◆ **Promoting the positive.** Success breeds success. When you look out at motivated, fired-up, happy learners, be they kindergarteners or graduate students, it's a great shot in the arm for a teacher. Drink it in! Take the time to appreciate the happy, inspired learners that you helped create. Teachers' reinforcement rarely comes through monetary rewards; watching successful, eager learners is about the best reward a person can get.

Controlling Classroom Behavior

Teachers commonly complain about lack of control in the classroom. In many classrooms, students are inattentive, unwilling to participate, and distracted with side conversations. Worse, in some classrooms students are disruptive and even threatening.

You can keep yelling at disruptive students until you are blue in the face, but that only serves to further disrupt the lesson and takes time away from learning. You can use body language to unobtrusively control classroom disruptions. Here are a few of my favorite ways to control classroom behavior using body language:

◆ **Admonishing eyes.** If Johnny and Megan are carrying on a conversation, stare at them intently. Combine this with slow movement toward the disruptive pair and a scowl, so all but completely catatonic students will get the message. With a little practice, this visual rebuke can be pulled off without missing a beat in your lecture.

◆ **Cautioning kinesically.** A tilt of the head, a scowl, a little negative shake of the head, or a worried or concerned look cast in the direction of an offending student can be effective silencers. Combine these forms of body language with closer distances and eye contact for maximum effect.

◆ **Varying your volume.** To chastise chatty classes, doubling or tripling the volume of your voice will communicate clearly that you want silence. Try it while not missing a word of your lecture. This one takes some practice and isn't for the faint of voice. Talking softly or even whispering can be an attention-grabber, too.

◆ **Silencing spacially.** Moving closer to chatty or disruptive students is often enough for them to get the message to cool it with the conversation. If this fails, I have often walked right between a talkative twosome, forcing them to look and talk around me to continue their dialog. All but the completely clueless get this message.

◆ **Thwarting touches.** Sometimes when a student is acting out, making faces, or chatting incessantly, a touch can quell (and soothe). While continuing your lesson or discussion, slowly walk toward the offending student and place your hand on her or his shoulder. It is a powerful and silent message to call a halt to disruptive behavior.

CAUTION

Bodily Blunders _____

Some teachers use the pregnant pause to cope with a disruptive or talkative student or group. Often this is combined with a disturbed-looking facial expression and a direct glare. I have never been a big fan of this strategy because it stops the lesson or lecture cold. In fact, this strategy may empower clever, wicked students to use unruly behavior as a power trip to stop a lesson in its tracks by being disruptive. This form of body language can be effective, but at a price.

As with all body language, combinations of cues work best. People are most likely to "get" redundant and consistent body language. Thus, the most obvious way to deter a disruptive duo is to simultaneously use a whole array of nonverbal interventions. I absolutely guarantee that if you move close to a difficult student, while glaring at them with a negative expression on your face, and touch them on the shoulder as you talk louder, they will get the message.

Designer Classrooms

Classrooms are communication environments where talk and body language should thrive and prosper. Unfortunately, teachers are often at the mercy of architects and even janitors who determine the optimal classroom design and desk placement.

The traditional classroom with desks in rows that face forward is good for two things: exams and lectures. The fact that the front-facing classroom minimizes interaction makes them great for tests and poor for classroom interaction.

If you want maximum interaction among students, circular tables with half a dozen chairs at each works best. This is ideal for discussions, collaboration, peer instruction, or group projects. In these environments, the teacher has to trust the students that they will be independently productive, since a teacher can visit only one table at a time.

For class discussion the circular classroom works best. Here all of the students face each other, which is an optimal position for communication. Moreover, this arrangement facilitates just about every type of body language among students. This type of class needs to be kept small, preferably under 20 students, if you really want a class discussion. A circle of 100 is less ideal for interaction than a front-facing classroom of 30.

A hybrid version of the front-facing and the circular classroom is the horseshoe-shaped classroom, with a teacher at the opening of the horseshoe. This still permits somewhat of a teacher-centered classroom, with the instructor in the front, but the face-to-face position of the students facilitates discussion and enables the exchange of body language.

In all these arrangements, it is generally best to let students select their own seats, especially in high school and college. In each of these classrooms, there are some positions that facilitate interaction with the teacher, usually the one directly facing the instructor. Outgoing, extroverted students like this position and don't appreciate being stuffed into the corner of a class. Likewise, shy, reserved students don't want the high-interaction seats. Putting them in these seats won't make them talk more, but it will make them anxious and reduce the chances of their liking the class, you, and the subject. The best advice is to let students select the seats that are most comfortable for them and most suited to their personalities.

So the bottom line is that you need to decide what you want out of a classroom. Design the classroom environment to either facilitate or inhibit interaction and body language. And don't let the janitor decide your optimal classroom arrangement.

Of Chalk and PowerPoint

One of the cardinal sins in the traditional classroom is writing on the board. Some teachers spend several minutes, sometimes even half a class period, writing on the board. Don't get me wrong; blackboards or whiteboards can be used effectively. Put some stuff up there before class and cover it if you don't want students reading ahead. But rule number one is to do a minimal amount of writing and drawing during class. Watching someone write is dreadfully boring. Worse, the back of your head is just not as expressive as your face and eyes. Since you're in front of the class, your hands are occupied, and your body is turned away, you cannot send body language with gestures, eye contact, smiling, space, or touch. In short, all the stuff that this book is about becomes impossible.

When you're writing on the board, you cannot monitor your student's body language, either. A silent coup d'état, public nudity, or a mass exodus might have occurred, but you missed it because you weren't looking. Sending and monitoring body language is an essential instructional activity. So face the class to improve interaction and facilitate body language.

In the new millennium, people are clearly beyond the blackboard and into the PowerPoint era. In schools, businesses, and at conferences, the ubiquitous PowerPoint rules. Here are some handy-dandy recommendations for powerful PowerPoint presentations.

- ◆ **Look at your audience, not at the screen.** Just because this is a PowerPoint presentation, body language didn't become irrelevant. The key is still the speaker and the audience, and reading one another's body language is vital. Eye contact equals connection, so look at the audience.

- ◆ **Lights on.** Dimming the lights is fine, but turning the lights off is a dicey decision. What about taking notes? What about body language? And remember some of the

 **Bodily Blunders**

PowerPoint is wallpaper. So says communication professor Brian Spitzberg. Like the wallpaper behind a Monet in a gallery, PowerPoint should be in the background; you and your expressive body should be in the foreground. If your PowerPoint competes with you, you have a problem.

audience might not want to be there. Giving them the opportunity to sneak out or nap under the cover of darkness is risky.

◆ **Don't read your slide.** Reading your slides, especially off the screen, is about as lame as orally reading a report. PowerPoint is a visual aid, you are the speaker; otherwise we could have just shipped some slides to the students.

◆ **Four bullets per slide.** My rule of thumb is more than four bullets and 60 words per slide is a waste. It is confusing, boring, and worst of all, distracts the audience from you, the speaker, and your beautiful body language.

Images rule. In PowerPoint as in life, the image is king. Pictures, videos, pie charts, and bar graphs make great videos. Pages out of the company bylaws or the Chicago phone directory should really be avoided.

The Least You Need to Know

◆ Warm body language by teachers motivates and facilitates learning.

◆ Positive, enthusiastic body language facilitates learning.

◆ Face forward. Eye contact is essential for teachers.

◆ Body language can be used to keep order in the classroom

◆ Read your students' body language to maximize effectiveness.

Part 5

Crossing the Boundaries of Body Language

Can body language cross the borders between pets and people? Between men and women? From commercial images to image-conscious consumers? Across continents and cultures? Even between real and virtual people? Keep reading to find out.

Chapter 24

Animal Actions: Relating to Your Pet

- ◆ The close relationship between people and pets
- ◆ Demonstrative dogs and cuddly cats: pet communication via body language
- ◆ The dark side of dogs
- ◆ The therapeutic value of pets

Apart from actual human relationships, our closest relationships are with our pets. If you've ever had a pet, you know the bond can become intense. In many households, pets are truly members of the family. They share your home, work and play with you, provide companionship, and communicate through rich and unambiguous body language.

Pets come in many species from dogs to donkeys, from cats to canaries, from hedgehogs to horses. More than one third of all U.S. households have dogs, and nearly one third have cats, though cats outnumber dogs 70 million to 60 million. Nearly a million households have horses and more than a million have birds. Though our discussion will focus on dogs and cats, people share their lives with a remarkable array of expressive animals.

Animotions and Creature Cognition

We have come to recognize that the line dividing humans and animals is an artificial one; after all, people *are* animals. Most stuff that was once believed unique to people, animals can do, too. Like humans, research suggests that animals have emotions, use tools, engage in complex cognitive and mental activity, develop relationships, have some elements of language, and certainly can send and receive body language. It's enough to make you a vegetarian.

Demonstrative Doggies

There is a reason why dogs are one of America's favorite pets and called man's best friend. For thousands of years they helped on the hunt, provided protection, and even kept their masters (and mistresses) warm at night. Many millennia ago, when the first wolf left the pack and entered a campsite, the destiny of humans and canines were changed forever. Dogs were probably the first domesticated animals and served as the prototype for wave after wave of other kinds of animal domestication.

Canines communicate with fierce body language recognizable to people, other dogs, and most other species. As a result, dogs have been used for centuries as guards. Recent research by Adam Miklosi and colleagues at Eotvos University also reveals that unlike foxes, wolves, and even monkeys, dogs recognize human facial expressions and gestures. This is not because dogs are raised with humans—wolves and foxes that are raised with humans do not recognize human facial expressions. So, dogs are genetically programmed to recognize human facial expressions; their evolutionary history and body language is intertwined with humans.

Science is now confirming what Darwin postulated more than a century ago: that animals possess basic emotions and express them. Recent research in neurology, biology, and psychology suggests that dogs, for example, can read people's emotions (better than people can) and express their own emotions.

Dogs certainly can display affection and express it by "smiling," making eye contact, wagging their tails, and licking. It is their unrestrained affection that makes so many dogs wonderful companions and true friends.

Like many other animals, dogs can express fear. Running away with their tail between their legs may be a cliché, but that's exactly what dogs do. Dogs show fear with a pitiful yelp or whine, distinct from other vocalizations, an attentive, worried look, and defensive distancing. Because dogs are pack animals, when one dog displays this body language, the others will turn tail and run as well.

Fido and Rover can also display sadness. That hangdog, downcast demeanor, the sad eye, the whimper and whine are unmistakably sad body language.

Anger is unmistakable doggie body language that includes growling, barking, snarling, charging, a crouching posture, hair standing on end, and of course, the bite (I am scaring myself just thinking about it). Some dogs are bred for anger displays, others are trained to be vicious, but even the nicest dogs occasionally show anger.

Most dog owners know that dogs also experience and display loneliness, jealousy, pride, boredom, anxiety, guilt, shame, surprise, and excitement. Each expression is unique and can be easily read by people, other dogs, and of course, cats.

Dogs not only recognize facial body language, they have sensitive hearing and react strongly to the tone of our voices, too. If you say "I love you" to a dog in a loud, harsh, snarling tone of voice, the dog will react negatively, for they are sensitive to the non-verbal elements of the voice, but not to most words.

Dogs can detect dominant or submissive body language, affection, and hostility with their excellent eyesight and sensitive ears. Dogs also have a keen sense of smell, nearly 100 times as powerful as people. Much as you or I would give another person a visual once-over, dogs give people a thorough smell-over. Unrestrained by puritanical rules and human norms of politeness, dogs sometimes go overboard by sticking their nose in the most private places.

Cuddly Cats

Any cat owner can recognize a contented cat. Curling up on a lap, responding to gentle strokes, cats purr blissfully, smile, rub, and roll.

Felines can also clearly display anger or hostility. Hissing, snarling, open-mouth displays, an arched back, and an erect, bushy tail are all hostile forms of cat body language. Kittens appear humorous when they act angry. Despite this fierce Halloween-cat display, these cuddly critters are not very scary to people. However, the angry body language of their cousins, such as panthers and tigers, is nothing to laugh about.

Cats that are exploring something forbidden display guilty body language, including a crouching, creeping gait, a pitiful bleating

> **Nonverbally Speaking**
>
> I focused on dogs and cats in this chapter because they are the most common pets. This is no diss on horses, mules, goats, bunnies, rats, hamsters, gerbils, ferrets, birds, turtles, snakes, fish, and even hermit crabs, all of which can make wonderful pets and make their own unique kinds of body language.

meow, panicky retreats, and furtive, guilty glances. Cats are curious and get into anything that is new or arouses their curiosity. My cats look guilty a lot, which always makes me wonder what they've been up to.

Cats experience hurt and fear, both physically and psychologically, and will tell you so with their body language—which includes an abrupt meow, panicky looks, and rapid retreats. Cats are also incredibly jealous. The surest way to attract many reticent, aloof cats is to pet another cat. The unapproachable, prissy pet quickly becomes your new best friend, to make sure the other cat doesn't get all the attention.

Cats are playful, curious, and cuddly, but always on their own terms.

(Image courtesy of Peter Andersen)

Pet Relationships

Like our human relationships, relationships between pets and humans provide friendship, affection, love, trust, help, comfort, and companionship. Communication with a pet can be intense and captivating, but it almost exclusively consists of body language. Pets don't understand much actual language, though they can be trained to recognize a few words. On the other hand, their body language vocabulary is vast.

Some people think it trivializes human relationships to discuss pets in the same breath. But talk to any person who has spent part of their life with a special horse, dog, cat, or other animal and they will tell you

> **Nonverbally Speaking**
>
> We constantly read of heroic dog rescues. Not just of trained dogs that track lost hikers or save skiers buried in an avalanche, but stories of pets pulling their human partners from a burning building, rescuing a drowning child, or capturing a robber. Their ability to read distressed body language, sense danger, and act intuitively is truly amazing.

of a wonderful bond that equals some of our closest human relationships. Animals are work partners, daily companions, and playmates for us.

Joy, closeness, and exchange of affectionate body language characterize the relationship between people and their pets.

(Image courtesy of Peter Andersen)

The Dark Side of Dogs

The most intense relationships humans have are with their loveable dogs. Unfortunately, they also constitute a major national health hazard. Each year there are about 6 million dog bites in the United States alone, afflicting over 2 percent of the entire American population. Nearly a million dog bites require medical attention, over a third of a million, or about a thousand a day, require a trip to the emergency room. Worse, children are the victims of the vast majority of dog bites. This is an intolerable situation that causes suffering, disfigurement, and a massive burden on the nation's soaring health bill.

Any walker, jogger, or parent with a stroller can recount scary stories of dogs that appear to be vicious, charge, bark, snarl, and generally scare the heck out of innocent passersby. Barking dogs are often a neighborhood nuisance that disturb the peace and annoy neighbors.

It's ironic that we tolerate behavior from dogs and dog owners we would never accept from teens or children. If a specific age group or ethnic group caused millions of injuries each year, massive outrage and retaliation would occur. Dog owners need to take more responsibility for the actions of their pets, train them, restrain them, and contain them. Pets are an extension of their owners; it is their responsibility to control their injurious actions and bullying body language.

Dogs are both friendly and aggressive with children.

(Image courtesy of Peter Andersen)

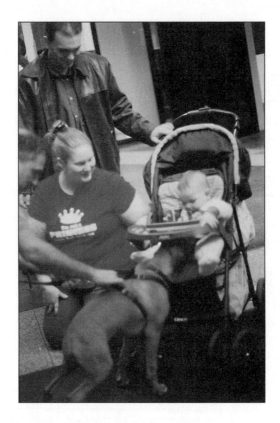

Pet Therapy: Healing and Restoration

Research demonstrates the therapeutic value of pets. One of the primary values of our animal friends comes from touch, the strokes that soothe. Throughout this book you've learned about the healing power of touch. Research shows that stroking a pet can lengthen life, comfort the dejected and distressed, create connection, and decrease depression and anxiety.

> **Nonverbally Speaking**
>
> Several studies show that children with Down's syndrome and other mental handicaps benefit greatly from petting and touching dogs or cats. Shyness diminishes, trust increases, physical coordination improves, and their emotional tone is more positive after interaction with animals.

The preferred playthings of infants are stuffed animals, which are really simulated pets. Teddy bears, toy cats, lions, otters, rabbits—almost any furry friend, reflects the almost innate connection between tots and pets. Furry pets, in particular, provide a rich tactile experience for people of any age, as they stroke, pat, caress, and cuddle. And many pets enjoy this mothering body language and respond with contented body language. Touch is a crucial connection that provides much of the value of our precious pet relationships.

Infants and toddlers are fascinated and elated with pets, whether they are living or stuffed toys.

(Image courtesy of Peter Andersen)

Pets can be of help to people living alone. Research suggests that for single seniors, sharing space with a pet has incredible value. Pets reduce feelings of loneliness and give the senior a sense of companionship. Some folks enjoy sleeping with a pet and experiencing the warm contact of that close connection.

Pets can open up severely withdrawn children, improve kids' self-esteem, decrease loneliness, heal patients after surgery, diminish the severity of minor aches and pains, reduce cholesterol, speed recovery from heart attacks, improve morale in nursing homes, decrease the pain in burn patients, increase optimism following illness, cut down violence among prison inmates, and reduce patients' trips to the doctor. Studies have shown that petting an animal can slow heart rate and reduce blood pressure, soothe and relax, and decrease depression and anxiety. That's quite an impressive list of accomplishments for our furry friends!

Nonverbally Speaking

Can pets harm our human relationships and decrease the need for other people, thereby increasing loneliness and isolation? Evidence suggests this is not the case. Good relationships with pets and good relationships with people appear to be correlated.

Horses are amazingly loyal and popular with people of all ages and among the four most common pets in the United States.

(Image courtesy of Peter Andersen)

Plants, hobbies, and even television can provide comfort to people, but the two-way interaction between pets and people seems to add value. Body language provides a two-way connection that just isn't possible between plants or paintings and people.

The Least You Need to Know

- Dogs are the only animal to read human facial expressions, which explains our close relationships with them.

- Demonstrative dogs and communicative cats send body language and read your body language.

- Pets can be dangerous. Avoid your dog's dark side by being a responsible pet owner.

- For many people, especially children and the elderly, pets have huge healing powers.

Commercial Cues: Selling Images

In This Chapter

◆ How images trump logic

◆ Sex sells

◆ Powerful appeals

◆ Arousing advertisements

◆ Sensational selling

If you want to learn about human beings' most basic and automatic psychological responses, watch television. Especially watch the commercials. The multibillion-dollar advertising industry tries not to waste its money. Ads on television and in magazines are targeted at the most fundamental cues to which humans respond: sex, power, excitement, and warmth. These are basic forces that make the world go around.

Media companies spend more money on the production of television commercials than on television shows. Similarly, movie producers spend as much money on trailers—the "coming attractions" that advertise a movie—as on the movie itself. You want to know what really makes people tick?

Study the advertisements, including TV commercials, movie trailers, billboards, and magazine ads.

It doesn't matter what you're selling, with a twist or two the same processes work. Whether you're trying to get people to buy prescription drugs, beer, cars, or clothes, the same kinds of cues grab our attention. And these principles work for health communication and public health campaigns, too. Some of the ads you'll see in this section are from a national cancer prevention campaign called GoSunSmart. It is an attempt to prevent high-altitude sunburning. But if those ads were selling winter vacations or snowboard equipment, many of the techniques would have been the same.

The Image Is Trump

Human beings process information in two primary ways: through the verbal world using thought and logic, and through intuition and image. Although research suggests we often use both processes simultaneously, the more primary, primitive, and powerful process is the image. Images defy logic and deter refutation. There is no rebuttal or counterargument to an image. Words have opposites; images do not. Images of beauty, strength, status, or wealth trigger automatic reactions.

Positive body images have long been used to sell products, and are now being used to sell healthier lifestyles. This sun safety ad is an attempt to persuade women that they can look good in a hat while being SunSmart.

(Image courtesy of Aimee J. Giese)

For thousands of years exciting body language has stimulated people to take action. Beautiful or handsome images have always been attractive to human beings and can produce sexual arousal that appeal to our reproductive instincts. Images of strength persuade us to follow leaders like parents and presidents, policemen and doctors.

Research on public health has shown the image trumps logic. Studies have found that condom campaigns are more effective if they show families coping with AIDS, or a sickly intravenous drug user with AIDS, as opposed to campaigns that list the health risks as stated by the U.S. Surgeon General or written descriptions of how AIDS is contracted or prevented.

This poster, from the GoSun-Smart campaign to prevent winter sunburning, uses images to defeat the long-held belief that the raccoon look is a winter status symbol.

(Image courtesy of Aimee J. Giese)

Commercial Sexploitation

Among your most basic psychological forces is the sex drive. Deep in your genes, you have a basic desire to reproduce. For men, minimal body language cues such as an hourglass figure, female breasts or buttocks, or a pretty face often triggers arousal. For women, tall, handsome, broad-shouldered, but compassionate men activate similar instincts.

Companies that sell sexy products have it the easiest. It's really pretty simple. To get the attention of men, they just need to show their sexy products in sexy ways. To get the attention of women, all they do is make women think their product will make them look like the same sexy women whom men look at. In fact, want to see the sexiest ads? Look in women's magazines. This isn't because most readers have latent lesbian leanings; rather, those ads are intended to make women want to look like the women in the ads.

There's nothing new about sexy ads, although their blatancy has steadily increased over the years. Today we are saturated with sex on billboards, in catalogs, in magazines, and of course, on TV. Have you watched a Victoria's Secret commercial on TV? I've seen R-rated movies that were less blatant! And for decades Calvin Klein has been selling jeans with prurient pictures of teen models. The ads incited public pandemonium and protests. Despite the controversy, the Klein ads have been wildly successful, particularly with the added star power of Brooke Shields, Marky Mark, Kate Moss, and Tyrese Gibson. Sex sells, and celebrity sex sells even better. (For the record, Calvin Klein says that all the models they use are over 18.)

Bodily Blunders

In mid-'90s, the FBI launched an investigation of whether or not Calvin Klein's jeans and clothing ads violated federal pornography or pedophile laws! In one image, a pubescent girl revealed white cotton panties under her short skirt. One critic called them the most disturbing ad campaign in history. Calvin Klein said all the models were over 18 and while they pulled this set of ads, they continue to push the envelope of public propriety.

Recently, Abercrombie and Fitch scrapped their winter sales catalog altogether. Parents across the country were shocked and amazed to see nude photos in A&F's Christmas magalog, a combination magazine and catalog that targeted the preteen, teen, and twenty-something set. In addition to the more typical response by religious groups and feminists, parents from across the country shrieked in protest, and even *60 Minutes* did a sexposé on the magalog.

Risqué ads have become almost commonplace in the last decade. Christian Dior's ads for their Svelte cellulite cream features lots of hips and buttocks in the buff. Fragrance ads are among the sexiest. For instance, J.Lo's Glow ads leave little to the imagination, and a naked Sophie Dawh is used to hawk Opium perfume. Perhaps the most blatant of all are recent Clairol shampoo ads, which depict a woman having an orgasmic experience while shampooing her hair!

Liquor ads aren't far behind beauty products when it comes to using sex to sell. Such advertisements often suggest that liquor will reduce inhibitions and enhance sexual enjoyment. Captain Morgan Rum ads use lots of sexual innuendo, but one featuring bikini-clad women with the caption, "catch of the day," has drawn criticism in several countries. Coors commercials often are blatantly sexual as well, culminating with the "twins" ads, which imply that if one girl is good, two are better.

CAUTION **Bodily Blunders** _____

Controversy over sexual ads is not just an American phenomenon. In Britain, lingerie company Gossard was ordered to take down posters of naked men and women pictured among their discarded underwear. The ads contained equally risqué captions. The English Advertising Standards Authority, which regulates ads in Britain, claimed they were sexually explicit, gratuitous, offensive, and unsuitable for outdoor sites, and ordered that they be removed.

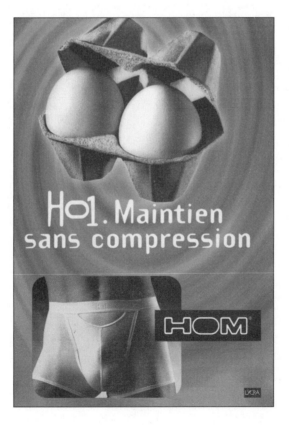

All across the world, sexual images are used to sell products like this French ad for underwear.

(Image courtesy of Aimee J. Giese)

Sometimes the product itself contains sexual suggestions, like the Barbie doll, whose unrealistic 39-23-33 proportions make her a hypersexual model for young women. At the other end of the advertising spectrum, ads use sex for products totally unrelated to the human body, like cars, trucks, boats, cigarettes, and vacations. Beyond the obvious attention that such ads attract, the implication is, of course, that these products will enhance your sex life.

Presenting Power

Besides sex, images of power and strength are probably used the most frequently to promote products. These sort of ads typically feature celebrity male athletes like Michael Jordan, Shaquille O'Neal, Mark McGuire, Junior Seau, and Howie Long. Like the sexy female ads discussed previously, these ads have a dual audience: Men who idolize these sports heroes and view them as physical role models, and women who think of these stars as the ultimate in power, status, and attractiveness.

> **Nonverbally Speaking**
>
> The images of sports stars gross about as much income as the Gross National Product of third-world countries! At the close of his career, Michael Jordan was making over $30 million per year in product endorsements. These numbers have been dwarfed by Tiger Woods, whose estimated endorsement earnings this year will be around 70 million before he ever hits a golf ball. Tiger, who has endorsement contracts with Buick, Nike, Rolex, American Express, Titleist golf clubs, and Asahi Breweries, is not taking on additional endorsements so as not to dilute the value of his image.

Of course, movie stars and rock stars have the most marketable images of all. J. Lo, Madonna, Britney Spears, Mick Jagger, Mel Gibson, and Ben Afleck transcend their own bodies and exist as images and icons that have a life of their own. These stars' images transcend their human presence, seemingly taking on a reality of their own.

The heroes in these sports power ads are mostly men, although soccer player Mia Hamm, tennis phenom Serena Williams, and sprinter Marion Jones have been featured in them. Usually, female sports ads appeal more to our sex drive than to our hunger for power. Tennis superstar Anna Kournakova, for example, who leads all tennis stars in endorsements, gets so much media attention because of her stunning beauty, not because of her average pro tennis ability.

> **Bodily Blunders**
>
> The anorexic image of Hollywood stars and runway models has long been known to be a factor contributing to women's eating disorders. The focus on fitness and male sports heroes has created similar syndromes in men. Men are becoming increasingly obsessed with working out and are suffering from the same anxiety, distorted body image, and insecurity that have typically been associated with women.

Former U.S. Senate leader and two-time Republican presidential candidate Bob Dole transformed his dour campaign image into a humorous and happy advertising image. He started as a spokesperson for the male potency drug, Viagra, but quickly parlayed that success into an advertising spot with Pepsi. In one Pepsi ad, senior citizen Dole does virtual backsprings on the beach and remarks that this amazing product makes him feel vital again. Dole reveals that the source of his vitality is his "little blue friend," implying Viagra, but a woman's voice says: "No, not that one; he's talking about Pepsi." Another Pepsi commercial shows several males, including Dole, going gaga over Britney Spears. In a clear double-entendre, Dole pets his dog while saying "down boy."

Superlative Stimulation

People are happiest and most comfortable at moderate levels of stimulation. Under-stimulated people are bored and are usually motivated to seek more stimulation. That's because the human brain is programmed for input and stimulation. Sensory deprivation experiments, where people are deprived of sight, sound, touch, and smell, typically produce an interesting effect: People start to hallucinate. The brain is designed to process incoming information, and when that data stops coming in, the brain will produce its own information, the hallucination.

Overstimulation also creates a negative reaction we variously call stress, pressure, anxiety, or tension. In today's fast-paced world, we are on the verge of constant over-stimulation: multiple deadlines to process, information overload, too much to re-member, and constant time demands. If you don't feel stressed out from time to time, you're not living in the twenty-first century.

One of the few times Americans really relax is in front of the television. In fact, Amer-icans are so overtired and overworked that many people fall asleep in front of the "tube," and those who are awake often fall into a quiet, trancelike state in which their heart rate falls and relaxation sets in. Television advertisers use sights, sounds, speed, and sex to jar viewers into paying attention. They can't afford to have us zone out dur-ing a half-million-dollar ad. Turn on commercial television at any moment and you'll see what I mean: beautiful, strong, vigorous people, all moving to a thumping beat, designed to capture your attention and evoke positive product images.

Arousing images go to the heart. They evoke emotions that viewers cannot control: fear, joy, lust, and power, to mention but a few. Some people especially love excite-ment. Lots of recent research has been done on these sensation-seekers, excitement-lovers who thrive on stimulation.

Sensation-Seeking and Advertising

You may have noticed the speed, excitement, and stimulation in television commercials has increased a lot in the last decade. Led by the Mountain Dew commercials that picture bodies in motion, usually of young men jumping out of airplanes and doing radical moves on mountain bikes, roller blades, and snowboards, other companies have attempted to ratchet up the stimulation level of their commercials. For instance, sport utility vehicles usually depict men driving over mountain ranges, tearing through swamps, or driving up a cliff.

Such action-packed commercials are a turn-off to senior citizens who grew up in the pre-TV era. Seniors can't process many of these commercials—they are too fast-paced—and when all is said and done they have little idea what the commercial's point was or even what product was being sold. So what's with these commercials that are missing a huge demographic?

It turns out that these fast-paced, bodies-in-action ads are targeted at two groups: young people and so-called sensation-seekers.

Young people, who grew up on TV and are often tuned in to several media simultaneously, have no problem processing these commercials. It's not unusual today to observe teens concurrently online, listening to CDs, and watching TV. Baby Boomers (ages 38–58) can multitask, too, but Generation Xers (ages 25–37) and especially Echo Boomers (ages 16–24) have taken it to a whole new level. It turns out that these high-action commercials are very effective at grabbing the attention and promoting products to a younger demographic. Not coincidently, with the exception of a few products like medication and travel, seniors are much thriftier than materialistic younger people who grew up in the wealthiest era in history. Selling to younger consumers has literally sustained the American economy for the past decade.

The fast-paced body language of extreme games, exploits of sports superstars, and radical actions especially appeal to another group, sensation-seekers. About 20 percent of the population are adrenaline junkies who are labeled "high sensation seekers" by social scientists. This interesting group consists of people of all ages and both sexes, but it is overrepresented by young males. These thrill-seekers engage in riskier behaviors, from unsafe sex to drug abuse, from problem drinking to using less sunscreen. We have also learned that these people will only tune in to messages that are exciting and stimulating. These exciting, high-sensation ads work just fine for most other people in these generations, the exception being seniors who were raised in the pre-TV era. So advertisers for trucks, soft drinks, and beer, as well as campaigns to prevent STDs, skin cancer, and problem drinking, are all using exciting, high-sensation ads.

In our GoSunSmart sun-safety campaign, we employ high-sensation ads with extreme body language, like this one, to appeal to sensation-seekers, especially young people, males, and snowboarders.

(Image courtesy of Aimee J. Giese)

The Least You Need to Know

◆ The image is trump. Image-based ads are more effective than ads that use logical appeals.

◆ The body images of celebrities are worth millions. A person's image may transcend the reality of their performance.

◆ Sex sells. Media of all types are increasingly dominated by sexually oriented ads.

◆ Power is an aphrodisiac and a huge moneymaker. Power sports images, celebrities, and politicians sell products.

◆ Fast-paced, stimulating ads targeted at sensation seekers dominate television advertising.

Chapter 26

Gendered Gestures: Masculine and Feminine Body Language

In This Chapter

◆ Why women are better at reading body language than men

◆ Understanding the mysteries of women's intuition

◆ The nature of gendered body language

◆ Dividing people into those who express their emotions and those who don't

People are fascinated with gender differences. We would love to understand what's going on with those strange people of the opposite sex. There are hundreds of ethnic groups, religious orientations, body types, and languages in the human race, but there are just two sexes, male and female. From the time we first realized this fact as children, we wanted to understand how the other sex thinks, behaves, and communicates.

In this chapter, we will consider whether men and women really are all that different. We will explore sex differences in people's ability to read and send body language. We will take a stab at explaining the mystery of women's intuition and try to explain some reasons why people are body language suppressors and others are body language expressers.

Men Are from Brooklyn, Women Are from Queens

Despite what you might have read, men and women are not from different planets. They're not even from different countries, or even different states. It's more like they come from different neighborhoods in the same city. Similarities between men and women completely outweigh differences, although you sell a whole lot more books if you sensationalize the differences and downplay the similarities.

> **Nonverbally Speaking**
>
> Polarizing portrayals of men and women are entertaining. However, by compiling all of the studies on sex differences in communication, Professor Dan Canary of Arizona State University revealed that men and women differ only by about 2 percent in their body language and in other communication behaviors.

Hundreds of studies on sex differences in communication have been combined into super studies. These super studies show that differences in the communication of men and women are small, with the exception of some medium-size differences in sensitivity to body language. But no matter whether we're talking about body language or spoken language, managerial communication or interpersonal communication, the real news is the substantial similarity—not difference—in men's and women's communication. Men and women are not from Mars and Venus—it's more like Brooklyn and Queens.

Inside Women's Intuition

Men and women speak the same language, and our body language consists of the same stuff—facial expressions, touch, gestures, and the like. One noteworthy exception to the massive similarities between the communication of men and women is in how we read body language. Guys, I am sorry! Across hundreds of studies on body language, the verdict is in: Women read body language better than men. Whether we study facial expressions, body postures, gestures, eye behavior, or whatever, the results are the same. As a group, women are much better people readers than men. Women have a particular advantage in reading facial expressions. A key to the mystique of women is understanding their enhanced social sensitivity, what most people call intuition.

Why are women better readers of body language? Where does this ability come from? Is it inherited or learned? Can guys be taught these skills? Let's take a closer look.

The Nurture of Nature

To really understand men and women and the differences in their ability to read body language, we need to delve into our past. Cut to 50,000 or even 5,000 years ago. Chances are your ancestors were hunters and gatherers living in small groups or tribes.

In those days life was short and nasty. Life expectancy was less than 30 years of age, and infant mortality was high. On the question of whether to make babies, unlike today, men and women had little choice: It was a matter of reproduction or extinction. Adult women were pregnant most of the time and those who weren't usually were carrying around and nursing small children. Close to a majority of our ancestors experienced skull fractures, suggesting hand to hand combat was common. These fractures were more commonly on the left side of the head, particularly among men, since club-wielding adversaries were mostly right-handed. This suggests that many of our ancestors were aphasic and probably couldn't talk, though their unaffected right hemisphere meant they could still communicate through body language (for more on left-brain/right-brain distinctions, see Chapter 2).

Since many women were nursing or expecting, they were usually less mobile than men. This resulted in a division of labor where women became the leaders in the village or campsite, tending to children, the injured, and the elderly. As leaders, the survival of the group depended on adult women's ability to send and read the body language of children and brain-injured, nonspeaking adults. Without communication and cooperation these small, isolated groups were doomed. Men were group leaders and caregivers, too, but not as frequently as women. For the more mobile men, hunting, gathering, combat, and finding mates from a different gene pool were more common activities, though women also ventured to do all of these things from time to time.

> **Nonverbally Speaking**
>
> All of our ancestors were survivors, and communication skills have always been pretty important survival skills. After all, humans are among the slowest creatures. With the exception of our big brains and incredible social skills, we're really a lot more like prey than predators. Your and my ancestors survived because they were clever and because they could communicate!

> **Positions of Power**
>
> Women do a lot of hinting and subtle communication through their body language. Men don't always pick it up. So here's a tip for women: Use words as well as actions. Men often appreciate direct communication.

Here is the bottom line: If a woman could read body language of her clan's kids, of the brain-damaged, of her mate, of other women and other men in the tribe, and use these skills to foster group cooperation, her tribe had a better chance of survival. That is one of the reasons that compared to men, on average, women of all ages and in all societies have better body language reading skills. And sex differences in non-verbal sensitivity are greater for boys and girls than for men and women, suggesting these might not be learned skills. When researchers find a difference that exists in many cultures and at all ages, we should suspect it has some evolutionary basis. As with all generalizations, there are numerous exceptions. Some men are highly sensitive to body language and some women are not. The average difference in sensitivity to body language between men and women is moderately large, but not so large that many of these skills can't be learned.

Guys, before you get too depressed or defensive, you need to know two things. First, the sex difference in sensitivity to body language can be overcome. Studies have shown that a single course in nonverbal communication for men can make men as adept as women in reading body language. And reading books like this one can result in a significant increase in sensitivity to body language. Second, studies show that men have far better spatial and navigational skills than women. They are better communicators across distances and in large groups, they read the body language of potential adversaries better than women, and they are just are as good or better at detecting deception.

> **Nonverbally Speaking**
>
> Though women have greater sensitivity to body language than men, men who major in social sciences like communication or psychology show no disparity from women. This suggests that body language reading skills can be improved upon.

The Nature of Nurture

Differences in men's and women's body language skills are due to both nature and how we are raised. It starts with parents' beliefs about boys and girls. Parents often believe that girls need more protection, and research shows that they are more likely to be kept indoors and closer to adults than are boys, who are thought to be more adventuresome and robust.

The different gender roles for boys and girls lay the foundation for many sex differences, including the ability to read body language. Research by Professor Judith Hall of Northeastern University has shown that some differences in sensitivity to body language start with parents' beliefs that girls should be more socially sensitive. She believes that these differences are a combination of nature and nurture.

From the start, parents train girls to think about interpersonal relationships and to be responsive to others. Traditional girls' games such as playing house and playing dolls, which emphasize relationships and people skills, may be training-grounds for learning to read people and their body language. Traditional boys' games like playing with cars, guns, and balls are more action-oriented and less social-oriented.

Little girls are also trained to be "sugar and spice and everything nice." This emphasis on manners and decorum may produce more attentive, mannerly adults who tune in to more subtle social cues. Little girls are more likely to be reprimanded for breaches of etiquette and rudeness than little boys, causing them to be more attentive to the subtleties of body language. So how we raise boys and girls is a key factor in their sex role socialization.

Another potential explanation for the gender gap in body language skills might be due to the gender difference in activity and power. Research suggests that men are trained to be proactive and powerful, whereas women are more reactive. To react competently women had to both read men's body language and react accordingly. Research has shown that less powerful people, in general, are much more attentive to the body language of their superiors than vice versa. These findings hold true in most cultures for organizational subordinates, lower-status racial groups, lower ranks in the military, and children. But considering that the women in powerful positions, such as executives, doctors, and professors, are often the best readers of body language, power discrepancies between men and women probably don't offer the whole explanation for sex differences in reading body language.

The oppression hypothesis stakes a similar claim. It suggests that the oppression of women in a patriarchal society has forced them to be subservient. Attentiveness to the body language of their oppressors became an important survival skill. Although many societies are patriarchal and oppressive toward women, there is little support for the oppression hypothesis. Because the gender difference in the ability to read body language appears early in life and is actually strongest for the youngest boys and girls, oppression would have to start early and then diminish as kids become men and women. In addition, the most educated women and the women who believe they are equal to men are the most sensitive to body language, not the least sensitive. Finally, women with the most traditional sex role attitudes are less sensitive than nontraditional women. So although socialization no doubt plays a part in developing the skill to read body language there, there is little support for the oppression hypothesis.

Positions of Power

One of the reasons women pick up more body language than men is that they look more. So here is a tip for men (and women): If you want to read more body language, look! Nearly 90 percent of body language is received visually.

Are You an Expresser or a Suppressor?

Research done at the University of Connecticut by Ross Buck has shown that we have two basic responses to our feelings: we internalize them, meaning that we suppress them, or we externalize them, meaning that we display them. At times we are all *internalizers*, sucking it up and suppressing our emotions, but men tend to internalize their emotions more often than not. Young men are told that only sissies show their feelings, "big boys don't cry," and to "be a man" when their feelings hurt or they are sad. Among 40 or so emotions researchers have investigated, only anger and dominance seem to be more frequently expressed by men.

Women are encouraged by society to express their emotions, especially positive ones, and therefore tend to be *externalizers*. Women express more joy, happiness, sadness, depression, guilt, shame, jealousy, embarrassment, warmth, affection, frustration, fear, and love than men.

The fact that men tend to be internalizers and women externalizers shouldn't be taken to mean that men experience fewer emotions than women, or experience the same emotions but to a significantly lesser degree. The big differences are in *expression* of feelings.

> **Body Talk**
>
> **Externalizers,** or expressers, are people who show their emotions. **Internalizers,** or repressors, conceal their emotions and as a result emotions cause internal responses such as higher blood pressure and a faster heart rate. Men are more likely to be internalizers and can hurt their health by raising their blood pressure and other internal stressors.

> **Nonverbally Speaking**
>
> Emotional suppression and internalization may be biologically based, because men seem to be more poker-faced worldwide. But it's important to note that not all men are internalizers and not all women are externalizers.

Check out these macho dudes. Their postures and lack of facial expressions are classically masculine.

(Image courtesy of Peter Andersen)

Gender Sending

Men and women use body language differently when they communicate. In general, women express themselves through body language more than men. Let's examine each component of body language with an eye toward gender differences.

What cues tell you whether this is a man or a woman?

(Image courtesy of Peter Andersen)

Spatial Signals in Men and Women

One of the most important aspects of your body language is how close to others you sit or stand. Males and females inhabit their personal spaces differently. Most people stand about the same distance—about an arm's length—from each other when they interact—most people, that is, except when men interact with other men. Men typically stand and sit more than an arm's length apart from each other. Spatially, man-to-man body language communicates low intimacy, aloofness, power, and defensiveness. Small wonder lots of researchers argue that male-male relationships are low in intimacy. Although this is accurate in one sense, an alternative kind of male intimacy involves sharing space while

Nonverbally Speaking

The fact that men stand farther from other men than women do from other women isn't just a function of the greater average size of men. Despite their longer arms, men interact at more than an arm's length and women at less than an arm's length.

Bodily Blunders

Men often read sexual meaning into women's body language, while women underestimate the sexual meaning of men's messages. Guys, if she makes eye contact or smiles at you, this is not necessarily a flirtation cue. Women, take note that many male messages contain more sexual intent than you think!

doing things together. Male bonding and intimacy are communicated through shared activities. Whether working on a car, going for a run, or playing softball, the body language of male intimacy is sharing activity.

Interestingly, despite many theories of male power dominance when men and women interact, men use the women's distance. This suggests that, at least in this situation, women have the power to alter the body language of men and in general can influence men to be less aggressive. For men, women don't constitute the potential threat that other men present. Interestingly, the closer distances maintained by females are found in females of all ages—even toddlers. This suggests that there's a possible biological origin to these distances. Yet, socialization happens early, and boys are allowed by parents to roam more than girls, suggesting that socialization may be at work after all. Women's close distances are a form of intimacy conveyed through the language of space. Moreover, the closer distances intensify other body language behaviors, such as facial expression and eye contact.

The Look of Gender

Women look at other people more than men, so they might observe more body language. And it's not just when they are talking that women look at people—they also look more when listening, and even during silence, further increasing their ability to read body language.

Women are also looked *at* more than men by both men and women. Men avoid looking at other men due to homophobia and masculine role rules. Women avoid looking at men because it might seem like a "come on." (As you learned in Chapter 17, men do often take engagement via body language as a sign of sexual interest.)

The most looking takes place between two women, which is why women often feel a special bond while interacting with other women. The least looking occurs between two men, and an intermediate amount between a man and a woman. The result is that men find interactions with women rich in body language and very intimate compared to men's interaction with other men. Some men find interacting with women to be too warm and personal. Women are sometimes disappointed by their interactions with men because of the lack of rich visual cues and body language.

In the Face of Gender

One of the clearest differences in the body language of men and women is in facial expressions. Women are much more likely to use facial expressions, especially those associated with happiness, guilt, fear, enthusiasm, sadness, shame, and love. Women are especially likely to communicate more positive emotions through facial expressions than men.

> **Positions of Power**
>
> When I coach high-level female executives in the corporate world, I tell them to keep smiling. Smiles are simultaneously positive, powerful, and persuasive and are one advantage for women in this still male-dominated world.

The largest gender difference among those expressions is in how often the two groups smile. Women are more likely to smile overall and especially more likely to smile when they are happy. This might give women a social advantage, since people like positive emotions.

Gendered Gestures

The differences in the hand gestures of men and women are not as extensive as differences in eye behavior or facial expressions. Some studies show no differences in gestural behavior. Most studies show that women gesture more than men, but that men use larger gestures than women. This seems to make sense; gestures with the fingers or wrist typically imply femininity. The term "limp-wristed" is a scornful, heterosexist term for feminine men. Full arm signals like a coach waving in a runner from third base, or a first-down sign in football have a distinctly masculine flavor.

The Touch of Gender

Many books and articles claim that men touch women more than women touch men and that men use touch as a power move to control women. Contrary to these stereotypes, there is slim evidence that touch is asymmetrical across gender. Men do initiate more touch early in dating relationships, but women initiate more touch in marriage. Research I conducted with Professor Laura Guerrero of Arizona State University suggests opposite-sex touch is almost entirely reciprocal. In all stages of relationships, from casual dating to engagement to long-term marriages, men and women touch each other about the some amount. Interestingly, this finding holds up regardless of the personality of the man and woman in the couple and regardless of their attitudes toward touch. And that says something about relationships: Relationships are powerful, so powerful that we adjust our body language to our partner and in some sense merge messages to accommodate him or her.

As for touch among people of the same sex, female-female touch is much more common than male-male touch in North America and Europe. These findings are also consistent with touch attitudes we discussed in Chapter 6; males are avoiders of same-sex touch, while women are same-sex touch approachers. Another way to look at these findings is that everybody avoids touching men. Studies suggest that men—especially single men and elderly men—receive so little touch they sometimes experience something called tactile deprivation. Such a lack of touch can create loneliness and cause health problems. So hug your bachelor brother or your grandpa today.

Walk Like a Man (or Woman)

Men and women have characteristic walks. Women are much more likely to take shorter steps, place one foot in front of the other when they walk, and swing their arms less. This style of walking causes women to swing their hips more than men. These are probably more learned than anatomical, since men can walk this way voluntarily. Interestingly, women are not conscious of the swing in their gait, although they can consciously exaggerate it if they want to. Men have a stiffer walking style, giving them a masculine image of power and rigidity. Some gay men display more hip movement and less arm swinging, giving them a less masculine image.

The Shape of Gender

Surveys done all over the world show that both men and women consider the hourglass figure to be the ideal female body type for women. Psychologists believe the universality of the preference for the hourglass figure is an innate mental mechanism providing a marker of female health and fertility. In fact, virtually everywhere in the world the *ideal* female image is perceived to be a .70 waist-to-hip ratio, but an .80 waist-to-hip ratio also sends very feminine cues. So, for an ideally beautiful body, a woman's waist should be about 70 percent of the size of her hips. Remember that is an ideal, not an average. In most countries even overweight women are perceived by men to be very attractive as long as they have the hourglass figure! Surveys show that the physical feature with which women are most dissatisfied is the size of their hips and buttocks. Young women should be taught to be proud of this profile since ample hips are a sign of health, fertility, and attractiveness worldwide. Only supermodels have no hips, and despite media hype, that body type is neither feminine nor healthy.

For men the v-shaped body is still the ideal. Muscular males are preferred by women worldwide as potential mates even at a time when brainpower is far more important than brawn. Like the hourglass figure for women, the v-shaped body is an unconscious sign of fertility fitness and health in men. Studies show that ideally attractive men should have no more than a more than a .90 waist-to-hip ratio. In other words, their waist size should be greater than 90 percent of the hip size to emit the maximum masculine gender cues.

The Least You Need to Know

- ◆ Men's and women's body language is more similar than different.

- ◆ Women's intuition is largely their sensitivity to body language.

- ◆ Gender differences in body language are both genetic and cultural

- ◆ Men are body language suppressors, which may damage their health.

- ◆ Body language is important to communicating your gender.

Chapter **27**

The Codes of Culture: Recognizing and Transcending Diversity

In This Chapter

- ◆ Cultural differences in nonverbal communication
- ◆ The body language of individualism and collectivism
- ◆ Cultural rigidity and body language
- ◆ The differences between nonverbal and verbal cultures

A while ago on a trip to Los Angeles, I hopped off the crowded freeway and drove on the surface streets through the belly the city. The city was teeming with signs in every language, smells of ethnic food, the dress of dozens of nations, and people of all colors and ethnicities. I could have been in Manila, or Bangkok, or Guadalajara. Los Angeles has become an international city.

California is the first state not to have white, European Americans as the majority, and as California leads in all trends, the rest of America will soon follow. Although we can never master 30 languages, we *can* develop an understanding of cultural similarities and differences in the most universal of languages, body language.

Second Nature: The Pervasiveness of Culture

Your culture is deep within you; nobody can really transcend it. Culture is so basic, learned so early, and is so taken for granted, it is often confused with human nature itself. The way your culture moves, dresses, drives, sits, cooks, and smells is thought to be the natural way. This sort of cultural myopia can only be resolved by education, by travel, or by living in a cosmopolitan area.

Until people communicate across cultures, they are unaware of their own body language. Culture is an implicit, spontaneous phenomenon, learned through image and imitation and body language. Cultural customs like how to wait in line, what food to eat, how to treat one's elders, what emotions to show, and how to greet other people are learned silently, by observing the body language of others.

The depth of culture means that it is hard to change important cultural customs including dress, gestures, tactile behaviors, religious customs, and language. People go to war to preserve their culture, and the aversion and fear of other cultures still plagues the planet. Someday we may transcend our cultural roots, but probably not in our lifetimes.

Cultural Time Warps

Cultures move at many speeds. Most of America moves fast. As a matter of fact, and Americans view time as commodity. We really think that we can save time, spend time, and waste time. America is a *monochronic culture* in a world that is mostly *polychronic*. Monochronic cultures schedule just one event at a time, start on time, and move quickly on to the next task. Polychronic cultures may schedule several things at once, may have no actual starting time, and allow events to naturally unfold.

The meaning of time is one of the biggest differences in body language across cultures. To people from the third world or even smalltown America, the freeways of Southern California or the subways of New York move at an unimaginable pace.

Monochronic cultures come from Northern Europe and today are likely to be found in England, Germany, Finland, Norway, Sweden, Switzerland, New Zealand, Canada, and the United States. In these countries, time is money and schedules reign supreme.

In most of the lesser-developed world, minutes and hours mean little or nothing. They exist polychronically and simultaneously, taking life as it comes. It is safe to assume when visiting any third-world culture that all your assumptions about time are wrong. So take a Mexican moment, experience Polynesian paralysis, and kick back a few notches when visiting a polychronic culture. They will not adjust to you, and if you don't adjust to them, your body language you will make you seem impatient, uptight, and generally annoying.

Nonverbally Speaking

A wonderful old story illustrates the different attitudes about time across culture. A family of Midwesterners are vacationing in the Southwest and go to visit a remote Indian reservation. Their tour book says that March is when Native Americans do a rain dance that is very beautiful and not to be missed. The tourists arrive in their station wagon with cameras ready but no rain dance is happening. The father approaches a distinguished looking tribal elder and says, "What about the rain dance?" The chief, arms folded across his chest says, "The time is not right." "Well," says the tourist, "when is the right time, today, tomorrow, when?" "The time is not right," repeats the chief. The tourist, obviously getting slightly impatient, tries again, "Well when will the time be right to dance?" The chief slowly replies, "When the birds fly to the north, when the day and night are the same length, when the clouds appear in the south, then we will dance."

The Space of Place

North Americans' body language is standoffish, because we have relatively large personal space bubbles of around an arm's length; only in a few Northern European countries do people stand farther from each other than we do. In the Mediterranean, the Middle East, and Latin America, interpersonal distances are so close that in America such distances would be considered sexual come-ons or the distances at which only the closest member of your family would sit or stand.

When you travel to many parts of the world, your personal space bubble will shrink. Like other Americans, I was shocked by the compressed space of trains in Tokyo, busses in Russia, and subways in Mexico City. In all three of these places, people are so compressed that any sense of personal space or modesty is gone. It's not unusual in these situations to be pressed against others' bodies almost to the point of pain, and certainly to the point of embarrassment. In Tokyo, conductors often push the last commuters onto the train with their hands and feet so they can close the door. This isn't rude spatial behavior—at least not in their own culture; it's literally a case of different strokes for different folks.

Touching Travels

Speaking of different strokes, touch varies greatly in many parts of the world. My colleague, Ed McDaniel of San Diego State University, and I have conducted field studies on difference in intercultural touch. We found that Asians are extremely unlikely to touch in public, even when they are saying farewell to a loved one they may not see for months or years. Americans, once thought to be a low-touch culture, are actually pretty high in touch, although people from Latin America, the Middle East, and the Mediterranean show the most public touch.

Touch is particularly culturally variable among men. Except for the handshake, the only situation in which most American men touch each other much is during celebrations at sporting events. In other parts of the world, touch among men is common. Men kiss each other in places as varied as France, Yemen, Italy, and Pakistan. In Eastern Europe men frequently hug, and I've observed Nigerian men walking while holding hands. American men are "too cool" or just plain too homophobic for that kind of display. The exception, of course, is when men play sports. During athletic contests, butt slaps are common after home runs, kisses are ordinary body language following soccer goals, and head rubbing and hair tousling often follow goals at hockey games.

Positions of Power

When it comes to touch, go with the flow. Look around. Notice who touches whom. When in Rome, make like a Roman. In China, touch like the Chinese. It can be interesting to experiment with new rules of touch.

Cultural Kinesics

Kinesics, or how people move their bodies, vary greatly across the world. In general, Northern Asians, Northern Europeans, and North Americans tend to be more restrained in their facial expressions, body movements, and gestures. To Africans, Mediterranean people, and Mexican Americans, the body language of the northern peoples seems pretty uptight and kind of square.

Nonverbally Speaking

The Pioneer 10 and 11 spacecrafts contain an etching, designed by American astronomer Carl Sagan, of a naked man and woman along with math formulae and a picture of the solar system, just in case any aliens find it. The man has an upraised arm with an open palm, a gesture of peace and greeting all over the world. Some religious groups objected to the nudity and some women's groups thought the woman should be gesturing, too. I'm sure it will be equally controversial on Alpha Centuri.

Disparate Gestures

Most gestures have meanings unique to each culture throughout the world. In much of Southeast Asia, pointing is reserved for pets, not people. In parts of Asia, the left hand is considered unclean and never used for handshakes or other interpersonal touch. (Toilet paper is not widespread in many parts of the world, and the left hand might literally be unclean!) In Japan, "come here" is communicated with beckoning fingers and the hand facing down, in American the hand is extended up. "No" is signaled by shaking the head in America; in Japan an upraised right hand, turned to the left, is moved back and forth in front of the face. In many of the islands of the Mediterranean, "no" is signaled by brushing the chin several times with the hand.

A few gestures are universal, like the hand shrug to indicate uncertainty, and the open palm, which is a universal sign of greeting or peace.

Bodily Blunders

In 1958, Vice President Nixon visited Venezuela, thought to be a friendly ally of the United States. As he got off the plane he raised both hands high in the air and made the "OK" sign by circling the thumb and first finger. Little did he know that in many parts of the world, that sign is the same as an upraised middle finger. In the riots that ensued, Nixon barely escaped with his life.

The gestures that Americans take to mean "okay" have different meanings in other cultures.

(Image courtesy of Robert Avery)

The Sharing of Smell

Americans aren't into sharing smell, unless the scent is provided by Ralph Lauren, Esteé Lauder, and the like. However, in much of the rest of the world sharing smells—including body odor and the smell of a person's breath—is just fine. As a matter of fact, the feel and smell of another person's breath, considered rude and obnoxious in America, is considered an affiliation cue—like eye contact or shaking hands—in the Middle East.

In Northern Europe, Canada, Australia, New Zealand, and Japan, people smell a lot like we do in the United States—that is, not much at all, except for deodorant or cologne. In the Mediterranean, most of South Asia, Africa, Latin America, and the Middle East, the body language of smell is quite apparent. Smell is covered in much more depth in Chapter 9, but suffice it to say that in many places smell is a real channel of communication that communicates sexual attraction, positive and negative emotions, and even cues about a person's health.

Eyeing the World

Across the world eye contact is an invitation to communicate, but differences exist in how it is used and interpreted. In much of the world, including Latin America and Africa, lower-status people are not supposed to make eye contact with those of higher status. Reports of teachers in the Peace Corps indicate some cultural confusion when they ask students to look at them and pay attention. These young students take a quick peek and then avert eye contact again. Teachers often report that such students are disobedient and impolite, when in reality they are trying to be very polite, according to the rules of their culture, by averting eye contact.

American women visiting France and Italy are often taken aback by the ogling eye behavior of men in that region. In America, a fleeting glance at a woman's body is all that is appropriate (we have excellent memories in America), but in the Mediterranean a man's gaze might linger at any part of a woman's anatomy.

Physical Appearance

When you visit another country, the first and most obvious difference in body language you'll notice is how people adorn themselves. Clothing and hairstyles vary greatly around the world. Consider, for instance, an international airport with Tongan men and women both in long bright ceremonial dresses, Hasidic Jews in blue yarmulkes with long beards, Sikhs in white turbans, Africans in Dashikis, Indian women in sarongs, and California girls in shorts and bikini tops.

Although business suits have become the uniform of the business class throughout the world, and blue jeans are found almost everywhere, there is still a lot of variety in how people dress. For example, in many Islamic countries, women must keep their bodies, including their faces, covered. In many Muslim countries, American tourists and businesswomen are considered rude and even indecent in their normal attire. Shorts are not acceptable attire for men over five years old in many parts of the world. When traveling to a foreign country, research the clothing customs of that region. Shoes are not worn indoors in many countries, heads must be covered or uncovered in many shrines or temples, and casual clothing may be considered inappropriate or insulting.

CAUTION

Bodily Blunders _____

On a visit to Russia several years ago, Russian men roundly scolded me in their language while pointing at my Bermuda shorts. Since I don't speak Russian, I have no idea what they said, but based on their body language—which included angry facial expressions, a sharp tone of voice, and pointing—it was probably something about being out on the street in my underwear.

Before you pack your bags for international travel, it pays to check out the "dress code" of the region you'll be visiting.

The Invisible Culture of Individualism

One way to help get a grip on a culture's body language is to determine if it is collectivist or individualist. Collectivist cultures emphasize community, collaboration, shared interests, harmony, tradition, and maintaining face. To make another "lose face" by embarrassing, shaming, or insulting them is a major faux pas in these places. Gerte Hofstede has done an extensive study of world cultures and believes that whether a community is individualistic or collectivistic is the most important factor that generates cultural differences.

In individualistic cultures, the ties between people are loose, personal rights reign supreme, and people value space, privacy, individual expression, freedom, innovation, and personal preferences. America is the most individualistic country on earth, so our body language is going to seem pretty weird in most of Asia, the Middle East, South America, Africa, and Eastern Europe. In short, we seem weird in much of the world, where collectivism rules.

In individualistic places like the United States, Canada, Australia, and most of Europe, emotional expression is an individual thing; you express your own emotions. In collectivistic countries, it may seem childish to express your own emotions; instead, people attune their emotions to the group. As a consequence, Americans and other people from other individualistic cultures display, but don't necessarily feel, a much greater range of emotions than do collectivist peoples.

Body language tends to be more coordinated and synchronized in collectivistic cultures, and people are more likely to mirror one another's facial expressions, body postures, and movements. To communicate politeness and interpersonal harmony, people smile more in Asian culture. Either that or everybody is really happy in Japan and China.

Positions of Power

Asia is the most collectivistic place on earth. When in Asia, you'll fit in a lot better if you follow these simple guidelines: Smile and bow to everybody, including corporate executives, street sweepers, housekeepers, and everybody else. Go with the flow; if everyone is walking on the left, walk left. Smile all the time except when everyone is showing another expression, such as concern or surprise; then show that emotion. Harmony is everything in Asia, so blend in and get in sync. Avoid confrontations, especially in public; they are much less common in collectivistic than in individualistic cultures.

Space is prized in individualistic cultures but not in collectivist ones. So on your trips to the collectivist world, get ready to have people touch, crowd, invade your space, and have strong body odor.

Individualistic people are concerned about image. They pay a lot more attention to attracting others, since dates and mates are an individual concern. As a result, Americans and other individuals put a lot more effort into various aspects of body language, including flirting, dating, makeup, and hairstyles. Our relationships are more casual and transient than collectivist peoples and, as a result, in the United States we enact body language rituals of initial acquaintance over and over again.

Storming the Caste

In some countries, social class and the cultural power structure is rigidly defined. In India, although they are officially outlawed, castes based on ancestry and race are so inflexible that people from different classes don't associate with one another and may not touch each other. Nations such as the Philippines, Mexico, Colombia, Venezuela, Brazil, Singapore, Hong Kong, and France are also places where social class is rigid and difficult to transcend and power is distributed unequally. Places where class matters little include Austria, Israel, Denmark, Sweden, Norway, Finland, New Zealand, Ireland, and Switzerland, a list dominated by cultures

Nonverbally Speaking

Sunlight makes people happy and brings out the body language in people. In sunny seasons and in sunny places, people touch and smile more and maintain closer distances than people in cooler and cloudier places.

of Northern Europe. Indeed, researchers have found that people in northern countries seem to be much more egalitarian than people from the tropics.

Body language is vastly different in countries with rigid class systems. Between classes, body language, including touch and eye contact, might be carefully proscribed. In these countries people from the lower classes are always expected to show positive emotions to their supervisors. Communication via touch between castes is greatly curtailed in Indian culture. The continuous smiles of many Asians are a cultural custom intended to appease superiors and smooth social relations, behaviors that are appropriate to a more stratified culture.

Interestingly, in countries where political authority is highly centralized, singing voices are tighter and the voice box is more closed, whereas people in more permissive societies produce more relaxed, open, and clear sounds. Cultures that value equality and individuality are more likely to employ loud tones of voice that may be offensive to others.

Rigid and Tolerant Cultures

Some cultures like change and ambiguity; others value stability and have rigid rules of behavior. A culture's predisposition to take risks and accept ambiguity has definite impact on people's body language. As you've probably guessed by now, body language is more rigid in cultures where rules are more rigid.

The most rigid rule structures are found in Greece, Portugal, Belgium, Japan, Peru, France, Chile, Spain, Argentina, and Turkey. Most of these cultures originated in the Mediterranean region. The 10 countries that are least rule-driven and most tolerant and innovative are Denmark, Sweden, Hong Kong, Singapore, Ireland, Great Britain, India, the Philippines, the United States, Canada, and New Zealand. This list is dominated by Northern European and South Asian cultures, many of which were formerly part of the British Empire.

Body language in more rule-governed countries is more rigid and people are less free to improvise. In rigid countries, emotional displays by young people are not appreciated or tolerated.

People in highly rigid cultures have more stylized and ritual behavior, so we should expect that nonverbal behavior is more prescribed in these cultures. When people from the United States communicate with people from a country such as Japan or France, the Americans may seem unruly, nonconforming, and unconventional; whereas their Japanese or French counterparts might seem too controlled and rigid to the Americans. The ultimate in prescribed, rigidly defined body language is the Japanese tea ceremony, where every movement is defined.

The ultimate in controlled, prescribed body language is the Japanese tea ceremony, where every gesture is carefully choreographed.

(Image courtesy of Peter Andersen)

Getting Close in a Contact Culture

Cultures in which close distances and interpersonal touch are the norm are called contact cultures. In these cultures, close distance is often accompanied by the exchange of olfactory cues from the body and breath. Smiling, touching, eye contact, and more vocal animation are also more prevalent in such societies.

Contact cultures are generally located in warmer countries nearer the equator, and low-contact cultures are found in cooler climates farther from the equator. Body language in cooler-climate cultures tends to be more task-oriented and interpersonally "cool," whereas cultures in warmer climates tend to be more interpersonally oriented and emotionally "warm." Even within the United States, the warmer latitudes tend to be higher-contact cultures with warmer body language. These differences have been shown to be due to energy level, climate, metabolism, and sunlight.

The body language of southerners is more expressive than northerners within many countries. Data from within Belgium, Croatia, France, Germany, Italy, Japan, Serbia, Spain, Switzerland, and the United States all show this pattern. Likewise, there is a large overall north-south difference within the entire northern hemisphere. In warm climates, people are

> **Nonverbally Speaking**
>
> In our survey of American universities, the highest-touch universities were in the sunbelt, including San Diego State, Arizona State, and Auburn University in Alabama. The Universities of Washington, Minnesota, and Maine were least touch-oriented; not surprisingly, all three of these universities are located in areas where winters are either long and cold or rainy and overcast.

more likely to interact with neighbors and less likely to be confined to the house. They are more likely to be socially extravagant and flamboyant, and to use expressive body language. In northern latitudes, societies are structured, more ordered, more constrained, and more organized.

High-contact cultures include most Arab countries, including North Africa; the Mediterranean region, including France, Greece, Italy, Portugal, and Spain; Jewish cultures in Europe and the Middle East; Eastern Europe and Russia; and virtually all of Latin America. Australians are moderate in their cultural contact level, as are North Americans.

Low-contact cultures comprise most of Northern Europe, including Scandinavia, Germany, and England, and the Anglo culture of the United States), and virtually every Asian country, including Burma, China, Indonesia, Japan, Korea, the Philippines, Thailand, and Vietnam. Recent research suggests the biggest differences in contact are between the rest of the world and Asia. Asians, as a group, are the least expressive and most controlled people in the world. Southern people, modern countries, and non-Asian cultures are the most expressive, spontaneous, and antimated.

Verbal and Nonverbal Cultures

Cultures in which communication is implicit, or unspoken, are called nonverbal cultures or *high-context cultures*. In such cultures, meaning is usually conveyed in the conversational context or by body language, so it doesn't have to be expressed linguistically. Cultures in which communication is explicit, or spoken, are called verbal or *low-context cultures*. In verbal cultures, a lot of stuff needs to be said because body language can't provide all the information.

In a nonverbal culture like Japan, meanings are often shared but unexpressed—people implicitly understand what others are thinking without having to say it. Like many people in nonverbal cultures, most long-term married couples or old friends skillfully use body language that is nearly impossible for an outsider to understand. The situation, a smile, or a glance provides meaning that doesn't need to be articulated. In nonverbal cultures, information is integrated from the environment, the context, the situation, and body language cues that give the message meaning that is

Body Talk

The great anthropologist Edward Hall first recognized high-context and low-context cultures. In high-context or nonverbal cultures, implicit communication and body language rules. In low-context or verbal cultures, explicit communication and language is more important.

unavailable in explicit verbal communication. In verbal cultures, most people communicate using explicit, or spoken, messages. Verbal messages must be detailed, crystal clear, and highly specific.

There is vast cultural variation in the degree to which language and body language are used in everyday communication. The most verbal cultures include the Swiss, German, North American, and Scandinavian. These cultures communicate using the spoken word, specific details, and precise time schedules at the expense of context and body language. Verbal cultures use traditional logic and talk more than nonverbal cultures.

The most nonverbal cultures are found in Asia and include China, Japan, and Korea. Although most languages are explicit, verbal communication systems, in China even the language is an implicit system. To use a Chinese dictionary, one must understand thousands of characters that change meaning in combination with other characters. Zen Buddhism, a major influence in Asia, places a high value on silence, lack of emotional expression, and the unspoken, nonverbal parts of communication.

Bodily Blunders

Americans sometimes complain that the Japanese never "get to the point." What they fail to recognize is that a nonverbal culture must provide a context and setting and let the point emerge.

Cultures that have some characteristics of both verbal and nonverbal cultures include the French, English, and Italian, which are more nonverbal than Northern European cultures but not as much as most Asian cultures.

People from verbal cultures are sometimes perceived as complete idiots, excessively talkative, and belaboring of the obvious by people from nonverbal cultures. At the same time, people from nonverbal cultures may be perceived as sneaky, silent, incomprehensible, and mysterious.

Body language is valued even more in nonverbal cultures than in verbal ones. In verbal cultures like the United States, talk is valued and talkative people are more attractive and thought of as friendly. People in nonverbal cultures anticipate that communicators will understand unspoken feelings, implicit gestures, and environmental clues that people from verbal cultures do not process. Given that both cultural extremes fail to recognize these basic communication differences, intercultural attributes about behavior are often incorrect.

The Least You Need to Know

♦ In individualistic cultures like the United States, body language reflects the individual rather than the group.

♦ In more rigid cultures, body language is prescribed.

♦ High-contact cultures, usually located nearer the equator, employ closer distances than low-contact cultures.

♦ In class- or caste-oriented cultures, the powerful dictate the body language of the powerless.

♦ High-context cultures like the United States rely more on talk than low-context cultures like the Japanese, who rely more on body language.

Chapter **28**

Virtual People: Body Language in Cyberspace

In This Chapter

- ◆ The nature of virtual body language

- ◆ Reality vs. virtuality: How real is real?

- ◆ The immersive nature of telepresent body language

- ◆ The dark side of virtual reality

If the history of human progress were divided in half, history's midpoint would be about 1945. In technology, medicine, electronics, weaponry, transportation, and communication, as much innovation occurred after 1945 as in all history before 1945. Baby boomers, born about 50 years ago, have seen as many advances in technology as all of their ancestors combined.

And it continues. In every field, not only is change accelerating, but so is the *rate* of change. A hundred years ago nobody could have predicted automobile and airplanes would be commonplace. Fifty years ago it would have been hard to imagine how central the television would become in our lives—not to mention color television, cable television, and satellite television. A decade ago it would have been hard to predict that our primary communication media would be computers and wireless phones.

Crystal balls are always cloudy. But what they do reveal is a world vastly different than the one we inhabit, with a dramatically different environment, new urban landscapes, accelerating technology, and the continuation of a trend that has already begun: the virtual person. And with virtual people must come virtual body language.

Virtual Worlds in Cyberspace Environments

Humankind is entering the era of virtual reality. Virtual reality is the use of technology to create simulated environments that are impossible to tell from ordinary reality.

Like *The Matrix*, virtual reality is an artificial world, a consensual hallucination, in which those immersed in the virtual experience think that they are experiencing reality, not some mediated environment.

Science fiction like *Neuromancer* or *The Matrix* has given us a glimpse of possible futures. The confluence of four technologies has made virtual reality a possibility. First, we now have the ability to digitalize almost anything—the Martian landscape, the ocean bottom, the human body, whatever! Second, the huge computing power and memory of computers has enabled the creation of virtual worlds that require billions of pixels to create scenes that look real. We now have more computing power on our desktops or in our laptops than mainframe computers had a few decades ago. And supercomputers today dwarf anything we have known. Third, advances in simulation, animation, and digital reproduction are making possible augmented reality and virtual worlds. During the last decade, movies like *Jurassic Park* and *The Lord of the Rings* have created realistic-looking virtual worlds with realistic-looking virtual creatures. Fourth, massive increases in bandwidth, using fiber optics, wireless communication, and digital compression, have enabled the transmission of the huge amounts of data required to support virtual environments.

These advances have made virtual reality a reality! Architects and homeowners can walk through a virtual home before it is ever built to make sure that it meets their every desire. The military teaches its personnel using virtual submarines and virtual helicopters that are so convincing it's hard to distinguish them from the real thing. Perhaps most amazingly, doctors can now perform virtual surgery on real people, by using a digitalized image, without even being in the same state or same country.

Disembodied Body Language

With the assistance of head-mounted displays, data gloves, and cybersuits, you can enter an artificial world and interact with artificial people or real people in artificial bodies. Amazingly, some of these virtual people are indistinguishable from real people! Part of the reason it's so hard to distinguish virtual people from real people is that their body language is so lifelike.

Virtual Gesticulation and Facial Simulation

Virtual reality has the capacity to create three-dimensional body images. These images can replicate human physical appearance, gestures, and facial expressions. Such a virtual system has the capability to transmit an exact three-dimensional image of an actual interactant so that interaction can happen at a distance. Moreover, a person can adopt the visual image of another person or even an animal, as long as the image has been digitally stored. Because someone can adopt another person's image, this is like a tele-conference on steroids, with the added potential for identity theft and virtual impersonation.

Accurate, real-time images of both the bodies and body language of other people would permit you to transmit all of your nonverbal behavior over great distances, much like your voice, including tone of voice, is transmitted by phone today. In this sort of virtual cyberspace environment, all of your emotions, your interpersonal intimacy, dominance, submission, boredom, and interest, would be communicated via body language just as they are in ordinary, everyday reality.

Positions of Power

In the future, communicating with a friend in a vivid virtual environment may be as common as placing a phone call. However, you'll be able to literally reach out and touch someone, as well as hear, see, and (maybe) smell them. Or maybe you'll go see a Voomie, a virtual reality movie that will provide much more than just sight and sound.

Reach Out and Touch Someone

In virtual reality, like ordinary reality, you should be able to have a touching experience, whether or not the person you're interacting with is a virtual person or real. You should be able to virtually hug, digitally shake hands, and perhaps have cyber-sex with that individual.

The development of the data glove, the cyber-suit, and forced feedback devices, combined with high-speed, high-bandwidth communication, have made virtual touch a reality. For over a decade the military has used forced feedback devices in their simulators. These devices transmit tactile feedback through a hydraulic system in the cybersuit. These simulators were so real in communicating actual touch that in collisions, tank commanders suffered real broken arms in their virtual tanks. Obviously, when the military realized how potent their virtual worlds were, they scaled the simulators back a bit.

Haptic interfaces have been used by employees at nuclear power plants for years to virtually touch—but really move—radioactive elements and by doctors to examine highly contagious patients.

> **Nonverbally Speaking**
>
> Although the whole idea of virtual sex, especially a virtual sex industry, sounds sordid, virtual sex is the ultimate in safe sex. It might diminish the size of the huge and dangerous sex worker industry around the world and help reduce the spread of sexually transmitted diseases, including AIDS.

For the general public, perhaps the most interesting application of virtual haptic body language is to communicate intimacy and sexuality. Imagine being able to virtually hug a spouse or a child and have that touch seem real. Military personnel on long tours of duty could have their kids sit on their virtual laps or give them a virtual kiss goodnight.

Nearly every new communication technology—from the book to the compact disk, to the Internet—has been a channel for sexual content, and haptic virtual reality will be no exception. One day people might have sex in cyberspace, giving a whole new meaning to the expression "reach out and touch someone."

Your Virtual Voice

You probably never thought about it, but telephones are virtual voice. You really do not hear another person's voice over the phone; instead, you listen to an electronic replica of the person's voice. The replica is so accurate that you can recognize who the person is by their unique vocal style and intonation pattern. Moreover, you can recognize emotions, hear turn-taking cues, and recognize leave-taking cues much as you would in a real conversation.

> **Nonverbally Speaking**
>
> Telephones are a virtual voice, the first widespread virtual reality technology. The great popularity of the phone results from its ability to preserve both words and vocal body language, and to transmit them interactively in real time. The mobile phone cuts the tether, thereby making your virtual voice, just like your real voice, completely portable.

Just as our voices are an important part of our real body language, virtual voices will be critical elements of cyberspace body language. To be effective, virtual voices must reconstruct the pitch, rate, tone, intonation, and vocal variation of our real voices.

You might be surprised to learn that the technology already exists for reproducing human voices in cyberspace—it's called the telephone! When you hear a voice on the phone, you are hearing a virtual voice, reconstructed out of the electronics that flow along a wire, a fiber-optic cable, or radio waves. The telephone and all its descendents—the cell phone, the answering machine, and voice mail—are virtual voices.

Virtual Eye Contact

As you have read throughout this book, eye contact is a vital form of body language. It invites communication, creates connections, signals your attention, and provides feedback. Virtual reality of the future must be able to capture the minute and interactive changes in eye behavior that we take for granted.

Moreover, when you turn your head or shift your eyes in a virtual environment, the scene must change just as it does in ordinary reality. Since visual information is such an important aspect of both sending and receiving body language, realistic virtual vision will be an essential component of any virtual system. Any delay in the virtual environment when you shift your eyes or turn your head will be disorienting and unconvincing.

Olfactory Authenticity

In everyday reality, smells create a sense of authenticity and provide another source of sensory information. Mexico City, Tokyo, and Stockholm all smell completely different from my hometown of San Diego. Likewise, as noted in Chapter 9, smell is an important communication channel that repels and attracts. Obviously, the addition of smell sensations would improve the virtuality of any artificial reality.

Nonverbally Speaking

People have tried to incorporate smells into alternative realities in the past. In addition to being able to see and hear Borg Warner's environment chamber, people could also smell it. When passing a man cooking corned beef on the street, in addition to seeing it cooked and hearing it sizzle, visitors to the chamber would smell it. It took 30 seconds to clear the room of one smell, and then people would get another whiff, including the smell of fresh rain, a wet dog, or a woman's perfume.

How Real Is Real? Achieving Virtual Reality

People attempt to use media to recreate and augment reality all the time. The big screen of the movie theatre, complete with surround sound, makes you feel as though you are really present in the picture. Of course, IMAX, wraparound screens, and 3D movies make the experience even more lifelike, sometimes even hyper-real. Even television captivates us by transporting us to a virtual environment, like the White House, the Middle East, or the Super Bowl. It makes us feel like we are really there, sort of. Virtual reality researchers have studied media with an eye toward what makes a medium real, and here is what they found.

Immersion

In real life, we often become completely engrossed in what we are doing. Whether it is a conversation, a report we are completing, a game we are playing, we spend much of our life absorbed and immersed in activities.

One test of the virtual reality of any medium is how immersive it is. Movies head the list of immersive media and sometimes are so engrossing that we feel the heroine's fear when she's being stalked or the hero's exhilaration when he vanquishes his enemy. You know you've just watched an immersive movie when you became completely absorbed in it. Since ordinary reality has no frame, the next time you go to the theater try sitting close enough so the movie fills your visual field, so that you are *in* the movie, not at a movie. Likewise, seeing theatre lights and exit signs detracts from the immersiveness of a movie experience.

Television is also highly immersive, and even a good book can be engrossing, transporting us to another time or place. The telephone can be immersive, which is why it can be dangerous to use while driving, but so can a live conversation with a passenger, or any other activity that occupies our attention. Radio is less immersive, though in its early days it really absorbed many folks who would hang on every word of early radio shows like *The Lone Ranger*.

To immerse us, a media should make us feel like we're part of the situation.

Real-Time Interactivity

Virtual reality must be highly interactive. Real human interaction, including all of your body language, takes place interactively and in real time. If someone says something shocking, you gasp, smile, and raise your eyebrows in a manner that's carefully synchronized with your partner's body language.

One reason the phone is such a successful communication medium is that it allows us to talk to others in real time, just like a face-to-face conversation. The problem with the phone is that it relies on only one kind of body language—the voice. Picture phones, which have never achieved great popularity, would be more virtually real, and videoconferences, which are rapidly gaining in popularity, are getting closer and closer to mimicking real meetings.

E-mail and letters are interactive, but they lack the real-time interactivity of face-to-face conversations. Instant messaging, chat rooms, and blogs are highly interactive, though their reliance on written words eliminates virtually all body language and delays the immediate responses that are so much a part of face-to-face interactions.

Because e-mail contains virtually no body language, people use emoticons—those little smiley faces and such that appear in e-mail, though some people consider then pretty dorky. Likewise, people will highlight or capitalize words, use the bold key, color, or punctuation for emphasis. These are great attempts, but not nearly as effective as good old face-to-face body language.

Multiple Channels

Real body language that accompanies real communication uses a lot of communication channels: facial expression, voice, touch, space, time—all the stuff this book is about. Any attempt at virtual reality has to be multichannelled, too. To be like our real bodies, sight, sound, touch, and smell must all be present. Motion and taste wouldn't hurt, either, in achieving a complete multisensory effect.

Even the most immersive media, movies and television, use only two communication channels (sight and sound), and our virtual voice, the telephone, uses only one. Some of the major breakthroughs in creating virtual people with realistic body language will have to await multisensory technologies.

Telepresence

Virtual reality should be able to transport you to another place. Likewise, virtual people should be able to communicate their entire personae, complete with a full array of body language. Full telepresence makes you feel fully transported to a mediated physical and social environment; your sense of presence is not divided. During some mediated experiences you have divided presence. For example, when you are in the family room watching a baseball game, you feel as though you are both in a stadium and also at home. Media vary in their degree of telepresence, but for an environment to constitute a virtual reality, you must be fully telepresent, with little awareness of any reality other than the virtual one you seem to be in.

Body Talk

In the *Matrix* movies, the hero of the films, Neo, becomes aware that practically the entire society is physically telepresent in the Matrix with no awareness of their actual presence on Earth. Neo, Morpheus, and Trinity are transported back and forth from their "real" existence to the Matrix by means of a virtual-reality program. Many of the people, including the agents, are sentient programs, who create a sense of social telepresence in the Matrix.

Navigation

Human beings are not static objects, but unfortunately, virtually all media immobilize us. We sit to read, view a movie, watch TV, or surf the 'net. In virtual reality, we must be able to walk, run, ride, or fly and have control over our movements to simulate our everyday life.

At some health clubs, virtual-reality stairmasters and cycles enable the users to navigate virtual environments while exercising. Although low in vividness and only moderately immersive and not very telepresent at all, these machines enable totally free movement through virtual environments. This may be the wave of the future, with virtual tourism taking us to other continents or other planets, to the top of the Himalayas or the depths of the ocean, with us in control of what we see and where we go.

Vividness

The ordinary world is extremely vivid, composed of brilliant colors, clear sounds, and tangible touch. Any virtual reality must create a reality that is nearly indistinguishable from everyday reality. A black-and-white television is only moderately vivid; an IMAX film is very vivid. An old 33rpm record played on a monaural player is moderately vivid; a DVD played in surround sound is very vivid.

Vividness depends on the sophistication of the technology being used. People in a virtual environment should have active, well-animated body language that looks just like an ordinary person. These "high-definition" people must be capable of enacting all forms of body language for a virtual environment to be socially vivid.

The Dark Side of Virtual Interaction

Technology is our servant, but also our master. Media critic and philosopher Marshall McLuhan believed that while media extend our senses, we become slaves to the technology as well. He believed that the Eskimo is a servomechanism (in this case, a human motor) of his kayak, the cowboy of his horse, the businessman of his clock, the cyberneticist—and soon the entire world—of his computer. Today we are the intelligent operating systems of the desktop computer with which we spend so much of our time.

Internet Isolation and Information Overload

The world that McLuhan predicted back in the 1960s has arrived: People *are* the operating systems of their computers. Many of us spend endless hours typing on keyboards and reading off screens. While we are all connected to each other via this global nervous system called the Internet, we are in a sense more isolated than ever. Cornell psychologist Robert Kraut reports that the more time we spend online, the less satisfied we are with our relationships and ourselves.

A decade ago, Swarthmore psychologist Kenneth Gergen called our immersion in the swirling world of technology and social relations the saturated self. He described how so many of are inundated by television, radio, fax, mail, e-mail, telephone, billboards, express mail, and more. A proliferation of relationships, long commutes, school, work, churches, and clubs saturate our lives. A decade later, matters are even worse. The increase in technology foreshadows a future world of increased stress, driven by more technology.

Last year Americans attended a record number of movies, spent record numbers of hours on the Internet, bought a near record number of books, and continued to listen to the radio, view DVDs, and watch a huge amount of television. Old media never die; they just continue to make demands on our time. Perhaps because of all of these demands on our time, Americans sleep less than ever before, and one study found that dads spend an average of only 17 minutes a day with their kids!

In our world of material comfort and technological innovation, we need to tune in to what really matters. We need to remember that in ordinary reality it's so nice to share space with friends, hug our kids, spend time with an elderly relative, or exchange laughs with our spouse. As we move to a world of virtual body language, we should never forget our most precious means of connection, real body language.

Mediated Muggings

Once virtual sexual encounters become common, society will have yet another problem to deal with: Virtual sexual assault. Imagine donning your cybersuit and cozying up to your computer for a wonderful evening of sexual interaction with your partner halfway around the world. As you are logging on, a hacker appears with the intention of engaging in a virtual sexual interaction with you—without your permission! Or worse, a hacker logs on in the persona of your partner, and you end up having cyber-sex with a stranger. Additionally, black markets in computer images, available for cyber-sex, could include everybody, from celebrities and politicians, to you or me.

> **Bodily Blunders**
>
> In a virtual world, will unwanted visits from virtual guests become a major nuisance or constitute virtual trespassing? Already junk mail, terrible telemarketers, and Internet spam bombard us; could virtual intruders be far off?

Cyberspace interaction, with virtually real body language, raises all sorts of ethical questions: What is privacy in such a virtual world? Can anyone have a virtual interaction with you, much as anyone can send you an e-mail today? If virtual reality in cyberspace creates the global village, is everyone welcome around your campfire?

Nonverbally Speaking
Here is a paradox to ponder. Replicating virtual body language in a cyberspace environment means exactly duplicating all the forms of nonverbal communication from touch to facial expression, from appearance to gesture. When all is said and done, what you have simulated in cyberspace is what we already have in everyday life, human communication with all its rich body language.

Parting Words

Despite the troubles of technology, I don't believe we will be technologically terrorized or live in a virtual dystopia. These are exciting times, and few of us would trade places with people in any other era. Nonetheless, some things are cultural constants in any society, at any time. Perhaps the most invariable certainty of life is the importance of human relationships, established through our most basic connection, body language.

The Least You Need to Know

- Media are already creating virtual worlds with realistic relationships.

- Virtual body language must create, at minimum, realistic gestures, authentic facial expression, true touch, simulated smell, virtual voices, and interactive eyes.

- Virtual interactions need to be immersive, interactive, multichannelled, telepresent, navigable, and vivid.

- Virtual reality has a dark side, including Internet isolation and mediated muggings.

Body Language from A to Z

adaptors   Random self-touching or object-touching behaviors like brushing hair out of your eyes or playing with a pen.

affect cues   Body language that expresses emotional states.

anosmia   The loss of the sense of smell that may also reduce taste and diminish sexual desire.

analogic   Signs with direct intrinsic relationships to the things they represent. They are continuous messages that look or sound like things for which they stand.

aphasia   The loss of linguistic abilities such as speaking, writing, reading, and understanding sign language. It's due to an injury to the left brain hemisphere.

arbitrary symbol   A sign that has a direct, humanly-defined relationships with what it stands for. Most words in natural languages are symbols.

arms akimbo   The hands-on-hips position, a sign of dominance or power.

arousal   When a person is stimulated, activated, or feeling intense emotion.

attachment   Patterns of parent-infant interaction that establish close or distant adult relationship patterns, body language behavior, and relationship quality.

baby talk   A variation of high-pitched children's speech used mostly with infants and small children, though it is sometimes used between lovers.

batons   Naturally occurring gestures that beat the rhythm of speech.

body language   Technically called nonverbal communication; body language is all the messages we send without the use of language.

boomerang effect   When a persuasive campaign has the opposite effect than was intended.

buffers   Body barriers such as objects or limbs that prevent invasion of our personal space zone.

cerebral cortex   The part of the brain that governs higher mental functions. It's comprised of the right and left brain hemispheres and the corpus collosum.

chronemics   The study of people's use of time and the meanings they associate with time during interpersonal interaction, such as spending time, waiting time, talk time, and so on.

collaborative deceptions   When somebody picks up deceptive body language but chooses to ignore it.

combat ritual   Simulated fighting as a form of body language. Characteristic of contact sports and play fighting, this is also called a mock aggression display.

contact culture   Cultures with body language that involves close interaction distances and plentiful touching. These cultures tend to be located near the equator and the Mediterranean region.

consciousness   Awareness of your self, others, and your surroundings.

corpus collosum   A bundle of nerve fibers that connects the right and left hemisphere providing connections between body language and linguistic behaviors and perceptions.

courtship behaviors   Body language used to send affiliative messages between people who are dating and/or mating.

crowding   Perceived interpersonal density, a feeling of too many people in a given space, often resulting in defensive or avoidant body language.

cyber-sex   Erotic communication via the Internet

deception cues   Body language or verbal behaviors that are associated with lying.

deception detection   The ability to detect lying in others from their words or body language.

deke   A hockey term from Canada that is short for "decoy." It is a body language fake often used in sports, such as a fake pass, a fake steal, or a fake handoff.

density   An objective measure of crowdedness; for example, the number of people per square foot or square mile.

digital communication   Messages sent by arbitrary, discrete, all-or-nothing codes as opposed to the natural, continuous codes of analogic communication. Natural language is the highest form of digital communication.

display rules   Learned behavioral norms about how, what, when, and where we should show our emotions.

duping delight   Positive, happy body language that is produced by smug, joyful, overconfident liars.

elder speak   Speaking very loud and overpronouncing each word, which works for the hard-of-hearing, but which many elderly people find patronizing.

emblems   Gestures with dictionary definitions like the hitchhiker's thumb or the thumbs-down gesture.

emotional contagion   The spontaneous spread of emotions from one person to another person or group through nonverbal expressions.

emotional expression   Body language that reveals your emotional states, primarily, but not exclusively, expressed in the face.

emotional intelligence   Awareness and sensitivity to your emotions, your emotional body language, and the emotional body language of others.

externalizers   People, most often women, who express their emotions through body language, especially facial expressions.

eye contact   Simultaneous or mutual gaze. When two people look at one another's face or eye area at the same time.

face-to-face position   A direct body position, also called direct body orientation, that communicates interest, approach, and availability.

facial feedback hypothesis   The idea, supported by research, that your own facial expressions influence your mood. When you look fearful or happy, for example, you feel those emotions.

fakes   Sports body language that communicates one action while engaging in a different action, such as a ball fake in basketball or a fake steal in baseball.

flirting   Enticing, but ambiguous, body language that people use to negotiate whether to begin a more involved dating sequence that could lead to a long-term relationship.

forward leans   Inclining forward toward another person; body language that communicates interest and involvement.

gaze   Looking at another person, usually at their face or eyes. A mutual gaze is also called eye contact.

gender signals   Body language that communicates our sex or gender, such as masculine or feminine walking, gesturing, sitting, and facial expressions.

ghost skirt   The habitual, compact, knees-together, body position often displayed by seated women even when they are wearing jeans.

halo effect   When one good characteristic, such as physical attractiveness, generalizes to positive impressions of other characteristics, like competence or trustworthiness.

hair flips   Flirtatious, self-touching, preening behavior that is designed to attract attention; usually employed by females.

hand shrugs   Upward palm gestures that look like a person is unsure. Some studies have found it to be a deception cue.

haptics   The study or science of touch communication.

high tech/high touch   The belief that in a technological society, interpersonal communication and body language, like touch, is more important than ever.

high-context culture   In some societies meaning is usually conveyed by the communication context or by body language, rather than explicit language.

hunting ritual   Games, sports, or actual hunting that simulate the vital hunts of our ancestors.

iconic   Signs or signals that bear a direct, nonarbitrary relationship with their referent.

ideographs   Gestures that sketch an idea, a graph, or a relationship.

illustrators   Gestures that accompany speech.

inconvenience displays   Body language that simultaneously communicates humility, subordination, and politeness, such as serving or opening a door for someone.

immediacy behaviors   Body language that reduces physical and psychological distance, increases availability for communication, and communicates warmth and closeness.

internalizer   People, especially men, who hide their emotional body language, resulting in greater internal responses such as heart rate and blood pressure.

interpersonal distance   The common zone of interpersonal interaction used for most conversation. In North America it extends about 1½ to 4 feet from your body.

intimacy behaviors   Aspects of body language that create and enhance interpersonal closeness, friendship, and love. Examples include warm hand shakes, cuddling, or sitting by a fireplace.

intimate distance   A zone within 18 inches of the body reserved for very close relationships such as friends, lovers, children, spouses, and other close relatives.

intimidation   Powerful, dominant body language, such as angry stares and menacing gestures, that causes fear or submissiveness in another individual.

intuition   A heightened sense of perceptiveness that is often attributed to women. It is most likely due to heightened sensitivity to body language.

kinesics   The formal term for the study of body movements or body language.

kinetographs   Gestures that reproduce a bodily action or a physical behavior. Imitations of prior body displays.

language   A set of arbitrarily coded symbols with dictionary definitions that stand for people, things, and actions.

leakage   Unintentional body language that reveals a persons' real attitudes or emotions.

left brain hemisphere   The portion of the cerebral cortex that controls the right side of the body and is the primary location for language, speech, and logic.

low-context culture   Also called nonverbal cultures, these are societies where communication is explicit rather than implicit.

mesomorph   The muscular, V-shaped body type often associated with leadership, strength, and masculinity.

mindlessness   Lack of awareness of one's actions. Behaviors that are performed or perceived with little or no conscious awareness.

mirroring   Engaging in body language behaviors similar to another person; this is a sign of admiration, alignment, and rapport.

mock aggression displays   Play fighting, usually done by children and adolescents of humans and other species, especially males.

modular mind A theory of the human mind that says different brain structures are specialized for different functions and come to different decisions.

monochronic Cultures that schedule just one event at a time, start on time, and move quickly on to the next task. Most characteristic of Northern Europe and North America.

multichannelled A quality of body language in which a message is sent via multiple codes or channels, such as facial expression, touch, voice, and posture, that makes a message more powerful and believable.

negative reinforcement The removal of a painful or aversive experience that increases the occurrence of a behavior.

nonlinguistic communication The most accurate term for body language; it includes all communication that occurs without arbitrary symbols or language.

nonverbal communication The most widely used term for body language consisting of signs and movements that are analogic, nonlinguistic, and generally controlled by the right brain hemisphere.

nonverbal listening Body language behaviors that indicate you are paying attention to the communication of another person; these include vocalizations or head nods.

nonverbal receiving ability The skill of accurately interpreting the body language of other people.

olfaction The sense of smell.

olfactory communication Scents, including pheromones, emitted by one person that have meaning for or change the behavior of another person.

open palm A universal gesture of peace and greeting throughout the world.

outercourse Sexual activity that does not result in the exchange of body fluids.

Othello error When a truth-teller is falsely accused of lying based on body language cues such as anxiety or agitation.

overarousal Agitated, overstimulated body language.

paralingustics The study of the nonverbal elements of the voice, including vocal inflection, which is also called vocalics.

pass through When a baby rapidly swings its face from one side to the other right past the adult's face. This is overstimulated, annoyed, avoidant body language.

personal space   An invisible bubble that surrounds the body creating a boundary for most interactions. Invasions of this bubble result in retreats, buffering, and avoidance.

pheromones   External chemical messages that often act as sexual attractants.

physical appearance   An important aspect of body language and the basis of both stereotypes and initial impressions.

pictographs   Gestures that draw a shape or object in the air.

pillow talk   Soft, gentle-voiced talk and body language employed by lovers.

pointers   Gestures that indicate directions, command people go to in a specific direction, or direct attention to a particular task.

poker-faced   A term to describe any unexpressive person.

polychronic   Cultures that schedule several things at once, may have no actual starting time, and allow events to naturally unfold.

positive reinforcement   A satisfier or a reward that follows a given behavior, increasing the chances of the behavior being repeated.

power position   Any form of dominant, controlling, or high-status body language, such as standing over someone, a mean stare, a raised seat, or the arms akimbo position.

preening behavior   Tidying or adjusting behaviors that sometimes send flirtatious messages to other people.

public space   An interaction zone approximately 10 feet or more in diameter reserved for dignitaries and public speakers.

punishment   The administration of a painful, unpleasant, or critical stimulus that results in the reduction or elimination of the previous behavior.

pupil dilation   An expansion of the dark center of the eye that indicates interest or arousal. People with dilated pupils are considered warmer and more attractive.

quasi-courtship displays   Friendly or flirtatious behaviors that are not meant to be taken as serious sexual overtures.

reactance   A process of resistance to influence or coercion by individuals who value their independence and "react" to defend it.

redundancy   Repetition of information over time or modes. Body language communicates across multiple modes or channels with simultaneous redundancy.

right brain hemisphere　The right side of the cerebral cortex, primarily responsible for body language including touch, spatial relations, intonation, music, and physical appearance.

self-conscious emotions　Feelings that are always social in nature and are displayed during emotional experiences in social situations. They include guilt, embarrassment, shame, pride, envy, and jealousy.

self-touching　Tactile contact with one's own body. It's often intended to comfort, but is also a powerful courtship cue, particularly when visibly touching one's own face, neck, breasts, or thighs.

sensation-seekers　People who thrive on high levels of stimulation or excitement.

sexploitation　Taking advantage of or attracting someone with blatantly sexual body language or media.

sexual arousal cues　Signs of sexual excitement, including heavy breathing; erection of the penis, clitoris, and nipples; flushed skin, and passionate vocal behaviors.

sexual signals　Body language, including flirtation and sexual arousal cues, that indicate readiness for sexual interaction.

sign language　A formal gestural system that is really a language complete with vocabulary, grammar, syntax, and linear structure.

social attraction　The quality of another person or public figure, usually communicated through body language, that makes you want to be friends or hang out with that person.

social/consulting space　The zone, approximately 4 to 8 feet from the body, used by salespeople, teachers, and other professionals in their interpersonal interactions.

spatials　Gestures that indicate size or distance.

steepling　A power gesture by leaders in professional settings, where fingers are vertically and symmetrically raised together to construct a tower or phallic symbol.

strategic deception cues　Behaviors associated with lying that result from intentional changes in behavior during lying.

stripping　Removing one's clothes for the purpose of sexual arousal; a form of safe sex.

submission rituals　Powerless or subservient body language including lowering, kneeling, cowering, prostrating, bowing, or bending.

surrogate touch   The substitution of the comforting touch of animals, pets, toys, or blankets in the absence of human touch.

symbolic killing   Body language that celebrates the demise of an opponent, like victorious fighters who raise their hand in victory and tower over defeated opponents.

synchrony   Coordinated body language with other people that literally and figuratively says that you are on the same wavelength.

staring   A dominant, scrutinizing, prolonged, or intrusive form of gazing at another person.

tactile communication   Touch communication or touch messages.

tactile deprivation   A lack of touch that can leave an adult lonely, stressed, and in ill health. It's even more serious for babies and can result in their death.

task attraction   Being drawn to someone because they are competent and easy to work with.

teacher immediacy   Warm, friendly, enthusiastic body language by an instructor that results in increased motivation, positive attitudes, and increased learning.

territorial markers   Personal belongings or artifacts that are used to save a space or protect a territory.

territorial tenure   The belief that occupying a territory over a period of time reserves that space permanently.

territoriality   A fixed, or semi-fixed, home territory that people defend and protect against invasion by unwanted others.

tie signs   Body language used by couples or groups to show their connections to one another.

touch communication   The sending of messages through tactile interaction, for example with hugs, strokes, or handshakes.

turn-taking cues   Body language behaviors that signal turn switches in a conversation.

unconscious competence   Being able to perform an activity so well that it can be accomplished without thinking about it.

underarousal   A lack of stimulation that results in boredom, dullness, and monotony.

virtual reality   The creation of an artificial world or interaction, electronically or mechanically, that results in an authentic, immersive, telepresent, and vivid experience that seems like ordinary reality.

virtual voice   An electronic simulation of voice that is transmitted or stored; the telephone or voice mail, for example.

visual stimulation   Any visual cue that causes sexual arousal.

Appendix B

Learning More About Body Language

The following websites, books, and articles include some of the best information on body language available today, and form the basis for much of the information in this book. I hope you go beyond this book and explore the fascinating world of nonverbal communication and body language.

Websites

http://members.aol.com/nonverbal2/index.htm

David Givens Center for Nonverbal Studies. This is the best online resource for information on body language for the public, with a great body language dictionary and lots of information.

http://www3.usal.es/~nonverbal/introduction.htm

A very useful website on nonverbal behavior with more than 130 links to other pages.

www.natcom.org/ctronline/nonverb.htm

The National Communication Association website with links to material on nonverbal communication.

http://www3.usal.es/~nonverbal/books.htm

David Masip's wonderful website with links to more than 100 books on body language.

Books

Aiello, J. R., and A. Baum. *Residential Crowding and Design*. New York: Plenum, 1979.

Andersen, P. A. *Nonverbal Communication: Forms and Functions*. Mountain View, CA: Mayfield Publishing, 1999.

Andersen, P. A., and L. K. Guerrero. *The Handbook of Communication and Emotion: Research, Theory, Applications and Contexts*. San Diego, CA: Academic Press, 1998.

Bateson, G. *Steps to an Ecology of Mind*. New York: Balantine Books, 1972.

Berscheid, E., and E. M. Walster. *Interpersonal Attraction*. 2nd ed. Reading, MA: Addison-Wesley, 1978.

Birdwhistell, R. L. *Kinesics and Context*. Philadelphia: University of Pennsylvania Press, 1970.

Bowlby, J. *Attachment*. New York: Basic Books, 1969.

Brehm, S. S., and J. W. Brehm. *Psychological Reactance: A Theory of Freedom and Control*. New York: Academic Press, 1981.

Brydon, S. R., and M. D. Scott. *Between One and Many: The Art and Science of Public Speaking*. New York: McGraw Hill, 1994.

Buck, R. *The Communication of Emotion*. New York: The Guilford Press, 1984

Burgoon, J. K., D. B. Buller, and W. G. Woodall. *Nonverbal Communication: The Unspoken Dialogue*. New York: McGraw-Hill, 1996.

Darwin, C. *The Expression of Emotion in Man and Animals*. London: John Murray, 1904.

Ekman, P. *Emotion in the Human Face*. Cambridge, UK: Cambridge University Press, 1982.

————. *Telling Lies: Clues in the Marketplace, Politics, and Marriage*. New York: Norton, 1985.

Gergen, K. J. *The Saturated Self: Dilemmas of Identity in Contemporary Life*. New York: Basic Books, 1991.

Goleman, D. *Emotional Intelligence*. New York: Bantam, 1995.

Guerrero, L. K., P. A. Anderson, and W. Afifi. *Close Encounters: Communication in Relationships*. Mountain View, CA: Mayfield Publishing, 2001.

Guerrero, L. K., J. Devito, and M. Hecht. *The Nonverbal Communication Reader*. Prospect Heights, IL: Waveland Press, 1999.

Hall, E. T. *The Hidden Dimension*. New York: Doubleday, 1966.

————. *Beyond Culture*. Garden City, NY: Anchor Books, 1976.

Hofstede, G. *Culture's Consequences*. (Abridged Edition). Beverly Hills, CA: Sage Publications, 1982.

Holihan, T. A. *Uncivil Wars: Political Campaigns in a Media Age*. Boston: Bedford/ St. Martin, 2001.

Jones, S. E. *The Right Touch: Understanding and Using the Language of Physical Contact*. Cresshill, NJ: Hampton Press, 1994.

Knapp, M. L., and J. A. Hall. *Nonverbal Communication in Human Interaction*. 4th ed. New York: Harcourt Brace, 1997.

Korzybski, A. *Science and Sanity: An Introduction to Non-Aristotelian Systems and General Semantics*. Lakeville, CT: International Non-Aristotelian Library Publishing Company, 1933.

Kübler-Ross, Elizabeth. *On Death and Dying*. New York: Macmillan, 1969.

LaFrance, M., and C. Mayo. *Moving Bodies: Nonverbal Communication in Social Relationships*. Monterey, CA: Brooks/Cole, 1978.

Leary, M. R., and R. M. Kowalski. *Social Anxiety*. New York: Guilford, 1995.

Manusov, V. *The Sourcebook of Nonverbal Measures: Going Beyond Words*. Erlbaum Publishing, 2004.

McLuhan, M. *Understanding Media: The Extensions of Man*. New York: Penguin, 1969.

Mehrabian, A. *Silent Messages*. Belmont, CA: Wadsworth, 1971(a).

————. *Public Places. Private Spaces*. New York: Basic Books, 1976.

Milgram, S. *Obedience to Authority*. New York: Harper & Row, 1974.

Miller, G.R., and J. B. Stiff. *Deceptive Communication*. Newbury Park, CA: Sage, 1993.

Molloy, John T. *John T. Molloy's New Dress for Success*. New York: Warner Books, 1988.

Montagu, A. *Touching: The Human Significance of the Skin*. New York: Harper & Row, 1971, 1978.

Morris, D. *Intimate Behavior*. New York: Random House, 1971.

————. *Manwatching: A Field Guide to Human Behavior*. New York: Harry N. Abrams, 1977.

Patterson, M. L. *Nonverbal Behavior: A Functional Perspective*. New York: Springer-Verlag, 1983.

Poizner, H., E. S. Klima, and U. Bellugi. *What the Hands Reveal About the Brain*. Cambridge, MA: MIT Press, 1987.

Rosenthal, R. *Skill in Nonverbal Communication: Individual Differences*. Cambridge, MA: Oelgeschlager, Gunn, & Hain, 1979.

Rosenthal, R., J. A. Hall, M. R. Dimatteo, P. L. Rogers, and D. Archer. *Sensitivity to Nonverbal Communication: The PONS Test*. Baltimore, MD: Johns Hopkins University Press, 1979.

Siegman, A. W., and S. Feldstein. *Multichannel Integrations of Nonverbal Behavior.* Hillsdale, N.J.: Lawrence Erlbaum Press, 1985.

———. *Nonverbal Behavior and Communication.* 2nd ed. New York: Halsted Press, 1987.

Stern, D. *The First Relationship: Mother and Infant.* Cambridge, MA: Harvard University Press, 1980.

Tangney, J. P., and K. W. Fischer. *Self-Conscious Emotions: The Psychology of Shame, Guilt, Embarrassment and Pride.* New York: Guilford, 1995.

Watzlawick, P., J. H. Beavin, and D. D. Jackson. *Pragmatics of Human Communication.* New York: Norton, 1967.

Articles

Aiello, J. R. "Human Spatial Behavior." *Handbook of Environmental Psychology,* edited by D. Stools and I. Altmann. Vol. 1. New York: Wiley, 1987.

Andersen, J. F. "Teacher Immediacy as a Predictor of Teaching Effectiveness." *Communication Yearbook 3,* edited by D. Nimme. New Brunswick, NJ: Transaction Books, 1979.

Andersen, J. F., P. A. Andersen, and M. W. Lustig. "Opposite-Sex Touch Avoidance: A National Replication and Extension." *Journal of Nonverbal Behavior* 11 (1987): 89–109.

Andersen, J. F., P. A. Andersen, M. A. Murphy, and N. Wendt-Wasco. "Teachers' Reports of Students' Nonverbal Communication in the Classroom: A Developmental Study in Grades K-12." *Communication Education* 34 (1985): 292–307.

Andersen, J. F., and J. G. Withrow. "The Impact of Lecturer Nonverbal Expressiveness on Improving Mediated Instruction." *Communication Education* 30 (1981): 342–353.

Andersen, P. A., and J. F. Andersen. "Nonverbal Immediacy in Instruction." *Communication in the Classroom: Original Essays*, edited by L.L. Barker. Englewood Cliffs, NJ: Prentice-Hall, 1982.

Andersen, P. A., J. F. Andersen, and S. M. Mayton. "The Development of Nonverbal Communication in the Classroom: Teachers' Perceptions of Students in Grades K-12." *Western Journal of Speech Communication* 49 (1985): 188–203.

Andersen, P. A., S. V. Eloy, L. K. Guererro, and B. H. Spitzberg. "Romantic Jealousy and Relational Satisfaction: A Look at the Impact of Jealousy Experience and Expression." *Communication Reports* 8 (1995): 77–85.

Andersen, P. A., J. P. Garrison, and J. F. Andersen. "Implications of a Neurophysiological Approach for the Study of Nonverbal Communication." *Human Communication Research* 6 (1979): 74–89.

Andersen, P. A., M. L. Hecht, G. D. Hoobler, and M. Smallwood. "Nonverbal Communication Across Cultures." *Handbook of International and Intercultural Communication*, edited by B. Gudykunst and B. Moody. Thousand Oaks, CA: Sage, 2002.

Andersen, P. A., and R. J. Kibler. "Candidate Valence as a Predictor of Voter Preference." *Human Communication Research* 5 (1978): 4–14.

Andersen, P. A., and K. Leibowitz. "The Development and Nature of the Construct Touch Avoidance." *Environmental Psychology and Nonverbal Behavior* 3 (1978): 89–106.

Andersen, P. A., and K. K. Sull. "Out of Touch, Out of Reach: Tactile Predispositions as Predictors of Interpersonal Distance." *The Western Journal of Speech Communication* 49 (1985): 57–72.

Andersen, P. A., W. E. Todd-Mancillas, and L. DiClemente. "The Effects of Pupil Dilation in Physical, Social, and Task Attraction." *Australian Scan: Journal of Human Communication* 7 and 8 (1980): 89–95.

Andersen, P. A. "Nonverbal Immediacy in Interpersonal Communication." *Multichannel Integrations of Nonverbal Behavior*, edited by A. W. Siegman and S. Feldstein. Hillsdale, NJ: Erlbaum, 1985.

———. "Consciousness, Cognition, and Communication." *Western Journal of Speech Communication* 50 (1986): 87–101.

———. "The Cognitive Valence Theory of Intimate Communication." *Progress in Communication Sciences, Volume XIV, Mutual Influence in Interpersonal Communication: Theory and Research in Cognition, Affect, and Behavior,* edited by M. T. Palmer and G. A. Barnett. Stamford, CT: Ablex, 1998.

———. "Influential Actions: Nonverbal Communication and Persuasion." *Perspectives on Persuasion, Social Influence and Compliance-Gaining,* edited by J. S. Sieter and R. H. Gass. Boston, MA: Allyn and Bacon, 2004.

———. "The Touch Avoidance Measure." *The Sourcebook of Nonverbal Measures: Going Beyond Words,* edited by V. Manusov. Hillsdale, NJ: Erlbaum, 2004.

Berry, D. S. "Vocal Attractiveness and Vocal Babyishness: Effects on Stranger, Self and Friend Impressions." *Journal of Nonverbal Behavior* 14 (1990): 141–153.

Blanck, P. D., and R. Rosenthal. "Nonverbal Behavior in the Courtroom." *Applications of Nonverbal Behavioral Theories and Research,* edited by R. S. Feldman. Hillsdale, NJ: Erlbaum, 1992.

Bowman, A. "Physical Attractiveness and Electability: Looks and Votes." Paper Presented at the Annual Meeting of the Midwest Political Science Association, April, 1980.

Buck, R. "Individual Differences in Nonverbal Sending Accuracy and Electrodermal Responding: The Externalizing-Internalizing Dimension." *Skill in Nonverbal Communication: Individual Differences,* edited by R. Rosenthal. Cambridge, MA: Oelgechlager, Gunn, & Hain, 1979.

Buller, D. B., and J. K. Burgoon. "Deception: Strategic and Nonstrategic Communication." *Interpersonal Communication,* edited by J. Daly and J. M. Wiemann. Hillsdale, NJ: Erlbaum, 1994.

Buller, D. B., and J. K. Burgoon. "Interpersonal Deception Theory." *Communication Theory* 6 (1996): 203–242.

———. "Emotional Expression in the Deception Process." *Handbook of Communication and Emotion: Research, Theory, Applications and Contexts*, edited by P. A. Andersen and L. K. Guerrero. San Diego, CA: Academic Press, 1998.

Burgoon, J. K. "Nonverbal Violations of Expectations." *Nonverbal Interaction*, edited by J. M. Wiemann and R. P. Harrison. Beverly Hills, CA: Sage, 1983.

Burleson, B. R., and D. J. Goldsmith. "How the Comforting Process Works: Alleviating Emotional Distress Through Conversationally Induced Reappraisals." *Handbook of Communication and Emotion: Research, Theory, Applications and Contexts*, edited by P. A. Andersen and L. K. Guerrero. San Diego, CA: Academic Press, 1998.

Calhoun, J. B. "Population Density and Social Pathology." *Scientific American* 26, no. 2 (1962): 139–148.

Cappella, J. N. "Mutual Influence in Expressive Behavior: Adult-Adult and Infant-Adult Dyadic Interaction." *Psychological Bulletin* 89 (1981): 101–132.

Cappella, J. N. "The Biological Origins of Automated Patterns of Human Interaction." *Communication Theory* 1 (1991): 4–35.

Cappella, J. N. "The Facial Feedback Hypothesis in Human Interaction." *Journal of Language and Social Psychology* 12 (1993): 13–29.

Cappella, J. N., and J. O. Greene. "A Discrepancy-Arousal Explanation of Mutual Influence in Expressive Behavior For Adult and Infant-Adult Interaction." *Communication Monographs* 49 (1982): 89–114.

Egland, K. L., M. A. Stelzner, P. A. Andersen, and B. H. Spitzberg. "Perceived Understanding, Nonverbal Communication and Relational Satisfaction." *Intrapersonal Communication Processes*, edited by J. Aitken and L Shedletsky. Annandale, VA: The Speech Communication Association, 1997.

Eibl-Eibesfelt, I. "Similarities and Differences Between Cultures in Expressive Movements." *Nonverbal Communication*, edited by R. A. Hinde. London: Cambridge University Press, 1972.

———. "Universals in Human Expressive Behavior." *Nonverbal Behavior, Applications and Cultural Implications*, edited by A. Wolfgang. New York: Academic Press, 1979.

Ekman, P., and W. V. Friesen. "Nonverbal Leakage and Clues to Deception." *Psychiatry* 32 (1969): 88–106.

———. "Hand Movements." *Journal of Communication* 22 (1972): 353–374.

———. "A New Pan-Cultural Facial Expression of Emotion." *Motivation and Emotion* 10 (1986): 159–168.

Emmers, T. M., and K. Dindia. "The Effect of Relational Stage and Intimacy on Touch: An Extension of Guerrero and Andersen." *Personal Relationships* 2 (1995): 225–236.

Engen, T. "Remembering Odors and Their Names." *American Scientist* 75 (1987): 497–503.

Exline, R. V., S. L. Ellyson, and B. Long. "Visual Behavior as an Aspect of Power Role Relationships." *Nonverbal Communication of Aggression, Volume 2*, edited by P. Pliner, L. Drames, and T. Alloway. New York: Plenum, 1975.

Fehr, B. J., and R. V. Exline. "Social Visual Interaction: A Conceptual and Literature Review." *Nonverbal Behavior and Communication*, edited by P. Pliner, L. Drames, and T. Alloway. 2nd ed. Hillsdale, NJ: Lawrence Erlbaum, 1987.

Feingold, A. "Good Looking People Are Not What We Think." *Psychological Bulletin* 3 (1992): 304–341.

Flora, J. A., and E. W. Maibach. "Cognitive Responses to AIDS Information: The Effect of Issue Involvement and Message Appeal." *Communication Research* 17 (1990): 759–774.

Frank, M. G. "The Dark Side of Self- and Social Perception: Black Uniforms and Aggression in Professional Sports." *Journal of Personality and Social Psychology* 54 (1988): 74–85.

Gilbert, A. N., and C. J. Wysocki. "The Smell Survey: Its Results." *National Geographic* 174, no. 4 (1987): 514–525.

Guerrero, L. K., and P. A. Andersen. "The Waxing and Waning of Relational Intimacy: Touch as a Function of Relational Stage, Gender and Touch Avoidance." *Journal of Social and Personal Relationships* 8 (1991): 147–165.

———. "Patterns of Matching and Initiation: Touch Behavior and Avoidance Across Romantic Relationship Stages." *Journal of Nonverbal Behavior* 18 (1994): 137–153.

———. "The Dark Side of Jealousy." *The Dark Side of Close Relationships*, edited by B. H. Spitzberg and W. R. Cupach. Mahwah, NJ: Lawrence Erlbaum, 1998.

Guerrero, L. K., P. A. Andersen, P. F. Jorgensen, B. H. Spitzberg, and S. V. Eloy. "Coping with the Green-Eyed Monster: Conceptualizing and Measuring Communicative Responses to Romantic Jealousy." *Western Journal of Communication* 59 (1995): 270–304.

Hall, J. A. "Gender Effects in Decoding Nonverbal Cues." *Psychological Bulletin* 85 (1978): 845–857.

———. "Male and Female Nonverbal Behavior." *Multichannel Integrations of Nonverbal Behavior*, edited by A. W. Siegman and S. Feldstein. Hillsdale, NJ: Erlbaum, 1985.

———. "How Big Are Nonverbal Sex Differences? The Case of Smiling and Sensitivity to Nonverbal Cues." *Sex Differences and Similarities in Communication*, edited by D. J. Canary and K. Dindia. Mahwah, NJ: Erlbaum, 1998.

Hall, J. A., and A. G. Halberstadt. "Subordination and Nonverbal Sensitivity: A Hypothesis in Search of Support." *Women, Men, & Gender: Ongoing Debates*, edited by M. R. Walsh. New Haven, CT: Yale University Press, 1997.

Hess, E. H. "The Role of Pupil Size in Communication." *Scientific American* 232 (1975): 110–119.

Hess, E. H., and S. B. Petrovich. "Pupillary Behavior in Communication." *Nonverbal Behavior and Communication*, edited by A. W. Siegman and S. Feldsein. Hillsdale, NJ: Lawrence Erlbaum, 1987.

Hess, E. H., A. L. Seltzer, and J. M. Schlien. "Pupil Response of Hetero and Homosexual Males to Pictures of Men and Women: A Pilot Study." *Journal of Abnormal Psychology* 70 (1965): 165–168.

Jaffe, J. "Parliamentary Procedure and the Brain." *Nonverbal Behavior and Communication*, edited by A. W. Siegman and S. Feldstein. New York: John Wiley & Sons, 1978.

Jones, S. E., and E. Yarbrough. "A Naturalistic Study of the Meanings of Touch." *Communication Monographs* 52 (1985) 19–56.

Kenrick, D. T., and R. C. Keefe. "Age Preferences in Mates Reflect Sex Differences in Human Reproductive Strategies." *Behavioral and Brain Sciences* 15 (1992): 75–137.

Knapp, M. L., and M. E. Comadena. "Telling It Like It Isn't: Deceptive Communications." *Human Communication Research* 5 (1979): 270–285.

Kraut, R. E., and R. E. Johnson. "Social and Emotional Messages of Smiling: An Ethological Approach." *Journal of Personality and Social Psychology* 37 (1979): 1539–1553.

Kraut, R., M. Patterson, V. Lundmark, S. Kiesler, T. Mukophadhyay, and W. Scherlis. "Internet Paradox: A Social Technology That Reduces Social Involvement and Psychological Well-Being?" *American Psychologist* 53 (1998): 1017–1031.

Langer, E. J. "Minding Matters." *Advances in Experimental Social Psychology*, edited by L. Berkowitz. New York: Academic Press, 1989.

McCroskey, J. C., and T. A. McCain. "The Measurement of Interpersonal Attraction." *Speech Monographs* 41 (1974): 261–266.

McDaniel, E., and P. A. Andersen. "International Patterns of Tactile Communication: A Field Study." *Journal of Nonverbal Behavior* 21 (1998): 59–75.

McHugo, G. J. "Emotional Reactions to a Political Leader's Expressive Displays." *Journal of Personality and Social Psychology* 49 (1985): 1513–1529.

Mezzakappa, D., and P. A. Anderson. "Nonverbal Cues of Crime Victims: Perceptions of Convicted Criminals." Paper Presented at the Annual Meeting of the Western States Communication Association, Pasadena, CA, February, 1996.

Miklosi, A., E. Kubinyi, J. Topal, N. Gacsi, Z. Viranyi, and V. Casanyi. "A Simple Reason for a Big Difference: Wolves Do Not Look Back at Humans but Dogs Do." *Current Biology* 13 (2003): 263–266.

Palmer, M. T., and K. B. Simmons. "Communicating Intentions Through Nonverbal Behaviors: Conscious and Nonconscious Encoding of Liking." *Human Communication Research* 22 (1995): 128–160.

Patterson, M. L. "Functions of Nonverbal Behavior in Close Relationships." *Handbook of Personal Relationships*, edited by S. Duck. New York: Wiley & Sons, 1988.

Riggio, R. E., J. Tucker, and K. F. Widaman. *Verbal and Nonverbal Cues as Mediators of Deception Ability. Journal of Nonverbal Behavior* 11 (1987): 126–145.

Sjoberg, S. L., N. Townsley, and P. A. Andersen. "Touch, Relational Stage and Matching: A Study of Airport Arrival Encounters." Presented at the Western State Communication Association. Pasadena, CA, February, 1996.

Sorensen, G., and M. J. Beatty. "The Interactive Effects of Touch and Touch Avoidance on Interpersonal Perceptions." *Communication Research Reports* 5 (1988): 84–90.

Stacks, D. W., and P. A. Andersen. "The Modular Mind: Implications for Intrapersonal Communication." *The Southern Communication Journal* 54 (1989): 273–293.

Street, R. L. "Evaluation of Noncontent Speech Accommodation." *Language and Communication* 2 (1982): 13–31.

Toulhuizen, J. H. "Communication Strategies for Intensifying Dating Relationships: Identification, Use and Structure." *Journal of Social and Personal Relationships* 6 (1989): 413–434.

Vrij, A., and G. R. Semin. "Lie Experts' Beliefs About Nonverbal Indicators of Deception." *Journal of Nonverbal Behavior* 20 (1996): 65–80.

Wedekind, C., T. Seebeck, F. Bettens, and A. J. Paepke. "MHC-Dependent Mate Preferences in Humans." *Proceedings of the Royal Society* 260 (1995): 245–249.

Index